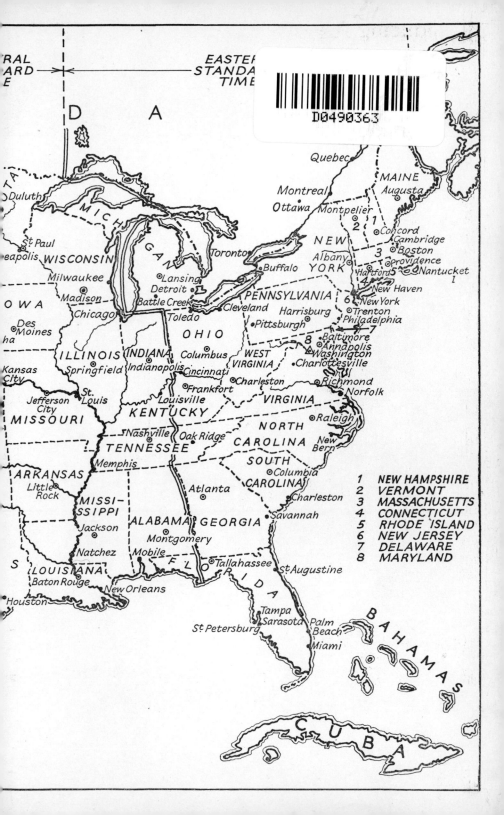

D0490363

RAL
ARD →
E

EASTER
STANDA
TIME

D   A

Quebec

MAINE
Montreal   Augusta
Ottawa   Montpelier
                    1
                2   Concord
                    Cambridge
                3   Boston
Albany   providence
Toronto   Hartford 5   Nantucket
Buffalo   NEW   4   I
          YORK   New Haven
PENNSYLVANIA   6   New York
Harrisburg   Philadelphia
Cleveland   Pittsburgh   7
                    8   Baltimore
OHIO   Annapolis
          Columbus   WEST   Washington
                    VIRGINIA   Charlottesville
Indianapolis Cincinnati   II
                Charleston   Richmond
          Frankfort   Norfolk
INDIANA   VIRGINIA
Louisville

Duluth

St Paul
eapolis   WISCONSIN
Milwaukee
Lansing
Madison   Detroit
Battle Creek
Chicago   Toledo

O W A
Des
Moines
ha

Kansas
City
Jefferson
City
St.
Louis   KENTUCKY
MISSOURI

Nashville   Oak Ridge
ARKANSAS   TENNESSEE
Little   Memphis
Rock
MISSI-
SSIPPI
Jackson
Natchez
S   LOUISIANA
Baton Rouge
Houston   New Orleans

MICHIGAN

ILLINOIS   INDIANA
Springfield Indianapolis

Atlanta
ALABAMA   GEORGIA
Montgomery
Mobile

NORTH
CAROLINA   New
          Bern
Raleigh

SOUTH
Columbia
CAROLINA
Charleston
Savannah

F L O R I D A
Tallahassee   St Augustine

Tampa
Sarasota   Palm
St Petersburg   Beach
Miami

B A H A M A S

C U B A

1   NEW HAMPSHIRE
2   VERMONT
3   MASSACHUSETTS
4   CONNECTICUT
5   RHODE ISLAND
6   NEW JERSEY
7   DELAWARE
8   MARYLAND

Introducing America

In this series

Introducing
AMERICA

by Barbara Kreutz
and Ellen Fleming

LONDON

METHUEN & CO LTD

36 ESSEX STREET, WC2

First published in Great Britain 1963
© 1963 by Barbara Kreutz and Ellen Fleming
Printed and bound in Great Britain by
Cox & Wyman Ltd., Fakenham.
Catalogue number 2/2515/29

Contents

v

Illustrations

MAPS

The maps have been drawn by Denys R. Baker.

Permission has kindly been given for use of photographs as follows:

Air Force Academy, Colorado, plate 10(a); David Barton, plate 16(a); Mrs Ellen Fleming, plate 15(a); Florida State News Bureau, plate 7; Pamela Moore, plate 6(b); The New England Council Inc., plate 2; United States Department of the Interior, National Park Service, plates 12(a), 13(a); United States Information Service, plates 5, 8(a), 9, 10(b).

Plates 3(b), 6(a), 11, 12(b), 13(b), 14(a), 14(b), 16(b) are from photographs by Free Lance Photographers Guild Inc; plate 1 by Fairchild Aerial Surveys, New York; plate 3 (a) by Associated Press Ltd; plate 4 by Pritchard Wood & Partners; plates 8(b), 15 (b) by Camera Press Ltd.

Introduction

America is different. It is not in the least like England, although many of its roots are English. It is not in the least like any other country in Europe, nor is it at all like other places where Europeans have settled. Unless a traveller goes prepared to find a foreign country, he will miss or misunderstand half of the United States.

Many things are done differently in America, and one must not immediately assume that this is a sign of inadequacy or lack of sophistication. Different challenges evoke different responses; what was esteemed a virtue in Boston, Lincolnshire, would perhaps have proved a considerable liability in Boston, Massachusetts. Americans therefore developed an entirely new hierarchy of public virtues and vices, in a manner either Utopian or materialistic, as you choose. And Americans still are either mad idealists or ruthless pragmatists, depending on how you look at them. You may agree with Compton Mackenzie and Mrs Trollope that it was appalling effrontery for nineteenth-century Americans to have called their totally uncivilized frontier outposts 'Athens', 'Syracuse', 'Paris'. Or you may be moved by the dream behind the deed. In any case, Americans are different, sometimes to an infuriating degree.

America is enormous. Into the single state of Texas you could fit the British Isles, Norway, Belgium, and Portugal, and still have room in the corner for Andorra and Lichtenstein. It took wagon trains four months to go to California from the rallying points in Missouri, already a third of the way across the continent; they had to cross almost two thousand miles, including a mountain range vaster than the Alps and day after day of trackless desert. Even now it takes longer to go from New York to California by train than from London to Moscow, or Copenhagen to Athens.

This book is therefore selective. We have tried to include all the most interesting places in the United States, but have had to bypass entire regions as well as several states which lie too far off the beaten path. We make no mention of Alaska or Hawaii, for example, and there are only brief generalizations about many other areas. Here and there we have deliberately omitted a place which we ourselves found disappointing, but many other omissions are simply the result of our need to compress. Anyone who knows and loves some particular corner may feel that we have been unpardonably superficial with his favourite section. We can only plead in return that the United States is altogether too huge and has far too many corners.

Many people on both sides of the Atlantic have generously given time and energy to helping with this book. We cannot hope to mention them all, but we are particularly indebted to Mr and Mrs Louis Benoist, Elizabeth Desan, Alfred France, Margaret Haferd and Sam Yates of the American Embassy in London, John Judkyn and Dallas Pratt of the American Museum at Bath, Somerset, Bertram K. Little of the Society for the Preservation of New England Antiquities, Helen Marshall, Mr and Mrs George Pierce, Dorothy Longaker and Polly Porter.

1 · General Information

CLIMATE

The tremendous size of the country means that there is no such thing as 'the American climate' either literally or figuratively. New Mexico is as unlike Connecticut as Denmark is unlike Greece. And while the weather in the north-eastern quarter of the United States is what is forbiddingly called by geographers 'Manchurian-Appalachian', in Florida and in southern California it is sub-tropical.

The pleasantest times to go to the United States are autumn and spring. October is clear and crisp, the hills and valleys a riot of red and gold. The maple trees in the north-east, and in the Rockies the cottonwood and the aspen, produce a wonderful burst of colour. Spring is lovely too: late March and April in the South, and late April and May in the North. Then is the flowering time for dogwood and redbud, wild lilac in California, and azaleas in the Carolinas.

But if you go in winter, anywhere north of a line running from Washington, D.C., through St Louis, or in the mountains and the high plateau country of the West, be prepared for deep snow and bitterly cold winds. Buffalo, New York, for example, is every bit as cold as Moscow in the winter, and Chicago and New York can be almost as bad. On the other hand, in full summer you must be ready to face really tropical heat, 90°F or more in the cities, very often for days on end. Once you have experienced the extremes of the American climate, you will perhaps understand better some features of American life. Americans walk less than Europeans not only because the distances from point to point are so much greater but also because the weather is so much less conducive to walking. Moreover, people who accustom themselves to heat in the summer then seem to crave it in the winter; hence central heating, very often in excess. Resign yourself, and for the colder months in the northern parts take very warm outer clothing and comparatively light indoor clothing. For the summer, take the sort of clothes one would take for Rome or Spain in July and August, or plan to buy them in the States. In the autumn and the spring, take what one would then want anywhere in Europe, but remember that in the South and in southern California it can sometimes be warm enough to bathe even in mid-winter. And of course in southern Florida it is always bathing weather.

THE STATES UNITED

The geographical and cultural complexity of the United States is compounded by the fact that there are fifty of them. To be sure, they are joined together in a federation; the Constitution shows that. But they are nonetheless quite separate entities. For example, the schools are entirely controlled and almost entirely financed by state and local governments; the standards, even the curricula, vary tremendously from state to state and town to town. In fact, not only is virtually every ordinary function of government seen to by state or city governments rather than the national government, but most of the laws which affect one's everyday life are state rather than national laws.

This means that once you are admitted by the United States immigration officer and cleared by the United States customs man, you will then have little further contact with federal officials. You will note, for example, that aliens who must register their whereabouts each year do so at the post office; it is the only branch of the federal government readily at hand. It is the states who will decide how fast you may drive, and when and where you can have a drink. State legislatures determine which holidays shall be celebrated, how each state's natural resources will be used, even whether or not to permit their courts to impose capital punishment.

The federal government is responsible for matters of common concern such as foreign policy, defence, foreign trade, immigration, the postal service, and ultimately for the national economy and welfare as a whole. In addition it is the federal government which must uphold the Bill of Rights, that section of the Constitution which spells out the civil liberties guaranteed to all Americans. And it is here, with its responsibility for safeguarding the rights of the individual, that the federal government has most often come into conflict with the states. For example, the state governments of the old Confederacy (the Southern side in the Civil War) had segregated school systems, Negro and white. The federal government decided that this was a violation of the Negro children's rights as individual citizens; the federal government therefore brought an action against those states in a federal court. Ultimately the case reached the United States Supreme Court, whose decision in such conflicts is always final. The Supreme Court decided that the civil rights of the Negro children were indeed affected, and to such a degree that the infringement outweighed any legal right the states had to manage their school systems in their own way. The Supreme Court thus decreed that segregation in the schools must cease. However, since no precise time-limit was set, the various Southern states through their state legislatures have now busied themselves trying to side-step the Supreme Court ruling by finding a formula which would permit segregation and yet not come into conflict with the United States Constitution. Quite apart from the moral issues involved, the school-segregation battle has furnished an almost classic example of federal powers and states' rights in America.

TRANSPORT

Perhaps because of the great size of the country, public transport in America has never been adequate by European standards. You can of course get from large city to large city quickly and easily without a car, and it is relatively simple to get about within the larger cities. But the moment you head for a small town not on any direct route between major cities, you are likely to run into difficulties. Moreover, many of the smaller cities lack an adequate city bus system, so once there you must either have a car or take a taxi.

The American businessman's solution to this problem is to fly to a town which he can make his headquarters, and then hire a car to drive himself wherever in that area he wants to go. You can fly almost anywhere in America, and in the larger cities there is even a moderately priced helicopter service available to and from the airports. For travellers who are not on an expense account, however, this combination of planes and hired cars is hardly an economical solution. In order to see what you want in a comparatively short time, you might well have to fly once or twice, and you would want to have a car occasionally, but it must be considered an expensive proceeding, to be planned with care. Mile for mile, flying is cheap in America, but the distances are so great that you are soon out of pocket anyway. Obviously one good rule-of-thumb would be to fly over the longest, dullest stretches of America, and some people will say this means that, going west, you should fly straight from the East Coast to the Rockies. But everyone should travel this distance on the ground just once, in order to comprehend the vastness, the incredible flatness, the special character of the central plains of the United States.

Other than going tourist-class, there are three ways to save money flying in America. One is to see if there are any special bargain rates which might apply: a special round-trip fare, or a 'family plan' arrangement which allows wives and children to travel more cheaply on certain days. Another is either to buy your actual tickets, or to buy an air-fare voucher, before you go to the United States. Like tickets paid for outside the country, the voucher avoids the American travel-taxes, currently 5 per cent of the fare. Once in the States, you simply present it at any airport or ticket office, and they will deduct from it the price of whatever ticket you are then buying. Any unused portion can be refunded when you return home. But you should make sure that the airline ticket man does not, after all, deduct the amount for taxes too.

The third way to save money on air fares is to travel on what are known as the 'supplemental' airlines, which used to be called the 'non-scheduled' airlines. These are small companies which fly older planes on a limited budget. Much of their business comes from chartering planes for special trips, but many of them do now have regularly scheduled passenger flights as well, usually at night, between four or five major American cities. One supplemental airline's flight from New York to San Francisco is not only $30 cheaper but also four hours shorter than a rival economy flight offered by one of the big, recognized airlines. On the other hand the supplemental airlines offer no frills and no 'family plans'; one must carefully weigh all the advantages and disadvantages before deciding which is really the most economical way in any one instance.

With short distances, the time consumed getting to and from the airports can make the overall trip take as long by plane as by express bus or train. But in America, where the distances can be incredible, the time one saves by flying can sometimes matter more than the cost. It takes six hours to fly by jet from New

York to San Francisco, approximately seventy-two hours all-told to go by train, and slightly more again by bus.

Hiring a car in America is far from cheap, unless there are two or three people to share the cost; then it becomes reasonably practical. Yet it would seem a pity not to have a car at least once or twice, to explore in New England, or Colorado, or Louisiana, or to drive along the coast road in California. Some leading car-hire firms, such as Hertz and Avis, have desks at every airport as well as offices in every town of any size. It is often possible to hire a car in one city, drive it as far as you like and leave it there, paying only a fixed extra charge, no matter what the distance. You can almost always be sure of getting some sort of car without a reservation, but it may not be possible to have the cheapest. In many cities there are now 'bargain' car-hire firms, cheaper than Avis or Hertz. Some are completely reliable, but one should always read the contract carefully, and ask questions about the insurance liability coverage.

Massachusetts is the only state in America which refuses legal recognition to foreign driving licences; in Massachusetts a foreign visitor is required to have an International Driving Licence, but this may change soon.

Anyone who contemplates travelling about in America for more than a month or two might seriously consider buying a second-hand car. It can also be sensible for any group of three or four people who would like to cover a lot of ground. Local Better Business Bureaux or Chambers of Commerce will suggest a reliable dealer. It should be possible to buy a perfectly adequate car for about $600, and then sell it again at the end of the trip, probably not losing very much.

When travelling by road, the magnificent turnpikes and 'thru-ways' of the East are well worth the tolls they charge, because they save so much time. There are many free super-highways too, including some which are part of the new federal Interstate Highway system. But all of America is not criss-crossed so splendidly, and while most roads are quite adequate there are, particularly in the West and the South, some back-country roads which are definitely not hard-surfaced. Furthermore, in the West you must take care not to run out of petrol; the towns and the petrol stations can be far apart. And for mountain or desert driving in the summer it is recommended that one should carry extra water for the car. Everywhere, pay attention to the speed restrictions. Some areas are stricter than others, but a fine can be crushing.

For those who want to try camping, general information issued by the National Park Service, and also specific brochures for individual parks, can be obtained from the Travel Section of the American Embassy (Vigo Street, London, W.1).

Americans themselves go camping principally in the West; where the largest National and State parks are to be found. In many places in the West it is possible to hire camping equipment, and some of the National parks have completely equipped cabins. The A.A.A. and Rand McNally both publish comprehensive camping guides to the United States. But National parks are by no means just for campers. Almost all of them have hotels and lodges as well as cabins and camp-sites.

Americans generally camp and picnic only at designated spots; people simply do not stop for the night just anywhere, at least not without making very sure it is allowed. You can picnic along the side of the road, and in some parts of the country this is to be preferred, but there are many regions where the official picnic place is much the most pleasant stopping place for miles, and is therefore supplied with picnic tables, water, litter bins, and public conveniences. In the National and State parks there is no choice; you can camp or picnic only in the special areas.

Visitors who are members of motoring organizations in their own countries are advised to get in touch with the American Automobile Association either before they go to America or after they have arrived (carrying their credentials). The International Travel Department of the A.A.A. is at 250 Park Avenue, New York City; their touring services, camp-site directory and guidebooks are excellent.

A Convention and Visitors Bureau, which provides a full information service, will be found in most towns of any size. In large towns they will probably have their own offices, but in the smaller ones they are often to be found at the local Chamber of Commerce. In the smaller towns the A.A.A. office frequently doubles as a general tourist-information office in association with the local Chamber of Commerce, supplying free city maps and guides. Petrol stations are also good sources of travel information; they are used to providing free road maps and route advice. The best inclusive road map we have found is the Rand McNally Road

Atlas. On the whole, most American maps are less accurate than good European ones, and the road signposting is often downright bad. It is hardly necessary to add that it is wiser for a stranger not to attempt to drive in or out of a big American city during the rush-hour.

One final word about motoring in the United States; in winter, from November to the end of March, there is always the likelihood that snow and ice will make driving hazardous if not impossible in the northern regions. Winter is not the season in which to contemplate a leisurely back-roads drive from Denver to Seattle, for example.

Not all visitors to the United States will want to drive themselves about in a car at any time of the year, and it would be foolish to imply that there is no other agreeable way to see the country. First of all, for those who fancy a guided tour within a city, there is Gray Line (not to be confused with the Greyhound Bus Company), which offers sight-seeing bus tours in all the major cities. In some instances they also run short trips out into the surrounding countryside.

If you are not planning to fly from city to city, there are trains and cross-country buses. The railroads in America are not government-owned, and the various lines differ considerably in the care and attention they lavish on passengers. Generally speaking, the trains in the West are more pleasant than those in the East. You must be prepared for the sorry fact that no railroad runs all the way from New York to California; to get west of the Mississippi, you must always change trains. It takes about eighteen hours to go from New York to Chicago and then another forty-nine hours or so from Chicago on to the west coast.

The majority of the trains which travel overnight have 'Pullmans', which in America specifically means coaches divided into sleeping compartments of varying size and cost. In addition, most of these overnight trains also include 'day coaches', ordinary coaches with unreserved seats only. Naturally there is a vast difference in cost between going 'Pullman' and going 'day coach'. There remains one other form of overnight train travel; some of the railroads have a few express trains which are all 'coach', but of a superior kind. A seat must be booked, and is designed to be more comfortable than the usual type. A journey on this special sort of train is slightly more expensive than the usual 'coach' fare, but it is of course pleasanter, and still much cheaper than going 'Pullman'.

Most American railroads are very generous with their round-trip routings: they will allow you to travel from Chicago to San Francisco, say, by the northern route and come back the southern, swinging in a wide arc both going and coming. You can also make stopovers along the way, and some of the railroads have 'family plans' like the airlines. Finally, it should be noted that rail fares in the East are in some instances double those in the West.

To stay on the ground but travel very inexpensively, one can go by long-distance Greyhound or Trailways bus. (To avoid confusion and adhere to American usage, the term 'coach' is used only to denote coach-type travel by rail or plane.) It would take three and a half days to cross America from east to west on a bus, travelling day and night with brief stops for food and leg-stretching. You would see a great deal of the country, but you would be more dead than alive on arrival. The sensible way to use long-distance buses is to plan your trip so that you travel only during the day, and stop at night in some city you wish to see. The large express buses are very comfortable, and the drivers are courteous and helpful. Luggage not needed in the course of the trip can be checked through to one's ultimate destination, by-passing stopovers. Special rates are sometimes offered to overseas visitors; it can be very much to your advantage to investigate this before going to America, since the bargain vouchers can only be purchased outside the United States.

Unaccompanied luggage can be shipped about the country through R.E.A. Express, which has offices at most railway stations. If you travel by train and take your luggage with you, it is much wiser not to have more than you can carry yourself; station porters are a vanishing breed in America.

Any Greyhound bus station can tell you about all bus schedules anywhere in America. But for air and rail information, it is simplest to go to a travel agent, since there are innumerable competing airlines and railways.

FOOD

In addition to the proper restaurants, there are two other indigenous sorts of eating places in America: the drive-in and the drugstore. Drive-ins are what their name implies; you drive in,

sit in your car, and eat hot sandwiches and the like brought to
you on a tray. Some are good; most are only passable. The
American drugstore probably needs no introduction; it has supplanted the old-fashioned 'general store' as the purveyor of everything to everybody. It is likely to be open from 8 or 9 in the
morning until 9 or 10 at night. Most drugstores have counters
where sandwiches and sometimes entire meals are served,
although their gastronomic speciality traditionally was and is
the milk-shake, the malt, the ice-cream soda and the ice-cream
sundae.

Ordinary restaurants tend to stop serving dinner as early as
eight o'clock at night in the smaller towns, and perhaps at nine
or ten o'clock in the big cities. Like everything else, food is far
more expensive in the East, around New York City, Boston, and
Washington, than it is in the West and the South. Even in the
East, however, with a little extra caution, you can eat three meals
a day for $5. In the West and the South, except for the fanciest
resort areas, $5 a day is ample for food.

Breakfast is almost never included in the price of an American
hotel room, however, in any part of the country. For value
received, it is far and away the most expensive meal in America.
A continental breakfast is, naturally, the least expensive, but even
this can prove costly if it is brought to your room. (In America
things are cheap, but *services* very dear; nowhere is this more
obvious than in an hotel.) It is quite usual for travellers stopping
at hotels to go out for breakfast to a drugstore or a luncheonette.

We have found, in addition to the A.A.A. guides, two reliable
single-volume guides to restaurants: *Duncan Hines* and *Gourmet*.
The first includes more eating places in more cities and towns;
the second is rather more selective.

–AND LODGING

Very few hotels in the United States have a distinct personality of
their own. From coast to coast you will find the same Gideon
Bible, the same 'sanitized' tumbler in a transparent paper bag,
the same imitation Dufy on the wall, the same brochure full of
advertisements for car-hire firms, night clubs, and discreet escort
services.

Hotel prices, of course, cover a wide range. The visitor looking
for good but less expensive rooms in large cities such as New

York, without going far from the centre of town, will have to pick a hotel with care and probably book in advance.

The least expensive but still respectable hotels generally have quite adequate rooms with private bath for $8 for two people, breakfast not included. Hotels of the middle sort, large and conveniently situated but not luxurious or fashionable, can usually supply a double room with bath for $10 or $12. (Few hotels in the big cities have rooms without a private bath.) Very seldom does one have to pay more than $12 for two in order to be perfectly comfortable.

Anyone driving through America should try to sample one really expensive motel, with a swimming pool and tiers of rooms. They are designed to give the tired traveller a delicious sense of luxury. Motels began as a cheaper and less formal substitute for hotels, but over the years their tone and their prices have gone steadily up. Meanwhile the price and the tone of hotel rooms has remained virtually unchanged everywhere but in the largest cities; it is usually considerably cheaper to stay in a hotel in some country town than in a motel. Even a simple unadorned motel will probably charge at least $6, or as much as $10 for two people. The cheaper motels and many small-town hotels will not be found in the A.A.A. guide, for A.A.A. standards are high. The lack of A.A.A. approval may mean the rooms are really dreadful, but on the other hand it may only mean that the place needs paint or there is no air-conditioning. Another inexpensive kind of night's lodging is a room at one of those private houses in the smaller towns which display signs saying 'Tourists' or 'Overnight Guests'; there will be pink-fringed lampshades and a chatty landlady, but the room will probably be both cheap and clean.

In the large cities, the Y.M.C.A. and the Y.W.C.A. usually have rooms available at a modest price. A few accept entire families, but most of them are run for either men or women, but with private rooms, not dormitories. You need not have Y.M.C.A. or Y.W.C.A. connexions in order to stay there, and all sorts of Americans will tell you that there is no pleasanter way to economize. To be sure of a room, however, you should write well ahead of time.

TIPPING

New York City is far and away the most tip-hungry part of America, as well as the most expensive in every other way. Unfortunately, since most visitors go first to New York, they acquire the impression that massive and constant tipping is expected everywhere in America, and this simply is not so. But of course everywhere in America tipping is expected to some extent, for waiters, porters and so on. On the other hand, one never tips at petrol stations, and one neither pays for theatre programmes nor tips the usher. Furthermore, it is becoming less and less usual to tip the chambermaid in an hotel, unless one has stayed a long time or asked for special service. In eating places one leaves the normal 10–15 per cent, but it must never be less than 10¢ (a dime). Only in the New York City area will you be expected to leave a tip at the counter in a luncheonette or a drugstore; in other parts of the country this is optional. For taxi-drivers in New York City a tip of 20¢ or even 25¢ is necessary (25¢ is called a quarter, being a quarter of a dollar.) In other towns the tip can be less, and in some places taxi-drivers charge a flat fee and expect no tip at all. The boy who has carried your suitcase up to your hotel room will be accustomed to getting at least 50¢ in the big cities, 25¢ in the smaller towns, and of course more if there are several cases. The same applies to the 'red cap' who carries your suitcase in a railway station. Most Americans give $1 to the Pullman porter who has taken care of them on an overnight train trip. A nickel, 5¢, is almost never an adequate tip.

MONEY AND BANKING

Credit cards are widely used in the United States to enable goods and services to be obtained on account, which means, among other things, that the traveller need not carry large sums of money about with him. The cards can be used instead of cash for almost anything. Often, if a credit card is used, no deposit will be required: for example, when hiring a car. At present cards issued in the United States are for Americans and Canadians only, but intending visitors should inquire at travel agencies in their own countries about firms issuing cards that they can use in America.

Banks in America usually open at 9.0 a.m., and shut at 2.0 or 2.30 p.m. from Monday to Friday. Some banks are open on

Saturday mornings in some parts of the country. Most banks will change foreign currency or travellers cheques, but if you are planning to use travellers cheques at hotels and motels here and there across the country, it is necessary to have the readily-recognized American Express dollar cheques.

While leading travel agencies have branches in many of the large centres, American Express remains the only nationally-known American travel organization, with offices in most big cities. It should be remembered that some travel offices outside the United States can issue tax-free transportation vouchers for foreign visitors to use during their trip.

Banks in America shut on New Year's Day, Washington's Birthday (22 February), Memorial Day (30 May), 4 July, Labor Day (the first Monday in September), Veterans' Day (11 November), Thanksgiving Day (the last Thursday in November), and Christmas Day. In many states, the banks are also shut on Lincoln's Birthday (12 February), and Columbus Day (12 October). Shops, however, do not celebrate nearly so many holidays; usually they are closed only on New Year's Day, Memorial Day, 4 July, Labor Day, Thanksgiving, and Christmas.

TELEGRAMS AND TELEPHONES

Telegrams are sent at Western Union offices, not at a post office. And you may well need to send telegrams, for letters move slowly in America; the post cannot be relied upon for quick communication.

Public telephones are most commonly to be found in a drugstore; they are known as the 'pay-phone'. For services and shops, consult the invaluable classified 'yellow pages' of the telephone directory. In large cities the 'yellow pages' are bound separately; in smaller towns they are at the back of the ordinary directory.

OTHER CUSTOMS AND CHARACTERISTICS

Electrical fittings are standard all over the United States; the voltage is 110. Cigarettes and tobacco are sold at drugstores, in hotels and restaurants and bars, in vending machines at petrol stations. Men's haircuts are extremely costly.

American terminology differs from British in many instances. For example, in America the ground floor is the 'first floor'; a return ticket is a 'round-trip' ticket; sewing cotton is 'thread' and is to be found in the 'notions' department; cotton wool is simply 'cotton'. 'Broiled' meat is what the British call grilled; an iron-mongers is a 'hardware store'.

In addition to the complications caused by 'daylight saving time' in the summer – complications because it is not everywhere observed – there are four time zones across the country, each one an hour behind the next in the following order: Eastern, Central, Mountain, Pacific.

'Coffee shop' in America does not mean a shop where coffee beans are sold. Instead it is a term usually used to denote the less expensive, less formal eating place in a hotel. It is not the same as 'coffee bar'; real coffee bars, specializing in Italian coffee in exotic combinations, are likely to be found only in the largest cities and the resorts.

Americans always give street directions in terms of so many 'blocks': 'go four blocks east and then turn left', or 'it's at the end of the block'. A block in America means one square of the grid which in most American cities provides the pattern of the streets. Hence 'four blocks east' means 'east to the fourth turning'. Within each American block, you will usually find the odd-numbered buildings on one side of the street, even-numbered on the other. One block will include all houses numbered from 1700 to 1769, for example, and as the numbering commonly jumps 100 at every block, the next block will begin with 1800; the intervening numbers are simply omitted. The visitor should remember that streets in American cities can be enormously long. In this book detailed directions are given where the visitor might otherwise do a great deal of unnecessary walking.

Laundry and dry-cleaning services are relatively inexpensive, good, and quick in the United States. You can always get some-thing washed or cleaned in the course of one day if necessary, and normally two or three days is ample time to allow. Travellers driving through the country find the countless launderettes a great help; most of them are open late into the night. American launderettes usually have no attendant, but the other customers are unfailingly helpful.

There are almost no public lavatories as such in American cities or towns. Instead one repairs to an hotel, to a department store, to a petrol station; but do not ask for the cloakroom or you will run the risk of being told that you may keep your coat with you. The operative word is simply 'ladies' room' or 'men's room'.

HAZARDS

A late-Victorian guidebook solemnly declares that 'Manhattan' is an Indian word meaning 'the place where everybody gets drunk'. The Indians perhaps were looking ahead to the day when unsuspecting foreigners would discover only too late that whisky in America is often 100-proof and that the dry martini there is likely to be at least four parts gin to one part vermouth, and even more potent because it is chilled. But drink can also be a problem in the United States for quite a different reason. Nation-wide Prohibition ended in 1933, but some few states still will not allow wine or spirits to be sold in public places; some will allow it to be sold by the bottle, in shops, but not by the glass; and even in 'wet' states there will be certain 'dry' towns, without bars or liquor stores. In such cities as New York or Boston or Chicago or San Francisco you will never encounter any of these complications, but if you venture into the agricultural states west of the Mississippi or into the South (areas where the non-conformist and Calvinist influence is great), be warned. If you will be desolate without a drink in the evening, you had better carry your own bottle with you into the hinterland.

In America, 'inn' and even 'tavern' do not always imply drink. They are merely designations that seem to Americans to have a pleasant, traditional ring to them, and anyone starting up a country restaurant is likely to call it 'The-Something-Inn'. It may not be licensed, it may well not have rooms for stopping over-night. It will probably have good food with a regional flavour: home-made hot breads in the South, good fish chowder in New England, and so on. The same sort of warning applies to 'tea-rooms' which, if they do tea at all, will do it only incidentally. The inclusion of 'tea' in the name of an eating place is merely to impart a homely quaintness; again, you will probably get a good regional meal, but the place may well be closed at tea-time!

On city buses you will in most cities be expected to board the bus at the front and pay the driver. He is usually harried, having too many jobs to do, and will like you better if you have the correct coin to put in his fare box. If you must hand him a larger coin or a dollar bill, he will simply change your money and give you back the whole amount in silver. You must then yourself abstract the correct fare and put it in the fare box; the driver will not have deducted it. You are usually meant to leave the bus by the rear door; sometimes to open that door you must step down on the inner step.

Anyone who plans to picnic in America or to walk in the woods should learn to recognize poison ivy (*toxicodendron radicans*). It is most often found east of the Mississippi, in woods, on banks, and along fences. It is trifoliate, and characteristically the stem of the centre leaf is longer than the stems of the other two. The leaves are reddish in autumn and spring, shiny and green in summer. It is not to be confused with Virginia creeper, a much more common and perfectly harmless plant whose leaves grow in groups of five instead of three. People vary in their sensitivity to poison ivy, but it may cause a severe, long-lasting and maddening irritation wherever it comes into contact with the skin. A pharmacist can give you various preparations to ease the discomfort; serious cases are best seen by a doctor.

At dusk, mosquitoes become a plague in many parts of the United States. You can, however, buy various sorts of mosquito-repellent, which are quite effective, and indispensable on summer evening picnics.

If you like to know about all possible hazards, you can bear in mind that there are only four sorts of poisonous snakes in America: the coral snake, found only in the South; the water moccasin or cottonmouth (which lives along the rivers but is very shy); the copperhead; and the rattlesnake. Most Americans live and die without ever seeing a poisonous snake, and it is not a danger one should worry about. Some natives of the Southwest say that one should never walk through the desert without high boots because of the rattlesnakes; others, equally experienced, say that this is ridiculous and that they have walked hundreds of miles in isolated country without ever seeing a rattlesnake.

This brings us logically to the subject of medical treatment in the United States. You must not believe all you hear about the astronomic charges of doctors in America. Nevertheless, specialists are expensive and hospital fees high, and it would clearly be a good idea for anyone going to America (as indeed on any trip away from home) to take out a health and accident insurance policy; anywhere, at any time, one can have a sudden illness or be injured.

There is one more hazard in the United States which must be mentioned: 'tourist traps'. America, with its love of extravagant advertising, seems to have more than its share of 'The World's Deepest Cave' and 'The Largest Miniature Village in the Western Hemisphere'. Particularly if you are motoring, you will be confronted endlessly with signs proclaiming the eighth wonder of the world just around the next bend. You must regard these lures as nothing more than that, and not succumb. The sad part of it is that in America one becomes so cynical about much-touted 'sights' that one is likely to resist even so legitimate a claim on the attention as that of the Williamsburg Restorations. (It is told of P. T. Barnum, the great circus impressario, that he once had difficulty getting the crowds to leave his Museum of Marvels so that new crowds could be admitted. Knowing his fellow Americans only too well, he solved the problem by putting up a sign over the exit reading TO THE EGRESS. The people poured out, ever eager for a new attraction.)

VISAS

All visitors to the United States, except Canadians, require a visa. By applying to the American Embassy you can obtain all the relevant details. A non-immigrant visa is free, and is usually valid for four years; and at the end of that time it can be renewed for another four years. In order to enter the United States you will have to have been vaccinated against smallpox within the past three years. When leaving America, anyone there on business will have to fill out a special federal income tax form if he has been in the United States for more than ninety days. Students who want to go to America to take a job during the vacation must apply for an immigrant's visa. This is rather more complicated, and fairly costly, but an identity card can be obtained with the visa, making it possible for a number of visits to be made without reapplying.

LAST WORDS

There is tremendous variety in the United States, and many of the most interesting places are still relatively unknown even to Americans; in a country so huge, no one person can know all of

it well. Even the excellent Federal Writers' Project guides, one
volume written about each state in the 1930's, do not include
everything, and of course for some areas they are now sadly out
of date. You can still be the first to discover, down some country
road in Ohio, the finest 'steamboat Gothic' house of them all, or
a ruined plantation house in the South never noticed by other
travellers. You can do many unusual things: take a week's trip
down the Mississippi in one of the old paddle-wheel steamers, or
go on a windjammer cruise off the coast of Maine, or spend a few
days floating through the Everglades swamp in Florida, to name
only three.

You should try regional American foods, such as steamed
clams, Indian pudding, Maine lobster, and jonnycake in New
England, corn bread, hot biscuits, Virginia ham, melon, tiny
Gulf shrimp, and gumbo in the South, sand dabs, Rex sole,
Chinese peas, fresh dates, fresh figs, Olympia oysters, abalone and
stone crab and the multiplicity of salads in California. If you are
in the Midwest or the West at the end of summer, go to a State
Fair if one is near. They are principally agricultural, but in addition to the farm exhibits and the livestock there are usually harness
races (the horses trot or 'pace', the driver riding in a skeletal
'sulky') and show-jumping. Rodeos small and large occur at
frequent intervals all over the West during the whole summer.
If you are in America in the autumn, you ought to see a college
football game; in the winter, professional ice hockey or basketball. And a night baseball game in the summer can be very
pleasant indeed. Purists prefer their baseball in the daytime, which
is more traditional, but non-Americans might find a ball park in
July or August too hot to bear except in the evening.

With the exception of isolated pockets of French and Spanish
settlements farther west, America had its beginnings wholly along
the eastern coast; almost everything beyond the Mississippi is
very new. You cannot help noticing the immense difference
between New England and California: people dress differently,
speak differently, build differently, eat differently, live differently.
This is partly the old-and-new variation, partly the result of topo-
graphy and climate. And climate has caused other regional
differences. For example, the climate of the South was good for
growing cotton, cotton meant slaves, slavery led to the Civil War
and so the dividing line between North and South east of the

Mississippi, the old Mason-Dixon line, hardened into a barrier which still separates two totally different worlds. Perched at the very edge of the continent, New York City itself is a-typical; like all great ports it is too international, touched by too many currents. Despite many obvious similarities, the various sections of the United States are in their way quite separate worlds, with their own distinct political and social characteristics. It is true that New York City influences the rest of the country, but it is not nearly so much the centre of everything as New Yorkers like to think, or as London is the centre of England and Paris the centre of France. The country is simply too big to have only one centre; you cannot dismiss San Francisco, for instance, as merely a 'provincial' city.

Naturally anyone who is planning a trip to America will be influenced by the time of year he is going and by his own preferences. For history, and the best art and music and theatre, for mellow beauty and a sense of tradition, for ties with Great Britain, one would go to New York and Philadelphia, to New England and to that part of the southern Atlantic coast which lies between Washington and the Florida border. New England is at its best from April to October; the 'old' South is at its best in October and November, March and April.

In the middle of the winter you might choose Florida, or New Orleans with its French and Spanish background, or California, which is actually the one part of the country with an equable climate all the year round. Southern California gets hot in the summer along the coast, and very hot indeed in the central valley, but one can then repair to the near-by mountains or to the region around San Francisco, always a pleasant temperature.

If you should after all find yourself in the eastern part of the United States in the middle of the winter, with no hope of Florida or New Orleans or California, with snow and ice apparently condemning you to be city-bound, we suggest that you somehow get yourself to one of the early-American reconstructions or open-air museums. Williamsburg and Sturbridge are the most complete, and would be the best for a visit in the winter. Like the open-air museums of Scandinavia, they have become a distinct and characteristic part of the American scene, and most of them are in an attractive setting in the country. In the winter they are seldom crowded, and they provide special winter entertainment. The open-air museums, the reconstructions, are not the same thing as Disneyland and the innumerable inferior mock-Disneylands. They are large-scale, historically-accurate recreations of the past which have in most cases been brought to life with the aid of some great foundation or some public-spirited multi-millionaire: the Rockefellers created Williamsburg, and Henry Ford was responsible for Dearborn Village near Detroit. This sort of reconstruction is not operated for profit; the admission fees are only to keep things up. In subsequent chapters we will mention the best ones; otherwise the genuine article has to be distinguished from the commercial imitation by the tone of the advertising.

For spectacular scenery and cowboys and Indians, one goes to the Rockies and to the Southwest. But this is high country, with an early winter and a late spring even at the southern end, only practical to visit from the end of May to the end of October. Even in early June and in October there may be sudden snow and bitter cold. The perfect time for this part of the West is late June and late September, before and after the great rush of tourists but generally safe as to weather.

The Midwest is always considered the most purely American part of the country, and as such it has its own special charm. The great farms and the great industrial centres of this region also make it interesting, and there is surprisingly good art and music in many of the cities.

The ideal itinerary must then include New York City, but it would also include at least a measure of New England, the South, the Midwest, and the West. After that, to be quite perfect, a taste of Alaska and Hawaii, but that is another book.

2 · New York

In the past, travellers had a wide choice of American ports from which to begin their tour of the United States. They could sail not only to New York, but to Boston or to Baltimore, to Charleston in South Carolina, or straight to New Orleans like the redoubtable Mrs Trollope. Nowadays one can indeed fly directly to all the largest centres, even from Europe to California over the Pole. But most visitors today start at New York City, and if they travel by ship the first thing they see against the breathtaking skyline of Manhattan is the Statue of Liberty, standing on an island in New York harbour, a gift to the United States from France in 1883. You may never come any closer to the Statue of Liberty than at this first glimpse, but remember her. She is significant.

Every American schoolchild used to memorize the poem inscribed at the base of the statue:

> *Give me your tired, your poor,*
> *Your huddled masses yearning to breathe free,*
> *The wretched refuse of your teeming shore,*
> *Send these, the homeless, tempest-tossed to me;*
> *I lift my lamp beside the golden door.*

Reciting the poem, he saw millions of ragged, bewildered refugees from a harsher world across the Atlantic, sailing boat-load after cramped boat-load into New York harbour to begin a new life with new hope, new happiness, in the United States. Never mind that for far too many of the immigrants, life turned out to be pitifully difficult in the New World as well. The Statue of Liberty symbolizes, for Americans, the concept of the United States as a place of refuge and freedom, of opportunity for the downtrodden of the world. The fact that it is possibly easier for the proverbial camel to squeeze through a needle's eye than for most immigrants to get into the United States these days is irrelevant too. The very people who are the most ardent supporters of the current immigration restrictions like best to talk about America as the historic sanctuary of the oppressed. Which is the more significant: what we are or what we believe ourselves to be?

You should think of all this when you see the Statue of Liberty, and it should remind you that only about one-third of the blood flowing through American veins today is actually British. In fact, the English were not even the first settlers. The Spanish were in Florida and in the American Southwest before the first English colonists came to the Atlantic coast, and the evidence is still plain; the architecture and the atmosphere of Texas, Arizona, New Mexico and California are certainly not in the least English. The French were busy too, leaving marked traces in the way of French place-names and family names and, even today, pockets of French-speaking people remain along the eastern Canadian border and near New Orleans. Then there were the Dutch who settled in New York City and the Hudson River Valley, and those Germans who came into the Pennsylvania area early in the eighteenth century (and became known as 'Pennsylvania Dutch'). And the Negro: the first recorded slave-ship reached the Jamestown settlement in Virginia in 1619. From then on the slave trade grew until in 1776 there were perhaps half a million Negroes in the United States; their importation was made illegal in 1807, but 'black-birders' continued to smuggle them in.

Of even greater importance, so far as the heritage of the average American of today is concerned, was the great wave of immigration in the nineteenth century. The first to come then were the Irish, who began to cross over in large numbers at the time of the Potato Famine (1845–6). Next came a new wave of Germans, particularly as a result of the social and political upheavals of 1848 in Europe; many of these German immigrants were men of considerable education, who brought with them strong ideas about the way citizens and governments should conduct themselves, quite unlike the earlier German groups, mostly simple, pious farmers. German Jews arrived at this time too, and a good many French political refugees. The general tendency of all of the immigration from Germany and France in this period was to raise the cultural sights of the communities in which these immigrants settled, particularly when they moved westward, where they added a new sophistication to several rough frontier towns. Scandinavians began to immigrate; most of them headed for what are today the states of Minnesota and Wisconsin, Iowa and

Nebraska and the Dakotas; rich farming country now, but only vast, lonely plains before these hardworking settlers arrived. After the American Civil War (1860–5) the great swell of immigration from Southern and Eastern Europe rolled in, until in the years before the First World War 2,500 immigrants a day were entering the United States: Italians and Sicilians; Slavs, Croats; Jews from Poland and from Russia.

The lot of the immigrants varied tremendously. Yet no matter how grim things were, there was always at least the sustaining idea that every hardship was worthwhile because life would be better here for their children. And by and large the next generation did achieve the sort of success and security they could never have dreamed of in the 'old country'.

You must remember all of this as you walk around New York City, and later as you travel through America. The reminders of America's English heritage are everywhere, but you can never understand the United States unless you are also conscious of all the other influences at work.

On your first day you might well begin by going to the top of the Empire State Building to see how New York City looks from above. There are two special observation areas, one on the 86th floor and one on the 102nd; the tickets are not cheap, but unless you are very hard-pressed it is worth the money.

New York City is actually made up of five boroughs: Queens, Brooklyn, The Bronx, Richmond, and Manhattan. However Manhattan is what most people have in mind when they talk about New York City. It has always been the centre of things. It was Manhattan Island that the canny Dutch bought from the Indians in 1624 for the equivalent of twenty-four dollars, thus establishing a Dutch colony which spread up the Hudson River and remained thoroughly Dutch in spirit long after the British assumed control in 1664. Manhattan is indeed an island, with the Hudson River on the west, the East River on the east, the Harlem River and the Spuyten Duyvil Creek to the north, and the harbour to the south. All of these rivers are easily visible, with the exception of the northernmost one, more than five miles beyond Central Park. Queens and Brooklyn are part of New York City, but lie east of Manhattan, side by side on the western edge of Long Island. The borough of Richmond is really Staten Island, in the harbour

1 Lower Manhattan, New York

2 The Green, Lexington, Massachusetts

beyond the Statue of Liberty. The Bronx is the only part of New York City actually on the mainland; beyond it stretch Westchester County and the way to New England.

The bridges connect Manhattan not only with the state of New Jersey, but also with three of these other metropolitan boroughs; before the bridges, there were only ferries. The Brooklyn Bridge was the first to be built, the first great suspension bridge in the world (1883), picturesque and impressive even today; from the Brooklyn end, in Brooklyn Heights, one has the most famous view of the Manhattan skyline. The George Washington Bridge (to New Jersey) is perhaps the most beautiful. The Triborough Bridge, as its name indicates, connects three boroughs: Manhattan, Queens and The Bronx.

There are other links between Manhattan and the surrounding area which you cannot see: the Lincoln and the Holland Tunnels go under the Hudson River to New Jersey south of the George Washington Bridge. The new Brooklyn-Battery Tunnel connects Brooklyn with lower Manhattan, and the Queens-Midtown Tunnel runs from Queens to Manhattan near the United Nations.

Look too at Central Park, its southern edge fringed by the most expensive shops and hotels in the city. To the east of it lies the most expensive residential section. Near the south-west corner the Lincoln Center for the Performing Arts is rising in an area made available through slum-clearance. It will provide a new Metropolitan Opera House, two theatres, and a concert hall, in a great complex of contemporary buildings designed by America's leading architects. Away to the north, at the top of Central Park, is Harlem, with Columbia University an oasis in the midst of it on the west side.

Fifth Avenue runs along the east side of Central Park, and then continues south until it ends at Washington Square. The other main north-south streets are also 'avenues', beginning with First Avenue near the East River. The cross-streets (when you go from east to west or vice versa it is called going 'cross-town') are also numerically designated but are called 'streets', beginning with First Street just a bit below Washington Square and continuing north until one finally reaches 220th Street at the uppermost tip of Manhattan. One speaks of east or west in Manhattan in relation to Fifth Avenue. 'Uptown' is north, 'downtown' south.

Now look south, at the tip of Manhattan Island, the one area

c

in which the streets are not arranged according to the tidy grid
system so characteristic of the rest of the city. That is where New
York City began; where the first Dutch settlers had their houses
and farms. As in London, the financial district has remained in the
oldest part; Wall Street was once an actual wall, separating the
tiny Dutch settlement from the wilderness to the north. The
village in those days was called New Amsterdam. It was controlled by the Dutch West India Company from 1626, when
Peter Minuit, the first governor, bought it from the Indians, until
1664 when the last Dutch governor, the irascible Peter Stuyvesant,
watched in helpless rage as the townspeople surrendered to the
British without firing a shot. The British forces had been dispatched by the future James II, then Duke of York, to whom
Charles II had graciously granted a sizeable chunk of America,
including land the British did not really own. Apparently the
New Amsterdam burghers felt that any new ruler was bound to
be preferable to the interfering, domineering Stuyvesant, but
today the proudest old New York families are those, like the
Roosevelts, who can trace their ancestry back to the original
Dutch settlers.

A little to the north of the financial district are the city government buildings. You can probably see City Hall Park, and just
to the south-west of it the Woolworth Building, the first of New
York's great skyscrapers. It was the tallest from 1913, when it was
built, until 1929, when the Chrysler Building went up.

Down there too is the Bowery, in the mid-nineteenth century
the roaring centre of the theatre and music-hall district, but latterly
only the bleak last refuge of down-and-outers. In the beginning it
had been an Indian trail, and later acquired its name as the path
leading to Peter Stuyvesant's farm (*bouwerij*). To the east of the
Bowery lies what is known as the Lower East Side. As fashionable
New York moved north in the early nineteenth century, the
immigrants poured into this part of Manhattan. The Irish and the
Germans now have vanished from there almost without a trace.
But the Italian section and the Jewish section and the Polish section and 'Chinatown' on the other side of the Bowery are still
there, even if they are no longer as distinct or as colourful as they
once were. And now a new wave of immigrants has washed over
the Lower East Side, this time of Puerto Ricans, so that the old
Slav and Jewish and Italian and Chinese shops today sport signs

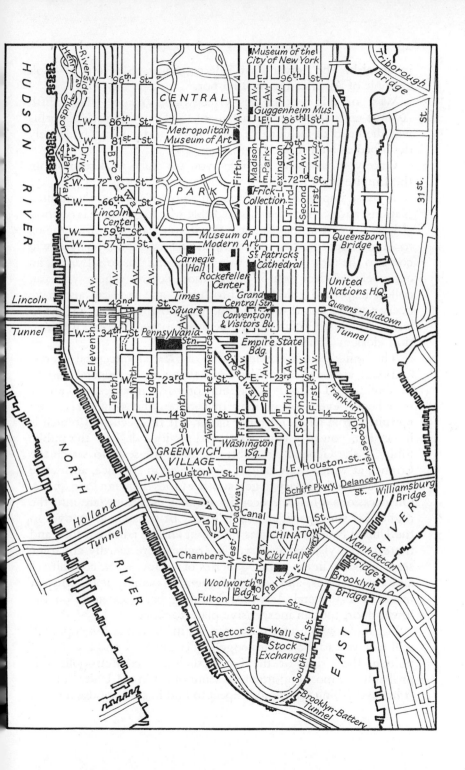

in Spanish. The Lower East Side continues to be a copy-book example of America-the-melting-pot.

West of this section lies Greenwich Village, where Fifth Avenue ends at Washington Square. In Henry James's day this was the heart of fashionable New York; today it can be loosely described as New York's Left Bank.

Once you have your bearings, you are ready to descend from the Empire State Building and plunge into the city.

A most important 'sight' on any visitor's list is the United Nations, and perhaps the most sensible way to get there is on foot, at least for part of the distance. For if you walk up Fifth Avenue to 42nd Street and then turn right, at 90 East 42nd Street you will come to the New York City Convention and Visitors Bureau, an extremely efficient tourist-information centre. There you can collect maps and guides and brochures, and you can also have every possible question answered, from how to charter a plane to where to buy chocolate ants. There is another, smaller, information kiosk at Times Square.

The United Nations buildings are of great architectural interest and there are excellent guided tours through the General Assembly building. The tours last about forty-five minutes, and a new tour begins every ten minutes or so; the guides themselves are recruited from all the member nations. If the Security Council is in session, you may apply at the admissions desk in the public lobby of the General Assembly Building for seats to watch the Council at work. Seats cannot be reserved in advance, and while they are sometimes easy to get, at other times there is a long queue. On occasions when the Security Council is sitting late into the night over some particular crisis it may be possible to go over to the United Nations as late as midnight and be admitted then and there to the visitors' gallery. Otherwise there usually are some seats available in the public galleries of various U.N. committees and commissions, and for the General Assembly itself when it meets. The General Assembly Building has a cafeteria on the lower floor, too: an inexpensive place for lunch.

For those who prefer museums, a Fifth Avenue bus 'uptown' will take you to the eastern edge of Central Park and the Metropolitan, the Frick, or the Guggenheim. The Metropolitan is probably the most important museum of art in the United States. It has everything one would expect to find in such a museum, and more. For example, in addition to the incomparable collection of European paintings, there is also a magnificent display of arms and armour. The Metropolitan has a fine collection of American painting, and in the American wing a series of reconstructed rooms illustrating the development of the decorative arts in America from the beginnings to the early part of the nineteenth century; this should not be missed. The Metropolitan also has a very pleasant restaurant for lunch or tea.

The Frick is a private collection made public, and must be one of the most charming small museums in the world. Henry Frick was the son of a German immigrant; an associate of Andrew Carnegie, he made a fortune in coal and steel. He had no children, and when he died he left his house and his pictures in trust, to be made available to the public. The house itself was built in that period just before the First World War when American architects seemed at last able to combine the desired feudal grandeur with beauty and utility; the most handsome great houses all date from that time, while those built twenty or thirty years earlier were often monstrous. Thus not only is the collection superb but the surroundings are delightful. In winter there are chamber-music concerts at the Frick.

The Guggenheim is famous as Frank Lloyd Wright's last major project. Devoted to contemporary art, it was opened in 1959, and while its collection is not as remarkable as others in New York City, it is well worth going to see for the sake of the building. Many people think it more successful inside than out, and the interior should not be missed.

The Empire State Building, the United Nations, and perhaps a museum are more than enough for one day, and the visitor will now be thinking about dinner. Meals in New York can be more expensive than anywhere in the world, or they can be very cheap indeed. A drugstore or any of the countless luncheonettes or cafeterias will feed you inexpensively; one good chain of 'quick lunch' places boasts the unwieldy name of Chock Full o' Nuts, and another, Prexy's, proudly claims 'the hamburger with the college education'. There are also the Horn and Hardart Automats, which resemble the *automaats* in Holland. The New York variety is somewhat more spacious, but as in Holland, you choose your food by peering through innumerable tiny glass doors; then you put the requisite number of nickels into the appropriate slots and the little glass door flies open so that you can take out your dish. You will not have an elegant dinner that way but neither will you spend very much, and of course it is very quick. If what you want is good American food at moderate prices, you might try one of the Schrafft's chain of restaurants. For a more elaborate or unusual dinner, consult *Cue*, which is published every week and is to be found on every news-stand. *Cue* gives information about all the cinemas, theatres and sporting events, and also includes a long list of restaurants with an indication of their prices.

After dinner, what? In most New York theatres, the curtain goes up at 8.40 p.m. Tickets for hit Broadway plays and musical comedies are usually impossible to get at short notice, but there are almost always some interesting plays being done 'off-Broadway'. Off-Broadway usually means in Greenwich Village. It also implies a limited budget, and experimentation with new forms and new ideas. This is not a new development in Greenwich Village: in the early 1920's the Provincetown Players gave the plays of Eugene O'Neill their first noteworthy productions there and changed the course of the American theatre. Off-Broadway theatres are not known for their comfort, but their smallness and intimacy gives them certain advantages, and their prices are pleasantly low in comparison to those of Broadway. Moreover, as Broadway productions have become more and more expensive and the Broadway managements less and less able to take risks, off-Broadway has become increasingly important not only as a testing ground for new playwrights but also as guardian of the theatre's past. Only there is one likely to find Shakespeare or Brecht or Chekhov being done in New York today. And since good plays and good roles tempt the best actors and producers, remarkable people contribute now to the off-Broadway theatre.

As well as the theatre, there is music. No city in the world offers greater musical riches than New York in the autumn and winter. Among the most obvious attractions are the Metropolitan Opera, due to move to its new home in Lincoln Center at the end of 1963, and the New York Philharmonic, with Leonard Bernstein its conductor, which has already moved to Lincoln Center from its traditional base at Carnegie Hall. In addition to the Metropolitan Opera season, there is opera at the City Center, more experimental and not so elaborately mounted. It is frequently delightful, but an even more celebrated tenant at City Center is the New York City Ballet, which has become America's finest ballet company with George Balanchine as its director and principal choreographer. In the summer in New York, there is usually no ballet and no opera, but there are open-air concerts then, at Lewisohn Stadium in The Bronx, and free open-air Shakespeare in Central Park.

There are in New York two other sorts of evening entertainment particularly characteristic of America: the jazz club and the supper club. These are not clubs in the usual sense: you do not have to be a member to get in. Nor do you have to have dinner there in order to watch the entertainment; in fact some of the places called 'supper clubs' serve only sandwiches and savouries. The jazz club is simply a bar or restaurant with good jazz as its attraction. The supper club is a form of cabaret; usually the star will be a monologuist like Mort Sahl or Shelley Berman, but sometimes there will be an entire small revue with satiric sketches and music.

Instead of a theatre or a night club, one can of course simply go on sight-seeing at night. From April to October there are fascinating trips all round Manhattan by boat, run by both the Circle Line and the Hudson River Day Line. Most of the trips are by daylight, but from late June to early September there is usually an additional one which starts as late as six in the evening. Since the trip lasts for three hours and darkness falls comparatively early in these latitudes, by the end the whole of Manhattan is shimmering with light.

You must of course see Times Square at the heart of the Broadway theatre and cinema district, which is tawdry by day but bursts into spectacular bloom by night. With the cascading fountains of light, the flashing, the colours, this is Chesterton's 'glorious garden of wonders . . . for anyone lucky enough to be unable to read'. Over the years it has become even more luxuriant. With Rockefeller Center, the United Nations, the Empire State Building, and the view of New York from the harbour, Times Square at night is something every visitor should see.

It is not only the bright lights that fascinate. The crowds themselves are endlessly diverting, the shops remain open until midnight, and there is frenzied activity in restaurant windows where doughnuts and pancakes and hamburgers and waffles are tossed and turned and fried and grilled before your very eyes.

Even a visitor with only two days in New York will want to spend part of one day in the vicinity of Rockefeller Center. This great complex of buildings on Fifth Avenue somehow typifies New York, and its central plaza is a delightful place to sit on a fine day. There are restaurants on either side of the plaza, and in summer one can eat at tables out of doors. In winter the central court is flooded and frozen for skating, and there is no pleasanter place for a leisurely Sunday breakfast than in the English Grill at a table by the window from which one can watch the skaters. One more among the many restaurants in Rockefeller Center which should be particularly mentioned is the Rainbow Room, high up in the R.C.A. Building. It is a fairly expensive place to dine, but one can also go up there for a drink before dinner, to enjoy the view. Rockefeller Center has a regular Observation Roof, and there are guided tours of the Center from nine in the morning to nine at night.

N.B.C., one of the three principal television and radio networks in America, has its headquarters in the R.C.A. Building; there are guided tours of the studios, and on the street level of the R.C.A. Building is the Exhibition Hall, full of gadgets including a device which enables you to see yourself on colour television. Recently the General Dynamics Corporation has also opened a scientific-historical exhibit, called 'Dynamic America', in its building in the Center.

On the Sixth Avenue side of Rockefeller Center is Radio City Music Hall, the largest cinema in the world, where the Rockettes high-step with guards-like precision in the flamboyant but innocent stage spectacles which accompany the films. At the other extreme, directly across Fifth Avenue from Rockefeller Center is St Patrick's Cathedral, the best-known and largest Roman Catholic church in the United States. And just north of Rockefeller Center is St Thomas' church, the most elegant Episcopal church in New York, superb imitation Gothic.

When you are at Rockefeller Center, Manhattan looks very prosperous. As an 1885 *Englishman's Guide to the United States* engagingly observed, 'The sights along Fifth Avenue must impress upon visitors from the old world the marvellous strides in the refinements of civilization America is continually making.'

With the exception of Lord & Taylor's at 38th Street, all the smartest large stores are on Fifth Avenue between Rockefeller Center and Central Park, and the cross-streets here, to the east of Fifth Avenue, have most of the expensive boutiques.

Everyone ought to window-shop along Fifth Avenue, but you might also bear in mind that the best museums for contemporary art and design are in this area as well as the best shops. The largest, the Museum of Modern Art, houses New York's most comprehensive collection of contemporary art and design. In the summer one can have lunch or tea very pleasantly in the Museum garden, and every day there is a showing of some film classic in the Museum cinema.

Back to back with the Museum of Modern Art is the Whitney Museum, solely devoted to contemporary American art. The Whitney 'annual' is New York's most celebrated showing of what is new (and currently favoured) in American painting and sculpture.

The Museum of Contemporary Crafts is just past the Museum of Modern Art, and the Museum of Primitive Art is almost opposite the Whitney. Both of these are striking new museums, which owe their existence to Rockefeller enthusiasms. Incidentally, contemporary American crafts are for sale at America House, a delightful shop across the street from the Museum of Modern Art. For other galleries and museums in the city *The New Yorker* provides an invaluable list.

Sometime during your stay in New York, perhaps after shopping along Fifth Avenue, walk east to Park Avenue. Here, on a street once famous only for the wealth of the people who lived there, are several of the most dramatic office buildings in America, including the Seagram building (Mies van der Rohe and Philip Johnson) at Park Avenue and 53rd Street, and at 54th Street, Lever House (Skidmore, Owings & Merrill). The Four Seasons, one of New York's most elaborate and expensive restaurants, is in the Seagram Building.

Beyond Park Avenue and Lexington Avenue comes Third Avenue. Third Avenue used to have an elevated railway and was dark and dingy; since the 'el' has been torn down Third Avenue has brightened noticeably, and now it has all sorts of smart little shops, roughly between 45th Street and 58th. You may not want to make a special trip all the way over to Third Avenue just to walk along it, but you might have dinner one night in one of the good French restaurants in that area.

Most visitors will probably spend the major share of their time in central Manhattan, but they will certainly want to make one or two expeditions to other parts of the city, and so on your second or third day in New York we suggest that you begin by taking a subway (underground train) to Wall Street. You can get there by bus (the Avenue of the Americas line) but it is a rather long and not remarkably interesting trip.

Wall Street is of course the heart of the financial district. The New York Stock Exchange (not to be confused with the smaller American Stock Exchange) is there, just east of Broadway; it has a visitors' gallery. The United States Treasury Building is almost opposite, at Wall and Broad Streets. It stands on the site of Federal Hall, the scene of the Stamp Act Congress, that first colonial protest gathering which antedated the Revolution by eleven years. Here too Washington was inaugurated, the Bill of Rights passed, and the Supreme Court organized. Now all that remains is a sad little museum beneath the stately entrance to the Treasury Building.

Most of the city's principal banks have their head offices on or near Wall Street. In the United States you will notice that every city and town has its own independent banks, connected and controlled only through the government's Federal Reserve Banking system. The major New York City banks, however, exert an undeniable influence on banking policies throughout the country.

Facing Wall Street, on Broadway, is Trinity Church, a dark Victorian Gothic building now dwarfed by the skyscrapers around it. There are of course hundreds of churches in New York City, but most of them are neither very old nor very new, and few have any marked architectural or historical significance. Trinity Church is one of the few which does warrant attention, both because of its situation and because of its historical associations. Many illustrious Americans lie buried in Trinity churchyard: Alexander Hamilton and Robert Fulton are probably the two whose names mean most today. Hamilton was the illegitimate son of a West Indies planter; he came to New York before the Revolution, married into one of the richest and most influential old Dutch families, and during the war made a splendid record as aide

to General Washington. Brilliant and strong-willed, he put the
young republic on its feet financially after the Revolution, but he
made implacable enemies on both Left and Right, and in 1804 was
killed in a duel with Aaron Burr.

Robert Fulton, ten years younger, was America's most interesting and original scientist after his fellow-Pennsylvanian, Benjamin
Franklin. As a young man he went to London to study portrait
painting with his compatriot Benjamin West, and there he met the
Duke of Bridgewater and James Watt and was induced to abandon art for engineering. At the turn of the century he was to be
found in Paris, experimenting in the Seine with his missile-firing
submarine *Nautilus*; but no one was interested. Finally, he
devoted himself to the work for which he is remembered today,
steam-driven boats, and in 1807 he saw his first steamboat, the
Clermont, start scheduled runs on the Hudson River between New
York City and Albany.

From Wall Street, one has a choice of at least three interesting
further explorations; on south to the Battery and a boat ride,
across the river to Brooklyn Heights, or back to mid-town Manhattan by way of City Hall and Greenwich Village.

If one opts for the Battery and a boat ride, one might walk to
Battery Park in a slightly roundabout manner in order to pass
Fraunces Tavern at the corner of Pearl Street and Broad Street.
The most notable pre-Revolutionary building in this part of the
city, this was first a house, built in 1719. In 1762 it became an inn,
and during the Revolution, while British troops occupied New
York, Black Sam Fraunces, the inn-keeper, made his hostelry the
rebels' best listening-post in Manhattan. Perhaps it was for this
reason that George Washington chose Fraunces Tavern for the
gathering which constituted his formal farewell to his officers at
the end of the Revolution. Fraunces Tavern today is still an eating
place, but the interior of the building is much altered.

Battery Park is in every respect the beginning of Manhattan;
it was here that Peter Minuit concluded his bargain with the
Indians for the island in 1626. It is a pleasant place to sit and
watch the ships, and it is also the embarkation point for the
Statue of Liberty boats and the Staten Island ferries.

One assumes that the beauty of Manhattan is its superb func-
tionalism, the purity of line of its tall buildings massed against
the sky. But this is not all; the very situation of the city is peculiarly

lovely. One hundred and thirty years ago, the usually acid Mrs Trollope was moved to say, 'I have never seen the bay of Naples . . . but my imagination is incapable of conceiving anything of the kind more beautiful than the harbour of New York . . . it rises, like Venice, from the sea, and like that fairest of cities in the days of her glory, receives into its lap tribute of all the riches of the earth.'

Boats leave for the Statue of Liberty every few minutes from nine to five in the summer, nine to four in the winter. The round trip, including a climb up into the statue, takes a little over an hour.

Ferries for Staten Island also go frequently, and the ride there and back is one of New York's greatest bargains. Staten Island is the Borough of Richmond, and it is pleasant to see a borough other than Manhattan. But while Staten Island is astonishingly rural in parts, and rich in lore, it is hard to see the most interesting parts of the island unless one has either a car or a considerable amount of time.

For a more limited exploration of another borough, you might take the subway (IRT line) from Wall Street to Brooklyn Heights, a once-fashionable section of Brooklyn now being rediscovered as a highly desirable place to live. All Brooklyn-bound IRT trains stop at Clark Street, the station for Brooklyn Heights. When you emerge into the street you will see part of the Brooklyn Bridge to the north. Walking towards it along Henry Street you will come almost immediately to Pineapple Street, where you can begin a serpentine trail which will show you a charming section of New York in the course of an hour's pleasant stroll, turning left at Pineapple Street, and then interweaving Hicks Street, Orange, Willow, and then Pineapple again.

On Orange Street still stands the Plymouth Church of the Pilgrims, famous all over America in the nineteenth century. The minister was Henry Ward Beecher, of a distinguished New England family; his sister was Harriet Beecher Stowe, author of *Uncle Tom's Cabin*.

At 13 Pineapple Street stands what must be the most pleasant old wooden house still to be found within sight of Manhattan, and with a delightful garden too. A few steps beyond it is the Esplanade, and here you should turn to the left, to go south along this charming walk to Pierrepont; but it is nice to sit on a bench for a while, to look at Manhattan across the river, and the boats coming and going. At Pierrepont you must leave the Esplanade (which becomes less interesting farther on) and head east to Willow Street. Along the block between Pierrepont and Clark on Willow Street are several particularly nice old houses. Prosperous merchants and shipowners lived in Brooklyn Heights a hundred or more years ago and there are a great many houses well worth restoring to their former glory.

The Botanical Gardens in Brooklyn are lovely, particularly in the spring when their remarkable cherry trees are in bloom. After exploring in Brooklyn Heights you could go on to see the Gardens by taking a train (subway) on to the Brooklyn Museum stop; the museum too is a good one, with a comprehensive collection which includes some fine pictures and a section devoted to American furniture and decoration.

A third choice of routes from Wall Street is to go back up Broadway towards central Manhattan. On Broadway, between Fulton and Vesey Streets, is St Paul's Chapel of Trinity Church, built in 1764 by a pupil of James Gibbs, the architect of St Martin-in-the-Fields in London. It is the oldest church still standing in Manhattan; its parent, Trinity Church, represents an older foundation (1697) but the original building burned to the ground and the present Trinity Church only dates from 1846. The official services following George Washington's first inauguration as President were held at St Paul's, and like Trinity Church it has innumerable other historical associations. It gives the peculiar impression of being St Martin-in-the-Fields dipped in chocolate, and the bonbon effect continues inside, where the succulent pastel colours of the walls suggest sugar-coating.

Just beyond St Paul's Chapel is City Hall Park, and on the other side of the park is City Hall itself. Neither City Hall nor St Paul's Chapel is commonly found in a list of famous New York sights; both deserve more attention than they ordinarily receive.

City Hall was begun in 1803, designed by a Scots-American named McComb. It is a rather unusual combination of disparate styles and materials, but is beautifully proportioned and altogether charming. On the ground floor is the headquarters of New York's city government; the Mayor's offices are here. Since the Mayor of New York has one of the most arduous jobs in the United States, and since New York City is always teetering between scandal and reform, the environs of the Mayor's office can be a fascinating place to loiter.

But the proper excuse for visiting City Hall is to see the state rooms on the floor above: the Governor's Rooms and the Council Chamber. The Governor's Rooms are at the head of the handsome circular staircase; the Governor of the State of New York uses these rooms on his official visits to the city. Most of the furniture was brought here from Federal Hall when that building was torn down: there are the desks of the first four Presidents of the United States, silver andirons cast by Paul Revere, and a splendid group of Trumbull portraits. Round the bend of the stairwell from the Governor's Rooms is the very handsome Council Chamber.

Continuing north from City Hall Park by bus along either Lafayette Street or Broadway, Chinatown, Skid Row, and the Lower East Side are to the right. To really see Chinatown, it is best to walk north-east from City Hall along Park Row until you come to Mott Street. Along Mott Street, and on Pell and Bayard which cross Mott, and along Doyers Street, is Chinatown. It is much smaller and not nearly so interesting as the Chinatown in San Francisco; New York's Chinatown seems less genuine, more for tourists, although there are sure to be some who will contest this. In any case, it has some pleasant Chinese restaurants as well as the usual shops.

A bus from the eastern edge of Chinatown will take you north up the Bowery, crossing Houston Street, which goes east into the centre of the old Lower East Side. The Bowery itself, along here, is Skid Row.

Above Cooper Square Park, at Astor Place, is Cooper Union, founded in 1859 as a technical college for poor boys, as an adult education centre, and to provide a forum for free and open discussion of all matters of public concern. It still fulfils all three functions, but the most notable speech ever delivered there was by Abraham Lincoln in the spring of 1860. Lincoln had at that time a considerable following in his native Middle West, but he was relatively unknown in the rest of the country. At the same time, the Republican Party was searching desperately for a man they could all agree on for their Presidential candidate in the autumn election: a man whom both the abolitionists and the moderates could trust. The Civil War was actually to break out within the year; already the controversy was intense. At this moment Lincoln came to speak at the new Cooper Union, and a great many of the influential people in the East came to hear him. The audience seem to have expected a very rough diamond, a clownish backwoods lawyer; instead they found a composed and confident statesman. If any single event can be said to have determined Lincoln's nomination, it was that speech.

From Astor Place it is only a short walk to the northern end of Washington Square, the heart of Greenwich Village. The Village is at its best in the late afternoon and evening; many of its shops are shut in the morning and open half the night. Places in the Village are also likely to be open on Saturday, and perhaps even on Sunday, but closed on Monday. Except on a Monday it is a good district for eating; many of the restaurants are Italian and most of them are relatively inexpensive.

At the time of the American Revolution, Washington Square was not only a potters' field but also the site of most public hanging. Later it was turned into a park, and slowly but steadily well-to-do New Yorkers began to build around it, until in the 1880's there was no more elegant address than Washington Square. Today the streets to the west are bustling with coffee bars, contemporary art and artifacts, exotic clothes shops, the best and the worst of modern design in America. On Sunday afternoons folk-singers congregate around the fountain in the centre of the square; their singing may be more earnest than authentic, but they are fun to see.

For a short walking tour of the Village, one might begin by going west along the northern edge of Washington Square, past the last of the elegant houses, to Macdougal Street. Turning right you will come almost immediately to Macdougal Alley, the smart mews behind those elegant houses. The next street to the north is West 8th Street, with several typical Village shops near the corner, but after a quick glance around, turn back and return along Macdougal Street to the Square, and then on beyond it. The purest essence-of-Village is to be found in the streets just to the south-west of Washington Square: off-Broadway theatres, shops selling sandals and Mexican baskets and esoteric paper-back books and the 'little' magazines.

Much of the area around Washington Square, particularly on the eastern fringe, is today part of New York University, N.Y.U.

This is one of the largest privately-supported universities in America, and one of the best, perhaps not as well known in other parts of the world as it deserves.

From Washington Square it is an easy trip on a Fifth Avenue bus back to midtown Manhattan.

Obviously, there are any number of other things to do and see in and around New York. No one guidebook can hope to include them all, and tastes differ. We have not even mentioned four of the most interesting museums: the Museum of Natural History with its dramatic African exhibits and the dioramas of American Indian villages and pueblos; the Museum of the American Indian with its own definitive collection; the delightful Museum of the City of New York, a light-hearted revelation of New York's past; and the Cloisters. The latter is under the aegis of the Metropolitan Museum and consists of parts of several medieval French and Spanish monastic buildings skilfully reassembled, complete with sculpture and tapestries, in a park on the heights of northernmost Manhattan overlooking the Hudson River. No doubt because each is so perfect of its kind, the Cloisters and the Frick tend to be the connoisseur's favourite New York museums.

You can take a helicopter ride over Manhattan; you can see Harlem by taking a number 2, 3 or 4 Fifth Avenue bus north all the way to Lenox Avenue, and then exploring from there. There are innumerable quasi-Disneylands in America; New York's is Freedomland in The Bronx. Its theme is American history, with stagecoach rides, a reconstruction of a mining camp, canoe trips past mock Indian villages, and a jouncing ride in an open mule wagon 'between the lines in the Civil War'. Freedomland is not as elaborate as Disneyland, but it is better than some of the other imitations and is amusing for children. There is also Coney Island, the giant amusement park at the far side of Brooklyn, and Palisades Park, a similar place across the Hudson River in New Jersey.

And don't forget Central Park. In good weather it is a delightful place for walks. You can birdwatch in the less frequented parts, or hire a boat and go rowing on the lake, or go to the zoo. New York's more famous zoo, and a fine one, is the Bronx Zoo, but the zoo in Central Park is pleasant. Horse-drawn hansom cabs stand at the entrance to Central Park nearest the Plaza Hotel of *Eloise* fame; if you have three dollars to spare, you can hire one

3a Eighteenth century houses on the Chesapeake and Ohio Canal, in Georgetown, Washington, D.C.

3b Upper Main Street, Nantucket, Massachusetts. Three identical houses, built by Joseph Starbuck in 1837 for his three sons

4 The White House, Washington, with the Washington Monument and the Jefferson Memorial in the background

for a half-hour's drive through the Park. Unhappily, it is not a good idea to go walking in Central Park after dark. There have been several unfortunate encounters there between unsuspecting visitors and knife-wielding street gangs.

Finally, there are day trips out of New York City, into Connecticut, out on Long Island, up the Hudson River, or over to Princeton in New Jersey. But these belong in the next chapter.

SPECIAL KNOWLEDGE

Anyone who arrives by ship will understand why Americans themselves are bitter about the conditions at the **New York City Docks**. The Customs men can be pleasant or cross, in the manner of Customs men the world over, but the porters who handle the luggage are exceptionally rough. Your cases may be thrown about a good deal unless you keep an eye on them and, if possible, move them yourself. And despite the notices to the contrary, the porters demand enormous tips.

If you come to New York by air and take a **taxi into the city**, you might ask the driver to go by way of the Triborough Bridge. Once he reaches Manhattan he can then either take you down to the centre of the city on Second Avenue, which will give you a glance at the Italian and Spanish sections of Harlem, or he can sweep you down the East River Drive and then come up into the city proper at the United Nations exit from the Drive. It is a slightly more devious route than most taxi-drivers would take if left to their own devices, but the view from the bridge and the trip through upper Manhattan make it worth the extra time and expense. However, you should agree in advance on the price. Altogether, if there are two people, taking a taxi all the way in from the airport should not be much more costly than taking the airport bus and then a taxi from the city terminal to one's ultimate destination.

By European standards, New York City **buses** are very expensive for short journeys, since the fare is the same for very short rides as it is for all but the longest trips. Moreover, some buses are privately owned and there are competing lines, which creates complications because of the transfer system. Since the buses tend to run only in a straight line, either north and south or east and west, one frequently takes one bus some distance north, for instance, and then transfers to a bus which goes east on one of the cross-streets. To manage this without paying two separate fares, one asks for a 'transfer' when boarding the first bus; the transfer then is used as a ticket for the second bus trip, and it will only have cost a few pennies more than one basic fare. However, one cannot transfer from the buses of one company to those of another, and, to cite only one example, the Fifth Avenue buses and the 42nd Street buses belong to rival firms. As if all of this were not bad enough, you must also remember the warning on p. 14 about the procedure for paying on American buses.

Since the city owns some of the bus lines and private companies run others, each organization shows only its own lines on its freely-distributed **maps**.

D

For a proper picture of the entire bus system, one must go to a bookshop or a news-stand to buy a Hagstrom map.

The **subway** (underground train) lines go up and down Manhattan on the east and west sides, but not in the middle. For long journeys, however, it is well worth the effort to get to a subway station. You must be careful to distinguish between 'local' and 'express' trains, and you must develop an eye for the all but imperceptible indications at street level that a subway station lurks below. They are poorly marked.

If you are **driving in New York,** note that along some of the avenues there are traffic lights only at every *other* cross-street. You must look ahead, however, and stop at the nearest cross-street when the lights go red.

What is known officially as the **Avenue of the Americas** is more commonly called Sixth Avenue.

There are several small, moderately-priced **hotels** between Fifth and Sixth Avenues, particularly along Forty-third, Forty-fourth and Forty-fifth Streets, a convenient location.

To be sure of seeing some celebrated **Broadway production,** it is best to write for tickets months before your arrival in America. The front section of *The New Yorker* has a full list of theatres. Prices are extremely high by European standards, and there are no unreserved gallery seats; for the impecunious late-comer there is only standing room, dealt out at the box office at opening time each morning. There is little point in going to an agency for **theatre tickets** in New York. All the larger hotels have a theatre ticket bureau in their lobbies, and there are several agencies in the theatre district itself near Times Square. But they all charge a considerable booking fee, handle only the most expensive seats, and are understandably prone to save tickets to the real hits for their regular customers. A stranger is really better off trying the box office direct.

The better **supper clubs** will almost always impose either a 'cover' or a 'minimum' charge. A cover charge is an additional sum over and above the cost of your drinks, like an admission charge paid at the end rather than the beginning. A 'minimum' simply means that the total bill cannot be less than the stated minimum charge multiplied by the number of people at your table. Some establishments have minimums which apply only to drinks; in other places sandwiches and the like count as well. Any place which has a minimum or cover charge must so indicate on a notice at each table. For aid in deciding which supper club or jazz place to patronize, consult the 'Supper Clubs' and 'Mostly for Music' sections in *The New Yorker*'s 'Goings on About Town' section.

SHOPPING

AMERICA HOUSE, 44 West 53rd Street. Contemporary American crafts.

BEST'S, Fifth Avenue at 51st Street. The traditional children's clothes shop. Also very good for clothes for teenagers.

BLOOMINGDALE'S, Lexington Avenue at 59th Street. A department store particularly recommended for its materials and for its special bargain basement.

BROOKS BROTHERS, Madison Avenue at 43rd Street. Men's outfitters, traditional and conservative.

FRIEDRICH'S RANCH SUPPLIES, 812 Eighth Avenue, between 49th and 50th Streets. They say this is where the real cowboys buy their fancy cowboy clothes when they come East for the big rodeo at Madison Square Garden.

THE HOBBY SHOP, 44th Street just west of Sixth Avenue. Antique guns, American Revolution and Civil War memorabilia, and a knowledgeable shopkeeper.

LORD AND TAYLOR, Fifth Avenue at 38th Street. A woman's dream-department-store, meticulously designed and arranged. In particular, you can find here the clothes one associates with New York career women: simple, practical; most departments not terribly expensive.

MACY'S, 34th Street at Herald Square. A giant department store, operated on the massive-sales, low-prices theory, with good value for your money. There are also some boutique departments, and in the household electrical section can be found appliances especially wired for British (230) voltage.

KORVETTE'S, Fifth Avenue at 47th Street. The biggest and best of the 'discount' shops; camera film, luggage, clothes, at lower than average prices.

OHRBACH'S, 34th Street between Fifth and Sixth Avenues. Very high-fashion women's clothes at very low prices.

POLK'S HOBBY SHOP, 314 Fifth Avenue. Three floors of models of all nations and all periods: trains, boats, cars, planes, soldiers.

THE RECORD HUNTER, Fifth Avenue between 42nd and 43rd Street. Gramophone records.

SAKS FIFTH AVENUE, Fifth Avenue at 49th Street. Women's and children's clothes at more or less the same price-level as Lord and Taylor; an excellent shop for lingerie, and, like Lord and Taylor, Saks has a good selection of moderately priced and attractive low-heeled shoes for women.

F. A. O. SCHWARTZ, Fifth Avenue at 58th Street. The traditional expensive toyshop.

WOOLWORTHS. One of the biggest is on Fifth Avenue at 40th Street.

In addition to those mentioned, there is a dazzling array of shops on Fifth Avenue between 52nd Street and 58th Street, with the most elegant nearest 58th Street. Most of the women's clothes shops there, like Henri Bendel and Bonwit Teller, have some departments which carry moderately priced things. Do not ask for the 'budget' section; this tends to mean really cheap clothes in America. Ask for the 'less expensive' dresses or shoes, etc., or look for a department that includes 'young' in its title – a kind of euphemism for inexpensive in American shops.

The shops along Third Avenue and those in Greenwich Village often keep strange hours; particularly in Greenwich Village you may find them closed until midday and then open half the night. They are also sometimes closed on Mondays. Most of the large department stores in central Manhattan are open on Thursday evenings until nine, and in July and August many of them are closed all day on Saturday.

NEW YORK CITY CONVENTION AND VISITORS BUREAU, 90 East 42nd Street. Daily 9–6.

TIMES SQUARE INFORMATION CENTER, Times Square. Monday to Saturday 10–9; Sunday 10–6.

BRONX ZOO (NEW YORK ZOOLOGICAL PARK), Fordham Road and Southern Boulevard in The Bronx. 16 February to 31 October, week-days 10–5; Sunday and holidays 10–5.30: 1 November to 15 February, daily 10–4.30. Admission charge Tuesday, Wednesday, Thursday.

BROOKLYN BOTANIC GARDEN, Flatbush Avenue and Empire Boulevard or Eastern Parkway and Washington Avenue, Brooklyn. Week-days 8–sundown; Sunday and holidays 10–sundown. Free.

BROOKLYN MUSEUM, Eastern Parkway and Washington Avenue, Brooklyn. Week-days 10–5; Sunday and holidays 1–5. Free.

CENTRAL PARK ZOO, Central Park East at 64th Street. Daily 10–5. Free.

CIRCLE LINE, Pier 83, West 43rd Street. 1 April to 31 October, 3-hour boat trips around Manhattan. At least five trips a day, starting at 9.45 Midsummer, one evening trip at 6.

CITY HALL, City Hall Park. Monday to Friday 9.30–4.

THE CLOISTERS, Fort Tryon Park. 1 May to 30 September, Tuesday to Saturday 10–6; 1 October to 30 April, Tuesday to Saturday 10–5; Sunday and holidays 1–5. Recorded medieval music, Tuesday and Sunday 3.30. Free.

EMPIRE STATE BUILDING, Fifth Avenue and 34th Street. Daily 9.30–midnight; 25 December and 1 January 2–10.

FREEDOMLAND, in The Bronx at Barstow Avenue Exit of the New England Thruway. Open daily during summer. Can be reached by subway or Gray Line bus.

THE FRICK COLLECTION, 1 East 70th Street. Tuesday to Saturday 10–5, Sunday 1–5. Closed August and holidays, except Labor Day. Children under ten not admitted; children ten to sixteen must be accompanied by an adult.

THE GUGGENHEIM MUSEUM, 1071 Fifth Avenue. Tuesday to Saturday 10–6; Sunday, Thanksgiving and 1 January, 12–6.

HELICOPTER RIDES, Manhattan Heliport, Pier 6, East River. Flights operate daily in summer; week-ends only in winter. For information telephone New York Airways.

HUDSON RIVER DAY LINE, Pier 81, West 41st Street. 1 April to 29 October, 3-hour boat trips around Manhattan. At least four trips a day. Midsummer, one evening trip at 6.

METROPOLITAN MUSEUM OF ART, Central Park, 5th Avenue and 82nd Street. Tuesday to Saturday 10–5; Sunday and holidays 1–5. Free.

MUSEUM OF THE AMERICAN INDIAN, Broadway at 155th Street. Tuesday to Sunday 1–5. Closed July, August and holidays. Free.

MUSEUM OF THE CITY OF NEW YORK, Fifth Avenue and 103rd Street. Tuesday to Saturday 10–5; Sunday and holidays 1–5. Free.

MUSEUM OF CONTEMPORARY CRAFTS, 29 West 53rd Street. Monday to Saturday 12–6; Sunday 2–6. Closed holidays. Free.

MUSEUM OF MODERN ART, 11 West 53rd Street. Week-days 11–6; Sunday 1–7. Classic films daily, 3 and 5.30.

MUSEUM OF PRIMITIVE ART, 15 West 54th Street. Tuesday to Sunday 1–5.

MUSEUM OF NATURAL HISTORY, Central Park West at 79th Street. Week-days 10–5; Sunday and holidays 1–5.

NEW YORK STOCK EXCHANGE, 20 Broad Street. Monday to Friday 10–3.30.

ROCKEFELLER CENTER, Fifth Avenue between 48th and 52nd Streets. Tours every fifteen minutes 15 June–14 September, daily 9.30–9; 15 September to 14 June, daily 9.30–5.30. Also separate tours of the broad-casting and television studios, daily 9–9. Observation roof open daily 9 a.m. to midnight.

ST. PAUL'S CHAPEL OF TRINITY CHURCH, Broadway between Vesey Street and Fulton Street. Week-days 7.30–6; Sunday 8–5; holidays 8–12.

STATUE OF LIBERTY. Boats go every hour on the hour from Battery Park daily 9–4; additional sailings April to October. A return trip takes 45 minutes; allow another hour if you plan to go up into the statue.

TRINITY CHURCH, Broadway at Wall Street. Sunday to Friday 7–6; Saturday 7–4.

UNITED NATIONS, First Avenue between 42nd Street and 48th Street. Daily 9.15–4.45. Closed 25 December and 1 January. Frequent guided tours. Tickets for the General Assembly and other sessions are not bookable, but are distributed, free, thirty minutes before the start of a meeting and thereafter additional tickets are handed out as seats become available.

WHITNEY MUSEUM OF AMERICAN ART, 22 West 54th Street. Daily 1–5. Closed major holidays. Free.

3 · Suburbia, Exurbia, and the Middle Atlantic States

Every day at five o'clock hordes of people pour out of New York City on their way home. It is said that only the very rich and the very poor live in Manhattan these days; everyone else commutes. They crowd into trains or they wedge their cars on to the park-ways, and they go east to Long Island, or north into Connecticut or along the Hudson River, or west across the river into New Jersey. Each of these areas has a distinct personality, and a visitor to New York can make very satisfactory excursions out of the city to see them.

In the course of this chapter we sketch two trips, one to Prince-ton in New Jersey and one up the Hudson River, which can be made in a day and without a car. We also suggest two other possible day-trips, an exploration of Long Island or an explora-tion of that part of Connecticut which is nearest New York City; but in connexion with these latter excursions, it must be pointed out that while one can see parts of Long Island without a car, you really must have one in order to look at Connecticut.

The remainder of the chapter is devoted to the farther reaches of the Middle Atlantic states: Pennsylvania, with Philadelphia at one end and Pittsburgh at the other, and what is known as 'up-state New York', which leads to Niagara Falls.

Two of New York City's boroughs are actually on the west-ern edge of Long Island, and more people who work in the city live out on the Island than in any of the other suburban areas.

Long Island today is a fantastic mixture of colonial America, wealthy aristocratic America, and suburban America Hollywood-style. For fifty years, more or less until the Second World War, 'Long Island' was synonymous in the popular press with 'the idle rich'. It was the setting for F. Scott Fitzgerald's stories, notably *The Great Gatsby*, and for an endless succession of drawing-room comedies. There were comparatively few people to the square mile on Long Island then, and although it tends to be flat and sandy from one end to the other, without great natural beauty, in those days the Island had a carefully tended tranquillity which offered a pleasant contrast to New York City itself. After the Second World War, however, a great many of the estates on Long Island were broken up, and since there was a tremendous demand for land within commuting distance from New York City, in no time at all the estates were gobbled up, and the population density of western Long Island doubled, tripled, quadrupled, soared out of sight.

The first of the great suburban housing developments built then was Levittown, in the centre of the western part of Long Island. Privately built, it benefited from a new scheme of loans guaranteed by the federal government to enable war veterans to buy houses. The Levittown idea, inexpensive houses in quantity, was soon extensively copied; it is almost impossible now to believe that this entire area could so recently have been rural and quiet. Eastern Long Island, less easy to reach, has not changed nearly so much, but the western half of Long Island is now just one town after another. The supermarkets carry everything from toothbrushes to yachts, and the used-car lots, filled with last week's iridescent playthings, are strung like opals along the Sunset Highway. This is suburban America Hollywood-style, one aspect of American life.

The Roosevelt Field Shopping Center, just off the Meadow-brook Parkway, is near Levittown. The concept of the shopping centre is a sort of corollary to the Levittown idea, particularly designed to appeal to young families living in a new district completely on their own, with not too much money. All sorts of shops are grouped together in the middle of an enormous car park on the fringe of a town, or perhaps even out in the country. All the young housewife needs is a car, and in an American suburb she will probably have one. Then she can drive to the shopping centre, park right in front of the shops, and not need to worry about how she is dressed or what to do with the baby; the shopping centre is highly informal.

This part of Long Island is a blend of the old and the new. At the Roosevelt Raceway, near Roosevelt Field, there are trotting races, which have rather the same appeal as greyhound racing in England. But, one of the few survivals of the old opulent days, on

summer Sundays polo is still played at Old Westbury. And along
the north shore of this part of Long Island there remain a few
regions which have not yet fallen into the hands of the sub-
dividers. For example, Theodore Roosevelt, a distant cousin of
Franklin Delano Roosevelt and President of the United States
before the First World War, lived at Oyster Bay on the north
shore. His big rambling family house, Sagamore Hill, is crammed
with mementoes of his fiercely active life. Open to the public, it
is delightfully situated, with a view of Long Island Sound. Still
farther out are three little towns which have been there since
before the American Revolution, Cold Spring Harbor, Stony
Brook and Setauket. Stony Brook today lures visitors with a
small but delightful museum which has an open-air annex in the
summer devoted to carriages and old steam engines. Setauket has
some nice old houses and a church built in 1729, which is known
as the Caroline Church because George II's queen helped to
endow it.

From Port Jefferson, just east of Setauket, there is a ferry
service in the summer to Bridgeport, Connecticut, across Long
Island Sound. Another ferry service runs from Orient Point,
much farther out on Long Island, to New London, Connecticut.
This latter service goes on even in the winter, with a reduced
schedule, but these ferries are most tempting in the summer,
when they provide a pleasant alternative to the usual route from
New York City to New England.

The eastern end of Long Island has changed much less than the
part nearer to New York City. Southampton, way out on the
island, is still the *ne plus ultra* in fashionable summer resorts. In
addition to smart shops, it has a good old car museum and an
admirable little art gallery, but most of Southampton's attractions are hidden, reserved for *habitués*. East Hampton, farther east,
is a more satisfactory place for a casual visit; it is more varied.
There is money in East Hampton too, but there are also handsome colonial houses around the Green, a good summer theatre,
and a considerable artists' colony. (Jackson Pollock lived here,
for example.) East Hampton in many ways seems very like New
England; it is in fact much closer to New England, across the
water, than to New York City. And there is another, smaller Long
Island town a few miles away which is also very reminiscent of
New England: Sag Harbor. Sag Harbor is much more homely.

Once a flourishing whaling port, it is now quiet and peaceful, with charming old sea captains' houses, a whaling museum, and a whalers' church.

Driving is relatively quick and comfortable on the parkways, except at summer week-ends and in the rush-hour, but the fact remains that Long Island is more than one hundred and twenty-five miles long. In only one day, you would have difficulty getting to the eastern end and back, unless you simply took the train to some one place like East Hampton. Of course if you had the time to spare, you might enjoy spending a night or two out on the eastern part of the Island; you could even drive all the way to the tip, Montauk Point, and go out on a boat to try deep-sea fishing. It should be made clear, however, that the eastern end of Long Island blooms only in the summer; in the winter months it is almost deserted.

In the summer there is one other possible excursion to Long Island; during a heatwave in New York City it can be both refreshing and interesting to spend part of a day at Jones Beach. There are public beaches all along the Long Island shore, but the most famous by far is Jones Beach, near Freeport, about an hour from New York City. The creation of a dedicated public servant named Robert Moses, who has also been responsible for the development of the parkway system around New York City, Jones Beach is actually not one beach but a whole series, each with its own changing houses, eating places, and car parks, all ranged along an enormous sandspit, without a house in sight. Every part of Jones Beach is kept scrupulously clean; Mr Moses believes in providing the people with every amenity but insisting that they take proper care of it. However, it is necessary to get there early in order to enjoy even a measure of peace in July and August, and it is madness to try Jones Beach at week-ends and holidays, when every parking space is filled by late morning and thousands of people are turned away. Most people go there by car, but one can also get there by train, taking the Long Island Railroad to Freeport where there are connecting buses to the largest beach areas. At the main beach, anyone arriving under-equipped can either buy or hire bathing suits and towels. In the height of the season the beaches are open until 8 at night, but it cannot be emphasized too strongly that the sun in this part of the world can burn you to a painful crisp in a terribly short time; it may seem unlikely, but New York City is in the same latitude as Naples and Istanbul.

To see a completely different sort of world, and have a very pretty drive as well, one can take the Merritt Parkway up towards Connecticut. Here, on either side of the New York-Connecticut state line, lies 'exurbia', where people who have come to New York and made their mark in the city spend their earnings playing at country life. 'The suburbs' suggests something more closely packed; hence 'exurbia', where there is a fine expensive feeling of space, with woods and hills and little lanes, and privacy.

This particular region was once the background for James Fenimore Cooper novels like *The Spy*; even today, on back roads here you can almost imagine you are in the Connecticut wilderness of the Revolutionary period, when this was a no-man's-land between the British and the American forces. Yet now this area is within commuting distance of New York City, and interspersed among its discreetly restored colonial farmhouses there are striking contemporary houses too. The old and the new are combined with taste and skill, the countryside is charming, and the little towns are extremely attractive.

For a sample of this region, you might take the Merritt Parkway across the Connecticut border, and then cut north along minor roads to Bedford Village and Pound Ridge, which are actually just within New York State but above this corner of Connecticut. Then from Pound Ridge head towards Wilton and Weston, and finally go back across the Parkway again to Westport. It is not in the least important to follow this route exactly; it is merely pleasant to explore some part of this area. Here, as on Long Island, you need a good map. On Long Island the map is necessary because the world-of-the-future aspect of the parkway system means that you must sometimes go north in order to go south. Here, however, a map is vital because this region is truly rural, and the minor roads wind and twist in a bewildering manner, with few signposts.

Westport is a good place to end your explorations because it is near the Parkway, for getting back to New York, and it is also more or less the 'capital' of this smart and wealthy region. One can easily while away an hour or two looking at the tempting wares of the Westport shops. Then, if it is hot, you might like to stop at the Old-fashioned Ice Cream Parlor for a delectable Victorian treat. Westport has a celebrated summer theatre too, and often a new play being tried out. There is also a season of Shakespeare every summer at Stratford, Connecticut, not far from Westport, on the other side of the ugly industrial town of Bridgeport. Most years, the Shakespeare productions at the Canadian Stratford have been the better ones on this side of the Atlantic, but sometimes Stratford, Connecticut, has done brilliantly, and the theatre at the Connecticut Stratford is a striking approximation of the Globe, pennants bravely flying among the trees.

The most popular and traditional day-long excursion from New York City is up the Hudson River. New Yorkers fondly remember a time when one could take a boat all the way to Albany, and fifty years ago businessmen commuted by boat to their offices in New York City; the land along the Hudson was the first 'exurbia'. These days there is only an excursion boat to Bear Mountain, but it is pleasant to go even that far on the river, particularly on a hot summer's day. The Hudson is a stately river which looks rather like the Rhine; the resemblance was strengthened in the nineteenth century when several rich eccentrics built mock castles on the heights above it.

Hyde Park, some seventy-five miles up the Hudson from New York City, has two noteworthy attractions for visitors. The best known is the country house of the Roosevelt family, where Franklin Delano Roosevelt was born, spent much of his life, and is buried. In addition to the house itself, there is a library-cum-museum, built to hold President Roosevelt's papers and acquisitions; he was an enthusiastic collector. The Roosevelt estate is attractive, quite apart from its historical interest, and it is well worth visiting.

The organized tours go only to the Roosevelt house, but also at Hyde Park there is a palatial, mock-Renaissance house built for Frederick Vanderbilt at the end of the nineteenth century. It is a stunning example of the way the great American millionaires of the last century imitated those Medici princes they so much resembled, and the house is now open to the public as a National Historic Site.

West Point was a strategically important fort during the Revolution, but its chief attraction today stems from the fact that since

1802 it has been the United States Military Academy, the American Sandhurst. Visitors are welcome to wander about the grounds and see some of the buildings; there is also a visitors' information centre which is open during the summer. Over and above its interest for anyone with a liking for military history, the situation of West Point, high above the Hudson, makes it worth seeing.

The cost of the organized tours, for two people, is only slightly less than the cost of hiring a car for a day's trip. Moreover there are several interesting things to see in this region which the tours do not include. If you are willing to forgo the boat ride, and are also willing to start early in the morning, you can have a rich, full day exploring the Hudson River valley.

The lands along the Hudson all the way to Albany once belonged entirely to a mere handful of Dutch overlords. Their feudal power waned towards the end of the eighteenth century, mostly because they adhered to the continental system of inheritance and with each succeeding generation the estates became more fragmented. Some few of them also lost their lands because they supported the losing side in the Revolution. The memory of the Dutch lives on in this part of the country, however, and two of the great Dutch manors on the east bank of the Hudson have recently been restored and are open to the public: Philipsburg, in North Tarrytown, and Van Cortlandt, a few miles farther north. (Unfortunately there is no practicable way of reaching either without a car.) In each case, what remains is only a fraction of the original estate, but the houses and some of the outbuildings are there, and the restoration-standard is as high as that of Williamsburg. Philipsburg has been restored to its seventeenth-century condition, while Van Cortlandt Manor today is substantially as it was in the eighteenth century. More of the arts and crafts of the period are demonstrated at Philipsburg, while Van Cortlandt boasts a small eighteenth-century inn on the site of an old ferry crossing, in addition to its manor house. It takes at least an hour to see either place properly.

As you drive towards these manors from New York City, along Route 9 on the east bank of the Hudson, you pass the entrance to Sunnyside, Washington Irving's house, at the southern edge of Tarrytown. Washington Irving was one of the first really successful American writers, in the early nineteenth century; he was also

American consul in England, and Minister to Spain. For 'The Legend of Sleepy Hollow' and 'Rip van Winkle' and the other stories in his *Sketch Book*, he drew on the old Dutch folklore of this region. Of interest chiefly to admirers of Washington Irving, the mock-Gothic house is open to the public; in fact it is the third of the 'Sleepy Hollow Restorations', Philipsburg and Van Cortlandt being the other two.

Driving north through Tarrytown on Route 9, you will see on the left a small park with a statue in it. It is the statue of Major André, marking the spot where that unfortunate British officer was captured during the Revolution. He was trying to get back to his own lines when he was stopped by an American patrol and found to be carrying in his boot a complete plan for the capture of West Point; the plans had just been delivered to him by the traitorous American commandant at West Point, Benedict Arnold. In the confusion which followed, Arnold himself escaped capture, made his way to a British ship, and spent the last twenty years of his life in London, 'sunk in melancholia', shunned by Americans and Englishmen alike. He had been one of the most brilliant and admired strategists in the American army, decisively defeating Burgoyne in the Saratoga campaign, but he was also vain, jealous, and extravagant, and apparently he defected out of pique and for money. The hapless, gallant Major André, who had wanted no part of this mission, was hanged as a spy a few days after his capture, across the river near Tappan.

Very near the turn-off for Philipsburg in North Tarrytown there is an old Dutch church on the east side of Route 9. It is a simple little stone building, with the graves of many Revolutionary soldiers in the churchyard.

The entrance to Van Cortlandt Manor is another ten miles farther on, just south of Croton-on-Hudson. On the way is Ossining, an attractive town with streets pitching steeply down to the river. Many people still prefer these quiet towns along the Hudson to any of the more recently fashionable regions. Ossining, like all of these older towns, is a good place to look for examples of that pleasant nineteenth-century architectural style called 'Hudson River Bracketed'; the distinguishing feature is a mansard roof which seems to be attached to the walls of the house with external wooden brackets, intricately carved. The style flourished all over the state of New York and in the older towns of Ohio, and it is

often charming. Ossining also has a solid example of more functional architecture: Sing Sing Prison is there.

From Van Cortlandt Manor it is another fifty miles up the river
to Hyde Park. Then, for the return to New York City, you can
cross the Hudson at Poughkeepsie, to go along the west bank.
Vassar, one of the best-known American colleges for women, is in
Poughkeepsie, but you will hardly dare take time to look at it if
you are trying to do this whole trip in one day. On the way back
towards New York City, along Route 9W, there is an opportunity
below Newburgh to go to the left and get closer to the river, on
Route 218. This is the old Storm King Highway, a winding road
cut into the cliffs above the river, and it is much the nicest way to
get to West Point. If you leave New York City very early in the
morning, with careful timing you may find yourself arriving at
West Point at just about 5.30. Then, if it is May or September,
and a Monday, a Tuesday, or a Thursday, there will probably be
a parade to watch. Afterwards it is pleasant to have supper at the
Hotel Thayer, in the grounds of the Academy, before driving back
to New York, along Route 9W and the Palisades Parkway to the
George Washington Bridge. There, confronted by all sorts of
confusing signs, you need only remember that to get to midtown
Manhattan you must follow the signs for the Henry Hudson
Parkway, which will take you south along the west side of Manhattan to the cross-streets leading to the centre of the city.

The state of New Jersey is immediately west of New York City.
It has a flat, sandy coastline dotted with summer resorts; it also
has several ugly industrial towns at the end nearest Manhattan,
and a great market-garden region in the centre. North-western
New Jersey, however, is quite different again, with rolling hills
and old farmhouses. On the fringe of this part of the state, half-
way between New York City and Philadelphia, lies Princeton, a
pretty, old town with a venerable university. It can be reached in
about an hour and a half by train or bus from New York City.

The place to start any tour of Princeton is at the university, and
the oldest part of the university is along Nassau Street. Nassau
Hall is the oldest building; it was finished in 1754. The university
was a hotbed of rebellion during the Revolution, encouraged by
its Scotch Presbyterian President, John Witherspoon, one of
those who signed the Declaration of Independence. Witherspoon

offered Nassau Hall to the Continental Congress for a meeting place, and they did use it for six months at the end of the war, in 1783. Through the years, however, Princeton has grown more conservative, as most radicals do. It has also acquired a reputation for a certain kind of sophistication; it is not as intellectual as Harvard nor as earnest as Yale. Nonetheless Princeton has had the rare distinction of seeing one of its Presidents, Woodrow Wilson, leave the university to become President of the United States.

Nearby, in Library Place, is Morven, a house built in 1709 and now the residence of the Governor of New Jersey. It is sometimes open to visitors on Tuesday afternoons. Farther along Library Place there are several handsome old houses, many of them Greek Revival in style, built in the early nineteenth century.

If you have come to Princeton by car, you might enjoy driving out along the Lawrenceville Road, a continuation of Stockton Street to the south-west. This was the post road at the time of the Revolution; on it you will pass an estate called Drumthwacket, with a very old lodge (1696) hidden in the trees, and a more recent and more visible house (1830). Just before the old stone bridge, beyond Drumthwacket, you should turn left again, to take the Princeton Pike and Mercer Street back into the town, passing an old Quaker Meeting House along the way. In 1777, during the Revolution, the American army under General Washington won an important battle here, defeating General Cornwallis and a contingent of British troops. Many of the soldiers from both sides lie buried near the Quaker Meeting House and in the grounds of Drumthwacket.

At the edge of town is Olden Lane, with Olden Manor, and behind it the Institute of Advanced Studies, whose director lives in the Manor. The Institute is not remarkable to look at, but it is one of the most interesting academic institutions in America. It is a non-teaching college, with Fellows elected so that they may pursue some independent line of research, in the humanities or mathematics or theoretical physics. It maintains its vigour by having only a very small number of permanent Fellows and a much larger number of Fellows elected only for one or two years. Albert Einstein remained a Fellow until his death, and among those who have been Fellows more briefly are C. V. Wedgwood, and George Kennan, the American scholar-diplomat. The Director of the Institute is Robert Oppenheimer, the atomic physicist.

The Institute of Advanced Studies is in no way connected with Princeton University, but the presence of these two institutions in the same town makes Princeton a very stimulating place in which to live, in addition to the charm of its situation and its quiet streets; through the years such figures as Thomas Mann have chosen to settle there.

Driving from New York City to Philadelphia it is pleasant to avoid the turnpikes and go instead along less-travelled roads, through Princeton, and then on across the Delaware River to New Hope in Pennsylvania. New Hope is in the heart of Bucks County, Pennsylvania, where many artists and writers have come to live, as well as a surprising number of people who commute every day all the way to New York City. Along almost every by-road in the Bucks County countryside there are charming old field-stone houses, for which the region around Philadelphia is famous. These are serious, solid houses which bespeak the mixture of English Quakers and Germans who settled this area.

Philadelphia itself, on the far side of Bucks County, can also be reached quickly by train or bus from New York City. It is not the capital of Pennsylvania; the capital is Harrisburg, farther west. But Philadelphia is Pennsylvania's largest city, and at the time of the Revolution it was the largest city in all of the American colonies, second only to London among the English-speaking cities of the world. It was established in 1682 by William Penn as the centre of his Quaker settlement in the New World, and the industrious Quakers soon made their region prosperous. They enjoyed excellent relations with the Indians, and they encouraged the coming of other hardworking settlers, no matter what their religious beliefs or nationality. Great numbers of dissenting Germans did come; in some instances entire German villages emigrated and then re-established their close-knit communities in Pennsylvania. Many other Germans came as indentured servants, worked their seven or fourteen years, and then struck out for themselves. Thus, while the English colonists in Pennsylvania were always in the majority, one must not forget the contributions of the dissenting German element, with their thrifty, industrious, pious ways, reinforcing the Quaker influences.

At the time of the Revolution, Philadelphia was not only the largest but also the most attractive American town in the opinion of most visitors: clean and elegant and cosmopolitan. Fifty years later the fractious Mrs Trollope was to find nothing to criticize here but the fact that chains were hung across the streets on the Sabbath to prevent the use of carriages; otherwise there was no evidence of religious inhibition, and the upper classes were 'most polished in manner'.

During this century Philadelphia has been noted for having some of the prettiest suburbs in the United States, where the old Philadelphia families lived comfortably and attractively but without ostentation. Yet until very recently Philadelphia has had little to boast of in the centre of the town. Now, however, it is engaged in a staggeringly ambitious programme of urban renewal, and the results are already exciting. The best of the old buildings have been preserved. You can still see Carpenters' Hall and Independence Hall, where the delegates from the thirteen American colonies met to organize a common resistance to Britain and then to hammer out first a declaration of independence and later a constitution for the new federated republic. Several other handsome and historic buildings still stand too, and any rows of old houses which could be rehabilitated have been spared, and are once again becoming fashionable places in which to live. But the rest of the old heart of the city has been pulled down, and carefully planned bold new buildings are going up. It is the most impressive project of this sort now under way anywhere in the United States.

The centre of Philadelphia can be roughly divided into three parts. To the west of City Hall is the Penn Center region, newly rebuilt. The 'Hospitality Center' is here, at 16th Street and Pennsylvania Boulevard; it is the principal visitors' information office. To the east of City Hall, along Market and Chestnut Streets, are most of the big shops, and beyond lies the section where you will find most of the historic buildings.

The most interesting historic building is Independence Hall, with its handsome pine-panelled rooms; the Declaration of Independence was signed here, and this is where the Liberty Bell hangs. At Independence Hall there is also another, smaller visitors' information office. On either side of Independence Hall are Congress Hall and the Second Bank of the United States and, farther along Chestnut Street, Carpenters' Hall; these are all worth noticing, and the buildings around them have now been

E

cleared away so that they stand out. In the Betsy Ross House on Arch Street, the first American flag was put together out of strips of petticoat and flannel; the house is minute, but well preserved and appropriately furnished. Just around the corner, off Second Street, is Elfreth's Alley, a narrow cobbled street with attractive small Georgian houses. Along Second Street is Christ Church, an impressive church, built around 1730, which has been very little altered inside. It still has the wine-glass pulpit and the original pews, one with George Washington's name on it. Many of the delegates to the Continental Congresses at the time of the Revolution worshipped at this church during the long months they were in Philadelphia. Unfortunately, at the moment the good buildings in this last part of the city are still smothered by old warehouses and other dilapidated structures. But just to the south of this region a large area known as Society Hill has been cleared for rebuilding, and this should in the end prove to be the most dramatic and successful of all the refurbished sections.

Like Boston, Philadelphia has a long tradition of support for the arts and sciences. The Philadelphia Orchestra is one of the three or four finest orchestras in the United States, and Philadelphia also has several notable museums. The University of Pennsylvania Museum has a fine archaeological collection, particularly notable in relation to such ancient cultures as the Babylonian, Sumerian, Assyrian; in these fields University of Pennsylvania archaeological teams have done much of the important work. The University of Pennsylvania was founded by Benjamin Franklin, eighteenth-century Philadelphia's most distinguished and versatile citizen, whose other lasting monument is the Franklin Institute, a science museum with an adjoining planetarium. The Philadelphia Museum of Art is, like the Philadelphia Orchestra, one of the three or four finest in the United States, with the magnificent Johnson Collection of Old Masters and the recently acquired Arensberg Collection of modern paintings.

The Museum of Art is situated at the south-eastern edge of Fairmount Park, which is in itself a tourist attraction. Fairmount Park is enormous. It covers 1,500 acres on both sides of the Schuylkill River, and it has everything: a zoo, and Robin Hood's Dell where outdoor concerts are held in the summer, and, scattered here and there in the Park, six handsome old houses, each in its day the elegant country seat of some eminent Philadelphia family. The houses vary in style and décor, but they are all eighteenth century. Each is now open to the public, and several of them are administered by the Museum of Art, which also sponsors bus tours to them for the benefit of visitors without cars. The tours are run in collaboration with the Gray Line organization, but the Museum supervises the training of the guides. Among these houses one might single out Mount Pleasant (1761), interesting for many reasons but especially for its fine examples of Philadelphia Chippendale furniture, sometimes called Philadelphia block-front. Mount Pleasant also has a fine view over the river and the Park.

Anyone who is interested in French Impressionist and Post-impressionist painting should know that the Barnes Foundation in Merrion, a Philadelphia suburb, has a remarkable collection. Merrion also boasts that rarity in the United States, a cricket club; we must confess, however, that cricket is now honoured there chiefly in the name.

About twenty miles west of Philadelphia is Valley Forge, where the colonial army encamped during the bleakest winter of the American Revolution, the winter of 1777–8. The first enthusiasm had worn off, the war was going badly for the Americans, enlistments had expired and thousands of General Washington's soldiers simply took their rifles and went home. For those who remained, there was no warm clothing and very little food. At Valley Forge they built rude huts, and waited, in the snow and the cold. Actually this was the turning point of the war, for in the spring news came that the French government had decided to send troops to help the Americans against the British; until then there had been only a few individual Frenchmen like Lafayette in the field with Washington's forces, and France had not taken official notice of their activities. This new assistance was to make all the difference. Nonetheless, if the ragged American Army had not held together at Valley Forge, no amount of French aid could have turned the tide. Valley Forge is therefore the great landmark of the Revolution, the most popular shrine. You can still see the encampment almost as it was that winter, with the little huts and the farmhouse General Washington used as his headquarters.

Going south from Philadelphia you soon cross from Pennsylvania into the state of Delaware. Delaware began as an independent Swedish settlement but it developed close ties with

Pennsylvania. Almost feudally controlled by a few families until well into the nineteenth century, it is now regarded as the fief of just one family, the Du Ponts. The centre of the Du Pont manufacturing empire is in Wilmington, the capital of Delaware, and between Wilmington and Philadelphia there are two celebrated examples of Du Pont munificence. One is Longwood, large and splendid gardens left by Pierre Du Pont a few years ago as 'a horticultural display for the benefit and enjoyment of the public'. It has an outdoor theatre, an ornamental lake, fountains and formal gardens, delightful 'natural' sections, and an enormous conservatory. The other monument to Du Pont generosity is Winterthur, nearer Wilmington. Winterthur also has a garden, designed to be at its loveliest in the spring, but Winterthur is chiefly famous for its collection of American furniture and decoration, which is much the finest collection of its kind in the United States. Experts and decorators and dealers come to do research at Winterthur, which consists of almost a hundred rooms, each one furnished in a different style characteristic of some period or region in America during the seventeenth, eighteenth, or nineteenth century. There are no rope barriers here; you can poke around in each room to your heart's content, but you must be accompanied by one of the guides, and must write to Winterthur well in advance for reservations. Only in late April and May is this stricture relaxed; then there is a sort of open season on the museum and a slightly lower admission charge.

Along the Brandywine Creek not far from Winterthur is the delightful little Hagley Museum, with working models of the first Du Pont mills and echoes of some of the other early activities in this region. The whole thing is unpretentious but extremely well done, and the situation is charming too: a wooded park with a few of the actual old mill buildings still standing along the river. Gray Line advertises an all-day tour to Longwood and Winterthur and the Hagley Museum.

West of Philadelphia is the Pennsylvania Dutch country. Many of the Pennsylvania colonists were German; other early settlers were from Holland and from the German-speaking part of Switzerland, and all of them came to be known as 'Pennsylvania Dutch'. Most of these German-speaking settlers were soon absorbed into the main stream of Pennsylvania life; only the German names here and there, and German dishes on restaurant menus in Philadelphia, commemorate them. But some of these settlers, members of strict religious sects, had fled to America in order to preserve their faith intact and their practices undisturbed; in Pennsylvania they continued determined to keep apart from the rest of the world. The most important of these groups were the Mennonites, and a kindred sect, the Amish. Unlike the rest of the German settlers, they have never been absorbed into the main stream of American life, and their customs have come to seem more unusual and more eccentric as the rest of the world has grown more worldly. Today, when someone mentions 'the Pennsylvania Dutch', he is probably referring to the Amish, 'the plain people'; the Amish are the most extreme of the surviving groups. Amish men have great beards and they wear broad-brimmed black hats and black suits or blue working clothes; the women wear close-fitting caps and long dresses, and the children are dressed in small versions of the adult costume. The Amish are pious, hardworking farmers, and they frown on all but the most wholesome pleasures. Moreover they eschew machinery and will not own cars or have telephones. They sometimes come into conflict with the state over schooling for the children, and over their refusal to take part in any government activity: they will not serve on juries nor join the army. But usually they manage to be left alone, and there are today about 50,000 Amish and strict Mennonites combined; they are best known in Pennsylvania but many of them also live in sections of Ohio and Indiana. They still speak a form of low German, and particularly in Pennsylvania they are famous for a distinctive sort of colourful, geometric decoration on the outsides of their barns and on their painted furniture, and for certain food specialities like shoo-fly pie.

If you take back roads in the area around Lancaster, you will very likely see an Amish farmer with his horse and buggy. And if you go into Lancaster itself on a Tuesday or a Friday or a Saturday, market days, you will no doubt see many Amish there too. In addition, five miles east of Lancaster, just beyond Paradise on Route 30, there is an 'Amish Farm and House' open to the public. This is not at all the sort of tourist trap one might suspect it would be, but a genuinely interesting place, run by people sympathetic to the Amish and anxious to explain their customs and beliefs.

About ten miles north of Lancaster there was once another German religious settlement, at Ephrata. Called the Ephrata

Cloister, it was a community of Seventh Day Baptists, both men and women, but celibate. As the Shaker communities in the next century were to win respect with their craftmanship and honesty, so the Ephrata Cloister members were admired as kindly, serious people who excelled in singing and in fine printing and manuscript illumination. Unfortunately, during the Revolution a typhus epidemic sadly reduced the numbers of the community, and in the nineteenth century it dwindled further to eventual dissolution. Today the Ephrata Cloister is owned by the state and open to the public, as a particularly good example of those Utopian religious communities which were so astonishingly numerous in America in the eighteenth and nineteenth centuries.

In Pennsylvania it is only a little way from Lancaster to York, and then a bit farther on in that direction you come to Gettysburg, the scene of the most famous battle of the Civil War. Under the brilliant leadership of Robert E. Lee, the Confederate armies had one success after another in the first years of the war, and now in 1863 they were penetrating deep into Northern territory. At Gettysburg, however, the tide turned; the battle lasted three days, with more men engaged on either side than in any other encounter of the war, and at the end the Confederates were forced to retreat back into Virginia. Both sides had suffered appalling losses. A few months later, Abraham Lincoln gave his brief and beautiful 'Gettysburg address' at the dedication of a memorial there. The National Park Service now administers the battlefield area, and guides can be engaged to drive with you round the twenty-five square miles. Opposite the graveyard is the privately run Gettysburg National Museum where a huge map dotted with electric lights illustrates the three-day battle while a recorded voice gives a running account.

It is pleasant to drive to Gettysburg on minor roads through the Pennsylvania Dutch region, but most people going there from Philadelphia take the Pennsylvania Turnpike. Built for the most part in the 1930's, this turnpike was the first great superhighway in the United States. It is still in many ways the most impressive. In the eastern part of the state it winds through rolling country dotted with fieldstone houses and farms. Between Philadelphia and the turning for Gettysburg, it comes close enough to Hershey, the town that chocolate built, so that the delicious aroma of cocoa beans sometimes wafts across the highway, and one is tempted to stop and tour the plant and see the model company-town.

Not far beyond the Gettysburg turning, the Turnpike goes through its first tunnel. There are six or seven tunnels in all, as the Turnpike pierces the Allegheny Mountains. The superb engineering rather softens the effect of these mountains, which used to seem a formidable barrier when one had to twist and climb for a hundred miles. This part of the Turnpike is very pleasant; the mountains are heavily wooded, with a blue cast to them except in the autumn when they are flaming red and gold.

The entire Allegheny region, extending well down into West Virginia, is coal-mining country. In the beginning many of the miners were Welsh and Scotch and Cornish, as some of the place-names indicate: Carnwath and Grampian, Crum Lynne, Treverton, Trevose. But in time many of these first miners made enough money to leave the hard life of the mines, or else moved on to the mining regions of the West. There were new recruits then from among the thousands of Central European immigrants who came to the United States in the years before the First World War, and the Allegheny coal fields became one of the great melting-pot areas. In this region arose many of the first great American labour leaders.

The heart of this area is Pittsburgh, which was Fort Pitt in the days before the American Revolution; it was then the key outpost on the western edge of British territory in America. The advantages of the site are obvious. Pittsburgh lies in a narrow valley at the confluence of the Ohio, the Monongahela, and the Allegheny rivers. You come down round a steep hill, and suddenly there before you is the iron and steel capital of America.

Pittsburgh was once one of the ugliest industrial cities in the United States, but it is now one of the most impressive. A few years ago, when industrial blight seemed about to devour it completely, the leading citizens decided that dreadfulness had gone far enough. Today, in a section which was formerly one of the worst in the city, where the Monongahela and the Allegheny come together to squeeze the heart of Pittsburgh into a point, there is now the Golden Triangle, a group of striking modern office buildings set round a little park. There is a wonderful view of the Golden Triangle at night from the top of Mount Washington at the edge of the city; one might go just for a drink to La

Mont or The Tin Angel, two expensive restaurants up on the heights.

Any city which calls its principal university building 'the Cathedral of Learning' must expect to have all its cultural institutions viewed with some scepticism. In fact, the Carnegie Institute, which combines a large library with a wide variety of collections, from pterodactyls to Perugino, does have some very good things. But obviously the most appropriate thing to do in Pittsburgh is to take one of the Wednesday tours at the U.S. Steel Corporation's giant works. You may also enjoy seeing one of the fashionable suburbs, Sewickley Heights perhaps, or Fox Chapel, or even Pittsburgh's beautiful exurbia around Ligonier, an hour and a half away to the south-east. The three rivers which come together at Pittsburgh have made deep valleys in the wooded hills, and the country around Pittsburgh is exceptionally pretty.

We abandoned New York State after the trip up the Hudson River. Now we must return to it in order to sketch in the void between New York City and Niagara Falls.

The Dutch flavour continues all the way up the Hudson to Albany, now the capital of New York State. There are a few links with the past in Albany: two eighteenth-century Dutch town houses, for example, which are open to the public. But most travellers rolling along on the New York State Thruway choose to by-pass the city.

North of Albany the Adirondack Mountains stretch to the Canadian border. Most of this region is part of a State Forest Preserve, and it is principally wooded lakes and hills, summer resorts and ski areas. The best known town is Saratoga Springs, which was an elegant spa in the late nineteenth century, 'the summer residence of the most refined circles of American society'. People lost interest in taking the waters, however, and Saratoga slowly declined; many of the delightful landmarks of the past have now been torn down. Nonetheless there is still a good race meeting at Saratoga Springs every year, and there are also yearling sales which attract large crowds of horse buyers.

Seventy-five miles north of Saratoga is Fort Ticonderoga, so handsomely situated on the far side of Lake George that one can enjoy going there even without a particular interest in history. Yet the fort was very important in its day. Captured from the

French by the British General Amherst in 1759, it was taken during the Revolution by Benedict Arnold for the Americans, and then retaken by General Burgoyne for the British; each side regarded it as vital to their defences. Today it is restored to its original state, and preserved as a National Historic Site.

At Massena, New York, about a hundred miles west of Fort Ticonderoga, where the St Lawrence River flows between New York State and the Canadian province of Ontario, are some of the most spectacular locks on the new St Lawrence Seaway. The Power Authority has arranged excellent exhibits in its Administration Building there, and one can take boat trips and bus tours. At the lower end of this stretch of the St Lawrence River lie the Thousand Islands, cool and pretty and popular in the summer.

West of Albany, the Dutch place names are intermingled with Indian names, and anyone who studies a local map will also notice that within a fifty-mile radius of Albany there is a Johnstown, a Fort Johnson, and a Johnsonville. This was Mohawk Indian country, and in the eighteenth century the greatest name in the Mohawk valley was that of Sir William Johnson. One always hears about men on the frontier who failed to understand the Indians, who tricked them and mistreated them; it is a pity that so few people have heard of this one remarkable exception. No other official of the Crown was ever so loved and trusted by the Indians as Johnson, and he in turn loved and defended his Mohawks. In time, he even took a Mohawk wife, the sister of a Mohawk leader called Joseph Brant; she was known as 'the brown Lady Johnson' to distinguish her from her paler predecessor.

Sir William's success in keeping the Mohawks pro-British is clearly one reason why he is so little known in the United States. Once you won over a Mohawk, he stuck like glue, and guided by Sir William's son, John, the Mohawks remained fiercely loyal to the Crown during the Revolution. In fact they took so many American scalps that the Johnson name became anathema in the region, and Sir John was forced to flee to Canada together with many of his Mohawk supporters.

For many years Sir William Johnson had lived at Fort Johnson, in a small stone house which is now the local museum. Later he had a manor house built for himself and his half-Mohawk family; called Johnson Hall, the house can still be seen in Johnstown. Most of the outbuildings are gone, and in some ways it is disappointing to visit, set as it is today in a tame park at the edge of a commonplace town. Yet what an anomaly it must once have seemed, neat and Georgian here in the wilderness, with Indians encamped in the grounds.

A two-hour drive west of Albany is Cooperstown, a pretty little town in rolling country on a pleasant lake with boating and a public bathing beach. Cooperstown is best known to Americans for its Baseball Hall of Fame, but it has many other attractions, including the delightful Farmers' Museum, run by the New York State Historical Society.

The first building of the Farmers' Museum contains a comprehensive collection of early farming tools and machinery which enthralls modern farmers. Beyond this lies an open-air museum which is a reconstructed village of the New York State of a hundred and fifty years ago. It is not as extensive as the village at Old Sturbridge Village in Massachusetts, but in some ways it is even more fun because of the enthusiasm with which the mock-inhabitants of the Cooperstown village play their nineteenth-century roles.

The headquarters of the Historical Society is at Fenimore House, across the road from the Farmers' Museum on the site of James Fenimore Cooper's house; the Cooper family, the leading landowners of the region, gave their name to the town. At Fenimore House today one can see a charming collection of itinerant paintings and other examples of early American folk art. The Historical Society also runs enjoyable week-long 'seminars on American culture' at Cooperstown every July.

The Baseball Hall of Fame, with memorials to all the great players of the past, is in Cooperstown because baseball began here; the first playing field was laid out in 1839 by one Abner Doubleday, a Cooperstown schoolmaster bent on devising a new sport for his boys. In the tourist season, multitudes of eager fathers can be seen propelling their sons from one exhibit to the next in the Hall of Fame, lecturing and admonishing. And perhaps a brief lecture on the subject should be given here; every visitor to America needs at least a rudimentary understanding of the national game.

Baseball is thought to have evolved from rounders. There are nine players to a side, nine innings, and four bases. The object of

the game is for a player to make his way from base to base until he
gets back again to 'home base' where he started; that scores a run.
If he can do it unaided, solely on the strength of his own hit, that
is a 'home run'. But he will consider himself fortunate even if he
gets only to first or second base through his own efforts. He can
then be helped along the rest of the way by those of his team-
mates who come up to bat after him, who will hope to drive him
on ahead as well as to get on base themselves. Baseball is a faster
game than cricket because the batter must run whenever he hits
the ball into the playing area, the 'fair' zone. And he has only a
limited number of tries. If the pitcher throws three good balls to
the batter and he fails to hit them, he is 'out on strikes'. He can
also be put out if he hits the ball but it is caught, or if he does not
succeed in reaching base before a fielder throws the ball there.
The pitcher too has his hazards; if he throws four bad balls to
a batter, he has 'walked' that batter, who can then go to first base
free. A team's share of the 'inning' is over as soon as three of the
men on that team have been ruled 'out'; the other team then has
its turn at bat, and the entire game is usually over in less than two
hours. The crowd at a baseball game loves powerful hitting, and,
particularly, home runs. But real devotees of the game admire
even more those skilful pitchers who can strike out batter after
batter, and the adept fielders who can make spectacular catches or
trap an opposing player between bases.

About a hundred miles west of Cooperstown are the lovely Finger
Lakes. One of the largest is Lake Cayuga, with Cornell University
handsomely situated at its southern end. At the foot of Seneca
Lake is the beautiful Watkins Glen, now part of a state park.
South of Watkins Glen is the town of Elmira, where Mark Twain
lived for many years after his marriage; he and his wife are buried
there, and one can visit his old studio, built in the shape of a
Mississipi river boat pilot house. West of Elmira is Corning,
where the Corning Glass Company turns out every kind of glass,
from Steuben, the most expensive decorative glass made in
America, to dishes for cooking and giant lenses for observatories.
The Corning Glass Center includes a splendid collection of ancient
and modern glass, and there are also demonstrations and films to
entertain and enlighten visitors.

·   ·   ·   ·   ·

Visitors to New York City sometimes arrive with the vague notion that Niagara Falls is just beyond the suburbs; actually it is more than four hundred miles away. It is easy to reach, however, by bus, train, plane or car. The quickest way by road is along the New York State Thruway. This follows the old route of the Erie Canal, which was cut through the state of New York from Buffalo to Albany in the 1820's, opening up a vast new area to trade and settlement. In its day, the Erie Canal was an even more momentous development than the St Lawrence Seaway promises to be in our own; it made New York City the most important port on the east coast of North America. Once the railways spread, however, the Erie Canal became less significant, and today it has almost disappeared; it has been blocked off, built over, and in some places combined with a newer canal. Yet here and there one still comes upon a stretch of it, all overgrown and sluggish, going through some sleepy little town like Canestota which once resounded to the cries of the canal boatmen.

There are several big industrial towns along the Thruway which owed their beginnings to the Erie Canal. The most interesting is probably Rochester, the Eastman Kodak headquarters. You can tour the Kodak works, and in George Eastman House there is an excellent museum of photography and photographic processes. Eastman generosity founded the Eastman School of Music in Rochester, too; it is one of the two or three best music schools in the country. In the late spring, Highland Park is famous for its lilacs; and there is also a pleasant example of Greek Revival architecture in Rochester: the Campbell-Whittlesey House.

Beyond Rochester, not far from Buffalo, anyone consulting a map may exclaim excitedly that there is an Indian reservation just north of the Thruway and another one nearer Niagara Falls. Actually, however, there is nothing to see. There are Indians, to be sure, but they dress like every other American, and live simply on small, scattered farms. Their most colourful characteristic is not visible as you drive through the reservation lands: many New York Indians have made a speciality of high construction work, on bridges and skyscrapers.

Buffalo has a fine art gallery, the Albright. Otherwise it is a big industrial city, best avoided; one can by-pass it and go directly to the chief attraction in this part of America, Niagara Falls.

Niagara Falls belongs both to Canada and the United States, and since the view from the Canadian side is superior one should certainly go to the Niagara Falls prepared to cross the border. For aliens, this usually means only that you must be sure to have your passport and visa and smallpox vaccination certificate with you. People crossing the border are usually also asked to show proof that they have some right to the car they are driving.

There is always a carnival atmosphere prevailing at Niagara Falls in the summer tourist season, and one is importuned on every side to take this or that guided tour and to stop at this or that motel or hotel. It is strongly recommended, however, that you choose only those tours and accommodation at Niagara Falls listed either by the A.A.A. or by the official Niagara Falls Convention and Visitors Bureau run by the local Chamber of Commerce. This carnival atmosphere is in fact nothing new; Niagara Falls has always been part circus and part natural wonder. In the nineteenth century the most respectable of people gathered here to see the incredible Blondin pirouette above the Falls on his tightrope, or to watch someone go over the Falls in a barrel. Niagara Falls had so much of everything, in fact, that it became a mecca for couples on their honeymoon. Sophisticated Americans now roar with laughter at the idea of going to Niagara Falls on a wedding trip, but many newly married couples still do go there.

The Maid of the Mist boat trip to the foot of the Canadian Falls is traditional and exciting, and can be done from either side. On the American side one can now also descend the cliff and take a guided walk in oilskins under the Falls. For that matter, one can walk from the Canadian to the American side on the Rainbow Bridge; signs point the way for 'Pedestrians to the United States'. On summer nights the Falls are illuminated with coloured lights, and in the winter they are spectacular in quite another way, with ice and freezing mist and blessedly few tourists.

The St Lawrence Seaway and the vast Niagara power project have resulted in new things to see in the vicinity of Niagara Falls: various aspects of the power project, and the Welland Locks on the Seaway. Anyone interested in these developments should go first to the Power Authority Exhibit Building in Niagara Falls.

For a totally different sort of outing, there is also Fort Niagara, on the shores of Lake Ontario. It is an eighteenth-century outpost, now colourfully restored and complete even to soldiers in period uniform.

SPECIAL KNOWLEDGE

Just as New York City is the most costly place in the United States for tourists, so **prices** are generally higher in the popular parts of New York State than they seem to be in any of the other tourist centres of the East, let alone the rest of the country. Choose carefully the places in this region at which you stop to eat and sleep.

You must also choose carefully the **sights** you see. Too often in New York State one leaves the highway to see some landmark, only to find it dreary and neglected, with a disagreeable guide-cum-ticket-taker who knows little and cares less. Or a noisily advertised place turns out to be only a remote approximation of the original thing, not worth the admission or the time. New Yorkers will object that this can happen anywhere, and of course that is so, but the fact remains that in New York one is lured with false promises more often, and is more often disappointed, than in any other state. In New York State, with the few exceptions we have mentioned, the scenery is far more satisfactory than the sights.

Buffalo, New York State

BUFFALO FINE ART ACADEMY, Albright-Knox Art Gallery, 1285 Elmwood Avenue. Monday, Tuesday, Thursday, Friday, Saturday 10–5; Wednesday 12–10; Sunday 12–6.

Cooperstown, New York State

FARMERS' MUSEUM, 1 May to 31 October, daily 9–6; 1 November to 30 April, Tuesday to Saturday 9–5 and Sunday afternoon. Closed Thanksgiving, 25 December and 1 January.

FENIMORE HOUSE, Opposite the Farmers' Museum. July and August daily 9–9; May, June, September, October, daily 9–6; November to April, daily 9–5. Write here for information about the Cooperstown summer seminars.

NATIONAL BASEBALL MUSEUM, Main Street. 1 May to 31 October, daily 9–9; 1 November to 30 April, daily 9–5.

Corning, New York State

CORNING GLASS CENTER, Centerway. Tuesday to Sunday, 9.30–1. Free.

Elmira, New York State

MARK TWAIN'S STUDIO, Elmira College campus. 1 June to 1 September, Monday to Saturday 1–4.30; 2 September to 31 May. Apply for key at Administration Building. Free.

Ephrata, Pennsylvania

EPHRATA CLOISTER, at the junction of U.S. Routes 322 and 222. Summer, Monday to Friday 8.30–5, Saturday 10–5, Sunday 12–6. Rest of year closes at 4.30 daily.

Johnstown, New York State

JOHNSON HALL, Hall Avenue. Monday to Saturday 9–5, Sunday 1–5. Free.

Fort Ticonderoga, New York State

Mid-May to 30 June and 1 September to mid-October, daily 8–5.30; 1 July to 31 August, daily 8–7.

Gettysburg, Pennsylvania

GETTYSBURG NATIONAL MILITARY PARK. This, the battlefield area, can be visited all the year round.

GETTYSBURG NATIONAL MUSEUM, on State Route 134. Winter, daily 9–5, spring and autumn 8.30–7.30, summer 8.30–8.45.

Hudson River, New York State

GRAY LINE TOURS, 245 West 50th Street, New York. Hyde Park, West Point, Bear Mountain tour: 26 May to 31 October, Tuesday, Thursday, Saturday, depart 8.30 a.m., lasts 10 hours. Reservation required.

HUDSON RIVER DAY LINE, Main Office: 303 West 42nd Street, New York City. Departure Pier: Pier 81, end of West 41st Street, New York City. West Point tour: 20 May to 30 June, Saturday to Thursday; 1 July to 10 September, daily; 11 September to 31 October, Saturday and Sunday. Depart 10, tour lasts 7 hours. Bear Mountain, West Point, Hyde Park tour, 20 May to 30 June, daily except Monday and Friday; 1 July to 10 September, daily; 11 September to 31 October, Saturday and Sunday. Depart 10, tour lasts 10 hours.

Hyde Park, New York State

FRANKLIN D. ROOSEVELT HOUSE, LIBRARY AND MUSEUM, 2 miles south of Hyde Park on U.S. Route 9. 15 June to Labor Day, daily 9–5; Labor Day to 14 June, Tuesday to Sunday 9–5. (Open Monday if a holiday; closed following Tuesday.)

VANDERBILT HOUSE, North of Hyde Park on U.S. Route 9. 15 June to Labor Day, daily 9–5; Labor Day to 14 June, Tuesday to Sunday 9–5. (Open Monday if a holiday; closed following Tuesday.)

Lancaster, Pennsylvania

THE AMISH FARM AND HOUSE, 6 miles east on U.S. Route 30, just beyond Paradise. 20 May to 9 September, daily 8.30–8; 10 September to 26 November, daily 8.30–5; 27 November to 17 March, Saturday, Sunday and holidays 9–5; 18 March to 19 May, daily 8.30–5.

Massena, New York State

POWER AUTHORITY ADMINISTRATION BUILDING, 1 July to 31 August, 8.30–8.30; 1 September to mid-December and 16 April to 30 June, daily 8.30–5; mid-December to 15 April, Monday to Friday 8.30–5.

Niagara Falls, New York State

MAID OF THE MIST BOAT RIDE, 1 July to 31 August, daily 9.30–8; 1 September to 30 June, daily 9.30–5.

SPANISH AEROCAR, 1 June to 31 August, daily 9–9; 1 September to 31 May, daily 10–5.

TABLE ROCK DESCENT, daily 9–5; in summer 9–10.

Old Fort Niagara, New York State

North of Youngstown in Fort Niagara State Park, 1 July to 10 August, daily 9–8.45; 11 August to Labor Day 9–8.15; Labor Day to 30 June, 9–4.30. Closed Thanksgiving, 25 December, 1 January.

Orient Point Ferry, Long Island

NEW LONDON FREIGHT LINES, INC., Dock Road, Orient Point, Long Island, New York. Ten round-trips daily from New London and Orient Point.

Oyster Bay, Long Island

SAGAMORE HILL (THEODORE ROOSEVELT'S HOUSE), 3 miles west of Oyster Bay: 1 July to 31 August, daily 10–5; 1 September to 30 June, Wednesday to Monday 10–5.

Philadelphia

HOSPITALITY CENTER, 16th Street and Pennsylvania Boulevard. Daily 8.45–5. Arrangements can be made for foreign visitors to meet Philadelphians in their homes.

BARNES FOUNDATION, Latch's Lane and Lapsley Road, Merion. Friday and Saturday 9.30–4.30. Closed July, August and holidays. Advanced reservation advisable.

BETSY ROSS HOUSE, 239 Arch Street. Daily 10–4.30. Free.

CHRIST CHURCH, 2nd Street, between Arch Street and Market Street. Daily 9–5. Services, Sunday 9 and 11.

GRAY LINE TOUR OF COLONIAL HOUSES IN FAIRMOUNT PARK, Pick-up service at all hotels three-quarters of an hour before departure times: 2 May to 5 September, Tuesday to Thursday 9.45, Sunday 2. Reservation required.

INDEPENDENCE HALL, Chestnut Street, between 5th and 6th Streets. Daily 8.45–5.15. Free.

MOUNT PLEASANT, East River Drive, Fairmount Park. Daily 10–5. Closed holidays.

PHILADELPHIA MUSEUM OF ART, end of the Benjamin Franklin Parkway. Daily 9–5. Closed holidays. Free.

UNIVERSITY OF PENNSYLVANIA MUSEUM, 33rd and Spruce Streets. Tuesday to Saturday 10–5, Sunday 1–5. Closed holidays. Free.

Princeton, New Jersey

MORVEN, Stockton Street at Library Place. Open sometimes on Tuesday afternoon.

PRINCETON UNIVERSITY, Visitors' Information Office, 2 North Reunion Hall, Nassau Street. Advance request for a student-guided tour is appreciated.

Rochester, New York State

CAMPBELL-WHITTLESEY HOUSE, 123 S. Fitzhugh Street at Troup Street. Tuesday to Saturday 10–5, Sunday 2–5.

GEORGE EASTMAN HOUSE, 900 East Avenue. Tuesday to Saturday 10–5, Sunday 1–6. Closed holidays. Free.

Sag Harbor, Long Island

SUFFOLK COUNTY WHALING MUSEUM, Main Street. 30 May to 12 October, Monday to Saturday 10–5, Sunday 2–5.

Setauket, Long Island

CAROLINE CHURCH, Main Street at Setauket Green. Daily 9–5.

Southampton, Long Island

LONG ISLAND AUTOMOTIVE MUSEUM, 1 mile west on State Route 39. 1 June to 30 September, daily 9–5; end of May and October, Saturday and Sunday 9–5.

PARRISH ART MUSEUM, Job's Lane. 15 May to 30 September, daily 10–5, Sunday 2–5. 1 October to 14 May, Thursday to Saturday 10–5.

Stony Brook, Long Island

SUFFOLK MUSEUM, Christian Avenue, north end of village green. 15 March to 20 December, Wednesday to Sunday, 10–5.30.

SUFFOLK MUSEUM (CARRIAGE HOUSE), State Route 25A. 1 April to 15 November, Wednesday to Sunday, 10–5.30.

Tarrytown, New York State

PHILIPSBURG MANOR, In North Tarrytown, on U.S. Route 9. Temporarily closed for archaeological research.

SUNNYSIDE, South of Tarrytown; West Sunnyside Lane off U.S. Route 9. Daily 9–5.

VAN CORTLANDT, South of Croton-on-Hudson, on U.S. Route 9. Daily 9–5.

Valley Forge, Pennsylvania

VALLEY FORGE STATE PARK. Daily 9–5.

F

West Point, New York State

VISITORS INFORMATION CENTER, near the Thayer Gate, open 1 April to 30 October, Monday to Saturday 9–5, Sunday 11–5. Parades: early September to early October, and May, Monday, Tuesday, Thursday 5.30. Reviews: Autumn and May, daily 1.10 p.m.

Wilmington, Delaware

HAGLEY MUSEUM, Barley Mill Road. Tuesday to Saturday 9.30–4.30, Sunday 1–5. Closed holidays. Free.

LONGWOOD GARDENS, PENNSYLVANIA, 13 miles north of Wilmington. Daily sunrise to sunset. Conservatories daily 11–5. Free.

WINTERTHUR MUSEUM, 6 miles north of Wilmington on State Route 52. Reservations for guided tours from H. F. Du Pont Winterthur Museum, Winterthur, Delaware, must be made in advance. Closed Sunday, Monday and first two weeks in July. Azalea Gardens and part of museum open without reservation, last week in April to 30 May, Tuesday to Saturday 10–4. Gardens only, Sunday 1–4.30.

4 · New England

New England is that group of states which lies in the north-east corner of the United States: Connecticut, Rhode Island, Massachusetts, Maine, Vermont, New Hampshire. The six states share a homogeneous tradition, a similar history.

Americans regard New England as the very well-spring of America, the embodiment of all the sturdy traditional American virtues. And yet Americans like to describe Boston, the capital of Massachusetts and New England's most important city, as very like London. This is not a contradiction, for many of the traditional American virtues were simply the virtues of rural, middle-class England in the early eighteenth century, Fielding's England. New England is as much heir to this as old England. Moreover, with the exception of a few Huguenot families in Boston (the Reveres, the Faneuils) and a scattering of French Canadians in Maine, the New England colonies remained almost purely English until the great rush of Irish immigration in the nineteenth century, followed later in that century by large numbers of Italians and Portuguese.

New England, proud of her English connexion, is even more proud of her share in the revolt against that connexion. Yet there is no real inconsistency here, for the New England Revolutionary leaders began by insisting only that a free-born Briton in the colonies must be guaranteed the same rights and privileges he would enjoy back in England.

Nowhere in the United States will you find more concern with tangible history, with the preservation of ancient monuments. It can go too far; you must use some discretion or you may find you have spent most of your New England hours in solemn consideration of rusty button-hooks and mildewed samplers. But the best of the old houses open to the public are charming. And time spent at such museum villages as Shelburne, Mystic, or Sturbridge is time well-spent; what one sees there is thoroughly American, but it also bears comparison with rural England in the seventeenth and eighteenth centuries, and hence is doubly fascinating. There is a useful pamphlet, published conjointly by the New England Council, the Boston Museum of Fine Arts, and the Society for the Preservation of New England Antiquities, which lists all the New England museums and historic houses open to the public, with their hours and a brief description. Anyone planning a tour of New England should try to combine the best of the old with a taste of the sort of holiday pleasures for which New England is also noted.

Boston is the heart of New England. It was founded in 1630, but to understand Boston one must begin outside the city limits and farther back in time: in 1620, to be exact. In that year one hundred 'pilgrims' embarked for the New World in the *Mayflower*. All of them were English, most of them were Separatists, and some of them had recently tried living as refugees in Holland. Their venture now was being financed partly by religious sympathizers, and partly by disinterested speculators who hoped only for a good return on their money.

From our superior vantage point today, it is hard to see how anyone could have thought that anything but trouble could come from letting the fractious, dissenting Separatists go off to settle the New World for England; it was simply sweeping gunpowder under the rug. But the attempts to settle the Virginia territory with more orthodox colonists had not been particularly successful; perhaps by 1620 England was grateful for any would-be settlers foolhardy enough to brave the voyage and the Indians and the American climate. In any event, the Pilgrims obtained land grants in the Virginia territory, and they set sail, ill-provisioned, ill-prepared for what lay ahead, but never lacking in courage and always sustained by their sense of righteousness.

Storms and haphazard navigation brought them ashore far to the north of the Virginia territory, but it was already mid-December so they decided they had better stay where they were. And stay they did, even though less than half of them survived that first grim winter. They had sailed from Plymouth in England; they named their landing place Plymouth, too, perhaps because the two harbours do bear a superficial resemblance to each other in shape. But there, today, the resemblance ends. The harbour at Plymouth, Massachusetts, has a navigable channel so narrow and insanely tortuous that twentieth-century sailors are very respectful

of the skill – or the luck – of the *Mayflower*'s crew. No wonder
the Pilgrims were convinced Divine Providence was on their
side!

Realizing that they were outside the jurisdiction of the Virginia
colony, the Pilgrim leaders drew up a rudimentary code on board
the ship and insisted that everyone sign it before disembarking; it
came to be known as 'the Mayflower Compact'. So there was
an independent government of sorts from the very beginning;
you might say that the American Revolution really began in
1620.

Ten years after the Pilgrims reached Plymouth, a much larger
group of Puritans, almost a thousand strong, landed twenty miles
farther up Massachusetts Bay. As they approached their new
world, their leader, John Winthrop, sat himself down in the cabin
of the *Arabella* and wrote a few words which three hundred years
later still keep their proud ring:

'. . . wee must consider that wee shall be as a citty upon a hill.
The eies of all people are upon us soe that if wee shall deale
falsely with our God in this worke wee have undertaken wee
shall be made a story and a by-word through the world.'

Under a charter which gave them fishing and trading rights for
the area and allowed them to organize local government as they
saw fit, they founded Boston and several smaller towns near by;
eventually the Plymouth group allied themselves with them. In
the years ahead, almost all the other settlements in New England
came into being as off-shoots of this Massachusetts Bay Colony,
with Boston as its centre. Some of these new settlements were
loyally patterned after the parent colony, but others were organized quite differently, by Massachusetts Bay rebels and outcasts.
People have always reacted strongly to Boston, and in the seventeenth century a good many could hardly wait to leave it. For the
Massachusetts Bay Colony was a rigid theocracy, administered
much like Calvin's Geneva. If you were one of God's elect, and
worked hard, you could expect to prosper; should adversity over-
take you, the community would care for you and your family. If,
however, you were a late-comer, you would have to prove your
conformity, your obedience, before you had any hope of accept-
ance. And if ever you dared to disagree with the elders of the
church, you could expect persecution, exile, even death.

Now let's drink a toast to old Boston
The home of the bean and the cod
Where the Cabots speak only to Lowells
And the Lowells speak only to God.

The Cabots and the Lowells may feel that this little verse is over-quoted, but there in four lines one does have at least part of the essence of Boston; first, homely, seafaring, colonial Boston, then the image of the proper Bostonian as the ultimate in stiff-necked American aristocracy, and last, but never least in Boston, God.

Obviously, then, the proper place to begin a visit to Boston is at the site of its first church, where Tremont and Park Streets cross at the edge of Boston Common. Boston is almost unique among large cities in still having its common, which is now at the centre of the city. It gives the city a quaint and friendly air, totally different from both the sleek impersonality of New York and the stateliness of Washington.

Where the first church once stood, there is now a newer building, the Park Street Church. Built in 1810, it was a centre of anti-slavery sentiment in the years before the Civil War. Today it is noteworthy as a leading example of the independent and evangelical sort of church so common in the United States; a church with only the loosest affiliation with any other church, with no governing body other than its own vestry, and with a minister who attracts vast crowds through the power of his preaching.

The Park Street Church is also the official starting point for the Freedom Trail, a suggested sign-posted walking tour which leads past Boston's most important historic sights. To follow the Freedom Trail in its entirety might involve too large a dose of rather repetitious American history. But both the start and the finish are interesting.

After the Park Street Church, the Freedom Trail leads north-east along Tremont Street to the Old Granary Burial Ground, just beyond the church. Several of the leading Revolutionary figures lie here, including John Hancock (who was the first to sign the Declaration of Independence, writing his name large 'so the King can read it without his spectacles') and Paul Revere. But perhaps the most famous grave is that of Mother Goose: Mrs Isaac Goose, she was, and she died in Boston in 1690; the rhymes she had recited to her children and grandchildren were collected and printed by her son.

A few steps farther on along Tremont Street is King's Chapel. The present building was finished in the middle of the eighteenth century. It was designed by Peter Harrison, one of the most celebrated architects of colonial New England; there is more of his work in Newport, Rhode Island, and Christ Church on the Common in Cambridge is his. The original church, built in 1688, was the first Church of England, or Episcopal, church in the Massachusetts Bay Colony, and as such it was bitterly resented by most of the colonists. After the Revolution, King's Chapel was re-dedicated as the first Unitarian Church in America. Wherever you go in New England, if you seek the oldest church, look for the Congregational Church; but the second oldest will very likely be Unitarian. The rigidity, the strictness of the Congregational Church (originally Puritan or Separatist) did not suit everyone, and Unitarianism won many adherents.

Everywhere in Boston you will be confronted by the Revolution, until the non-American may well weary of it. But the fact of the Revolution is as central to New England as the Stuart cause to Scotland, and you had better meet it head on.

The Pilgrims reached Plymouth in 1620; the Americans did not make their Declaration of Independence until 1776. Yet it would be a mistake to assume that all was serene in between those two dates. King's Chapel gave evidence of recurrent friction in New England over religious matters, and as the colonists became more ambitious in their trading and fishing ventures, they grew less tolerant of commercial restrictions imposed from London. The only thing which kept relations comparatively polite was the fact that Britain's problems in Europe kept her from paying much attention to the American colonies. Left to their own devices, the settlers prospered; particularly in New England, they simply circumvented those restrictions they found annoying. Then, in about 1750, England suddenly took cognizance of the fact that her American children were somewhat undisciplined, and she also noted that they were quite big and strong enough to be of considerable help to their mother, so the struggle over stamp duties and import and export quotas began. It was really too late now for firmness, which only aroused stubborn hostility and open defiance, but succeeding British governments persisted in trying, and made one tactical error after another. Only a few British leaders (Pitt, Charles James Fox, Burke) seemed to comprehend the seriousness and the complexity of the situation, and their advice was disregarded.

For thirty years before the Revolution, a Boston radical named Sam Adams had been speaking and writing against 'English tyranny'. The well-to-do merchants who by now more or less controlled Boston affairs paid scant attention to Adams and his 'rabble' until about 1760. Then, enraged first over the Writs of Assistance (unreasonable searching of ships, they thought), and later over the Stamp Acts (unreasonable duties imposed), many of them began to listen more sympathetically. The most important of the new converts was John Hancock, scion of one of the richest shipping families, and with him to several of Sam Adams's meetings came a distant cousin of Sam's, one John Adams, a studious, respectable young lawyer, tenacious to a fault. If one adds the name of the engraver and silversmith Paul Revere to this list, one has the four Revolutionary leaders from Boston whose names are best known today. And together they represent that cross-section of class and interest which, united, made success possible.

Everyone should see at least one of the buildings which figured so prominently in the struggles leading up to the Revolution, and the Freedom Trail markers lead to one of the best, the Old South Meeting House. The Congregational ministers were among the most ardent revolutionaries, dreading any extension of royal power for fear of Church-of-England control. So the Congregational meeting houses, and especially this one, welcomed mass meetings of the aroused citizenry. In 1773, the Boston Tea Party began here, at the end of a protest meeting, chaired by John Adams, which had failed to move the Governor from his determination to enforce the tax on tea and to compel the unloading of the two controversial shipments waiting in the harbour. Disguised as Indians, a large group of respectable Boston citizens proceeded to the ships and quietly threw all the casks of tea overboard.

Anyone passionately interested in the Revolution can continue on the Freedom Trail and see the charming little Old State House, and Faneuil Hall, the market house which sheltered many a patriotic meeting and is still the centre of market district. Two of the Boston restaurants most familiar to tourists are there, both specializing in seafood: the Durgin Park and the Union Oyster House.

Otherwise this seems the proper moment to head for one of the most interesting sights in Boston, the frigate U.S.S. *Constitution* known as 'Old Ironsides'. You can get there by underground train on the MTA, the Boston public transport system, going to the Navy Yard stop in the Charlestown section of Boston. The U.S.S. *Constitution* is the oldest fighting ship still afloat anywhere in the world; she was launched in 1797 and saw action in the war of 1812. She is now docked at the Navy Yard, where the Navy looks after her, and she is a delight to visit.

Paul Revere's house and the Old North Church lie in that rather shabby section of Boston which is just across the Charles River from the Navy Yard. You can walk there from the Common; they are at the end of the Freedom Trail. But it is a fairly long walk and not a particularly attractive one.

Paul Revere is most famous today for having ridden out to Lexington and Concord one night in 1775 to warn the leaders there that the British troops were on the march. The next day 'the shot heard round the world' was fired, in Lexington, and the Revolution had begun. But in his own day Paul Revere was far better known as a silversmith; he was a fine one, and his silver is tremendously sought after today. His house, which is open to the public, was built about 1680, and is an interesting example of simple domestic architecture and decoration in eighteenth-century Boston.

The Old North Church is the oldest church still standing in Boston (1723). In its steeple hung the lanterns which gave Paul Revere the signal to ride. The church and the house are in what is now one of Boston's principal Italian districts. You can sit in the little park behind the church and eat an Italian ice and watch the elderly Italians arguing fiercely over their checker boards.

But Boston has another, more recent past which bears investigation: nineteenth-century Boston, the Boston of Henry James's novels, the Boston where the Lowells spoke only to Cabots. This aspect of the city has been most consistently explored in our day in the novels of J. P. Marquand, which suggest that it is fading fast. Yet there is still no more pleasant walk in Boston than a stroll across the Common to the handsome 'new' State House and then down Beacon Street, itself a symbol of the world of the Boston

brahmin; the Athenaeum, that magnificent private library and
holy of holies, is just along it to the right when one reaches the
north-west corner of the Common, and downhill from the State
House lie the proper Bostonian town houses, in an area known as
Beacon Hill. (The name comes from the fact that once there was
an actual beacon at the top, a signal light made of rushes, ready to
be fired whenever Indians threatened or some dramatic event
needed advertising.) Here at the corner is the Saint-Gaudens
memorial to the young Union Civil War officer Colonel Shaw and
his Negro troops; one is reminded that the Boston brahmin is
after all descended from John Winthrop, and is not likely to 'deale
falsely' with either God or Man.

If you walk down Beacon Street from the State House, you
should glance at the windows of number 39 and number 40.
Some of the old panes are a lovely shade of mauve, from an ancient
impurity in the glass; these are only two of many houses in the
Beacon Hill district with this attractive irregularity; 31 Chestnut
Street is one of the best examples. At the heart of Beacon Hill is
Louisburg Square, reminiscent of a Georgian square in London,
although undeniably more plain, more Puritan. You can walk
through the Square to Pinckney Street, and then turn left down
Pinckney to Charles Street. Charles Street has countless antique
shops, and countless tea-shops and cafeterias. It is particularly
pleasant to walk through Beacon Hill in the dusk, just as the street
lights are going on, but you may then be disappointed on arriving
at Charles Street to find so many tempting shops to browse in,
all shut.

Modern Boston is still close to the Common, but on the south-
western side. If you go from Beacon Hill across the Common and
then across the adjacent Public Gardens, where children like to
ride in the swan boats, you come to the area of the most fashionable shops and hotels: 'Back Bay Boston'. In the midst of it, where
Boylston Street meets Huntington Avenue, is Trinity Church,
that incredible mass of Victorian Romanesque. South-west of
Trinity Church rises the great new Prudential Center, financed by
the Prudential Insurance Company, with shops and housing and
office buildings and an auditorium, all in one enormous plaza. On
the far side of the Prudential Center are those landmarks of the
Christian Science Church, the Mother Church, and the Christian
Science Publishing House. The latter is responsible for one of the

best newspapers in America, the independent *Christian Science Monitor*.

Huntington Avenue leads eventually to the main roads going out of the city to the south and west, but first it goes past examples of three of the things for which Boston is famous in America today: education, medicine, and music.

On Huntington Avenue two streets beyond the Prudential Center is Symphony Hall. The Boston Symphony, moulded by Serge Koussevitsky, is probably still the finest orchestra in America, although there are two or three other major orchestras to contest this. Next, along Huntington, the New England Conservatory of Music signals the beginning of that impressive collection of scientific and educational institutions between Huntington Avenue and The Fenway. Not all of the great teaching hospitals are here, and the two most famous universities are across the river in Cambridge, but nonetheless this area is the one most densely packed with doctors and teachers and students, thousands of students. A visitor with a professional interest might like to know that all of the big Boston hospitals are always ready and willing to allow such visitors to come and look over them; one need only telephone beforehand to the public relations office.

Next to Symphony Hall is Horticultural Hall, where flower shows are held. But any dedicated gardener who is in Boston at the proper time of year will want to go to the Arnold Aboretum, at the western edge of the city. Actually a part of Harvard University, used by Harvard botanists for experiment and demonstration, it is even more extensive than the fine Botanical Gardens in Brooklyn, and you can have a delightful picnic among the lilacs and azaleas and rhododendrons.

The two best Boston galleries are just a few streets beyond Symphony Hall: the Museum of Fine Arts on Huntington Avenue, and the Isabella Stewart Gardner Museum on the Fenway; they are not only the best in Boston, but among the finest in America. You can take an MTA bus from Copley Square (Trinity Church) out along Huntington Avenue to get to them, but it should be noted that the Gardner Museum has peculiar hours and on some days can only be visited on a guided tour.

The Gardner is a reconstructed Venetian palazzo, built as a town house for one Isabella Stewart Gardner at the turn of the century. Eccentric, beautiful, rich, and not-quite-accepted, she amassed a remarkable collection of art with the aid and advice of the young Bernard Berenson. Like the Frick in New York, this gallery is relatively small, but charmingly personal and rich in treasures.

The Museum of Fine Arts is many times the size of the Gardner, and completely different. It is a splendid and varied museum of art, second only to the Metropolitan in New York in the range and importance of its collections. In addition to the European and Graeco-Roman and Oriental sections, it has several excellent purely American treasures: Paul Revere silver, some fine examples of the work of Winslow Homer, and a series of rooms of early American furniture and décor. The Museum of Fine Arts has profited from centuries of collecting on the part of discriminating Bostonians; it has also profited through the years from the attentions of discriminating curators.

There is one other collection that should be mentioned for the benefit of those particularly interested in early-American architecture and artifacts. The Society for the Preservation of New England Antiquities, at its headquarters in the handsome old Harrison-Gray-Otis House at 141 Cambridge Street, has a good collection of china and glass, pewter, toys, ingenious displays illustrating early American building styles, and the like.

Boston would not be Boston without Cambridge. Cambridge is a separate city, not a borough of Boston, but it is just across the Charles River, a few minutes' ride on an MTA train to Harvard Square. The eminence of Cambridge began with the founding of Harvard College there in 1636; Harvard is the oldest university in America, antedating the College of William and Mary in Virginia by almost sixty years. It was founded by the Puritans themselves, to train teachers and preachers for the Massachusetts Bay Colony. Most of the Puritan leaders had been Cambridge-educated in England, and so the college town was called Cambridge, and the college itself was named for one of those Cambridge men, the young John Harvard, late of Emmanuel College, who had died after a few years' preaching in the Massachusetts Bay Colony and left what money and books he had to the new school. Harvard grew and prospered; it became more liberal, and attracted young men from the other colonies, and later from all the other states. In a frontier society, the lure of such a university town must have been overpowering for certain kinds of men, and Cambridge reached its zenith in the nineteenth century, when Longfellow lived there, and James Russell Lowell, and many men and women whose fame has dwindled, like Margaret Fuller, 'the female thinker'.

It is pleasant to walk from Harvard Square up Brattle Street towards Longfellow's house, past the precincts of Radcliffe, a woman's college which every year draws closer to the once thoroughly misogynist Harvard.

It is also pleasant to walk around Harvard itself. In the summer there are regular tours; the guide will be a Harvard undergraduate, and the tour a good one.

Massachusetts Hall in New Yard is the oldest Harvard building still standing (1720). Opposite it, University Hall (1815) was designed by Charles Bulfinch, who was also responsible for the central portion of the 'new' State House in Boston. The statue of John Harvard here is the work of Daniel Chester French, better known for the statues of Lincoln in the Lincoln Memorial in Washington and in Parliament Square in London. But one should see more of Harvard than this, perhaps going first to the Fogg Art Museum and the new Visual Arts Center, the first le Corbusier building in America. Then, you might walk down Boylston Street to Memorial Drive along the river and go east past Eliot House and John Winthrop House to Plympton Street, where you can turn north again and wind your way back towards Harvard Square. The river is particularly pleasant along here, with boating, walks, and bicycle paths along the banks.

The Harvard 'houses', Eliot and Winthrop and Lowell and all the others, are only for sleeping and eating; like most American universities, Harvard groups all its undergraduates together in one vast 'college of arts and sciences'. In the United States, there are usually separate colleges within a university only for those embarking on purely technical careers or learning to be teachers, and for those doing postgraduate studies.

But a technical college is not always part of a larger university, and one of the most prestigious independent technical colleges is the Massachusetts Institute of Technology. Sheltering a veritable pride of Nobel prizewinners, it too is in Cambridge, where Massachusetts Avenue crosses the river. There are tours of M.I.T. which include a look at its synchrotron and the lovely little chapel designed by Eero Saarinen.

As one might expect, there are several museums in Cambridge, most of them connected in one way or another with Harvard. The Fogg gallery is particularly strong in prints and drawings; the botanical section of the Harvard University Museum, familiarly called the Agazziz, seems destined always to be known chiefly for its intricate glass flowers; the Peabody is an archeological and ethnological museum; the Reisinger is devoted exclusively to Germanic art and sometimes offers German music in the background as well.

In early June, Boston has a two-week Arts Festival in the Public Gardens. And all summer long the new Cambridge Summer Theater flourishes on the banks of the Charles River; you can take a boat up the river to the performances, from the embankment in Boston.

For anyone who may have two or three days in Boston and wants to make a trip out of the city, one obvious possibility is a journey to Lexington and Concord. Concord is only twenty miles or so; Lexington is even nearer, in the same direction. There are organized bus tours which include them both.

If you have been to the Old North Church in Boston, you will have heard of the midnight ride of Paul Revere and you will remember that it took him to Lexington. In Lexington you can see the Hancock-Clarke house, his first stop that night in 1775. Expecting trouble, John Hancock and Sam Adams were staying here, out of Boston, out of sight; Paul Revere came to warn them that eight hundred British troops were heading that way. Today the house is interesting to fervent patriots for its historical associations, but it is also interesting simply as a good example of a plain colonial-Massachusetts dwelling house. Equally interesting is the old Buckman Tavern where seventy-odd Minutemen, the local militia, gathered later that night. The Tavern is at the edge of the green, where the militia met the troops the next day and gave way before them after several men on each side had been killed.

The British troops marched on from Lexington to Concord where there was rumoured to be a large cache of rebel arms, and at Concord Bridge they met the Concord Minutemen, who rather surprisingly forced them to retreat. The Revolution had begun in earnest.

But Concord has associations over and above the Revolutionary

ones. This is where the Little Women grew up; this is where
Louisa May Alcott lived. And Nathaniel Hawthorne lived here,
and Henry David Thoreau, and Ralph Waldo Emerson, whose
Transcendentalist movement was pure Concord. Cambridge was
an intellectual centre in the early nineteenth century, but Cambridge was too complacement to suit everyone; the iconoclasts
gathered in Concord.

Louisa May Alcott's father, Bronson Alcott, was an educator,
a philosopher, and an altogether endearing man, who was at one
time far more widely known than his daughter. He abhorred
violence and he had complete faith in the perfectibility of human
nature. The fact that he seldom succeeded in supporting his family
embittered neither his family nor his friends, who rallied round
with unfailing affection.

There are two houses in Concord in which the Alcotts lived:
Wayside, and Orchard House, next door to each other on the
Lexington Road. Of the two, only Orchard House is now open to
the public. The Alcotts moved from Wayside into Orchard House
in 1848, when Louisa May was sixteen; Hawthorne then moved
into Wayside. Emerson, 'the American Carlyle', in that day the
most famous of all the Concord figures, lived on the other side of
Concord, near the North Bridge; his house too is open to the
public. Thoreau lived on Main Street, and a mile or so to the
south of Concord is the still relatively unspoiled Walden Pond,
where Thoreau spent two memorable winters in the woods in a
hut he built himself. *Walden*, the book which resulted from that
experience, is an American classic.

Many of Bronson Alcott's Concord friends had also been
involved with him in either the Brook Farm or the Fruitlands
experiments in communal living and a return to a simple, agricultural life. Hawthorne, who spent one miserable winter at
Brook Farm, complained bitterly that after a day in the fields or
with the cows he was too tired to think or write clearly. Others
eventually grew impatient with the sacrifices demanded: one must
not wear wool, because it was unfair to sheep, or use oil lamps,
because they were unfair to whales. And then the amateur farmers
found that they were ill-equipped for competition with the rest of
the world, and the accounts suffered. So both Brook Farm and
Fruitlands in turn languished and died, but Fruitlands can still be
seen, in a lovely setting some twenty miles beyond Lexington and

Concord. There are several buildings there, scattered down a rolling green hill-side; in addition to the Alcott house there is a small American Indian museum, an excellent collection of early American paintings, and a Shaker house. For Fruitlands is at Harvard, Massachusetts (not to be confused with Harvard University at Cambridge) and Harvard had one of the most important Shaker colonies. Many of the Shaker buildings can still be seen, on the other side of Harvard village, and there is a Shaker burial ground there too, the grave markers looking like rows of lollipops stuck in the ground. None of these Shaker houses is open to the public; one must be content with visiting the one transported complete to Fruitlands.

The Shakers were one of those strange sects which seemed to flower in the New World. They combined an insistence on simplicity in dress and daily life with religious services which culminated in spontaneous ecstatic dancing, so they were known as 'shaking Quakers', and soon simply 'Shakers'. Strictly celibate, they nonetheless built mixed communities, with separate dormitories for men and women. They flourished principally in the nineteenth century, although a few elderly Shakers are still living in one of the seventeen original settlements. The sect might have been completely forgotten today were it not for the happy fact that the Shaker insistence on simplicity led to their making a special, recognizable sort of furniture, so plain and functional yet lovely that it now appeals to every sort of connoisseur.

If you have time to spare on the way back to Boston, you might stop at Lincoln, a pretty village with a small contemporary art gallery, the de Cordova. Or you might brave the industrial town of Waltham, to see either Lyman House, a late eighteenth-century country house by the brilliant Samuel McIntire, with a garden designed by a Scotch disciple of Repton; or Gore Place, considered the finest Federal-period country house in New England. What is known as Federal-period in American architecture and decoration roughly corresponds in date to that of Regency in England: in other words, the last ten years or so of the eighteenth century and the first twenty-five or thirty years of the nineteenth.

Lexington, and more particularly Concord and Fruitlands, lie well inland from Boston, in a pleasantly rural part of New England. Another good day's trip from Boston is along the more populous North Shore, where one can choose between Saugus, and Marblehead and Salem, and the pretty villages beyond Beverly, and Gloucester and Rockport, and Ipswich.

At Saugus they have restored America's first ironworks, which began operations in the mid-seventeenth century. The great forge hammer, the water wheels and the bellows actually work at set times every day when the restored area is open.

Marblehead is one of those towns considered tremendously picturesque, with rather too many people and cameras around on a summer afternoon, but it is deservedly popular. The Jeremiah Lee House, at 161 Washington Street, is one of the best colonial-period houses in New England.

Salem too has some fine houses open to the public, most notably two side by side on Essex Street, the Pingree House (Samuel McIntire) at number 128 and the Crowninshield-Bentley House at number 126. And at Derby Wharf, where today a submarine is berthed and open to visitors, one can still see the old Customs House where Nathaniel Hawthorne had a post. Salem was then a leading port, sending ships to the East Indies and growing rich on the profits. It was in fact a young Salem man, Nathaniel Bowditch, who in 1802 put together the classic *Practical Navigator*, to help the local sea captains. One can still see something of this aspect of Salem's past in the modern industrial town, but virtually no trace now remains of that dread Salem of the 1692 witchcraft trials, when the good citizens did to death twenty men and women before sanity prevailed. No trace, that is, unless one counts that great Salem tourist attraction, the House of Seven Gables, supposedly the inspiration for Hawthorne's novel of the same name in which the witch trials still cast a black shadow.

Beyond Salem, Route 127 leads north-east along the shore through a whole series of pretty places like Pride's Crossing and Manchester until it reaches Gloucester. Gloucester was the fishing port in Kipling's *Captains Courageous*, and it still has Portuguese fishermen and considerable character. It also has Beauport, a house-cum-museum with what is quite rightly characterized as 'an extraordinary and fascinating assembly of period rooms', the individual expression of one man, who left it at his death to the Preservation Society.

Rockport is out on Cape Ann, beyond Gloucester. Like Provincetown at the tip of Cape Cod, it attracts artists and also the

G

sort of people who come to stare at artists; it is suitably picturesque.

There is a nice beach which one can reach by back-tracking
from Gloucester, or by going due north from Salem: Crane's
Beach. And in the neighbouring town of Ipswich is still another
fine old house, the seventeenth-century John Whipple House
at 53 Main Street. The two most popular public beaches near
Boston are Revere Beach on the north and Nantasket Beach on the
south; one can even reach Nantasket Beach by boat, from
Boston harbour. But these two beaches are crowded and noisy,
and completely unlike the peaceful stretch of sand at Crane's
Beach.

Driving from New York to Boston, one has a choice of two main
routes: through Connecticut more or less along the coast, or
inland through Massachusetts. (It is also possible to go the length
of Long Island to Orient Point and there take a car-ferry to New
London, Connecticut, and thence to Boston; the ferries run all the
year round, and the A.A.A. can supply the schedule.)

The inland route is more direct and you can travel the entire
way on turnpikes; the coastal route will leave you at the mercy of
ordinary, old-fashioned roads once you reach the Connecticut–
Rhode Island border. The New Haven Railway goes to Boston
along the coast, with some fine glimpses of the sea near New
London; the fastest express buses use the inland route.

The coastal route follows the New England Thruway markers,
Interstate 95, out of New York City to the Connecticut Turnpike,
and for the first fifty miles goes through the older suburbs and
then that exurbanite area of which we spoke in the preceding
chapter. Only near New Haven does one begin to feel well away
from New York, well into New England.

New Haven is best known as a college town; Yale University
is there, founded by Connecticut Puritans in 1701. The name came
from Elihu Yale, a rather sour old man who had been so successful a Boston merchant that he gained royal favour and was
appointed Governor of Madras. He died and was buried in Wales,
leaving £560 to the new college, mainly to spite Harvard, which
he considered too liberal. Few people have bought immortality
so cheaply, and, as he would have wished, Yale has always considered itself Harvard's particular rival.

Yale is not nearly so handsome as Harvard, but it now has some fine modern buildings. Moreover, one can spend an agreeable hour or two in New Haven, starting at the green with its three handsome churches side by side on the north-west side. Behind Center Church (1814) is the grave of one of the men who presided at the trial and condemnation of Charles I. He and two others of the regicides fled to Connecticut after the Restoration and were hidden for several years in and around New Haven. A plaque on the outer rear wall of the church commemorates all three. North-east of the green along Prospect Street is the Grove Street cemetery, with the graves of several of those Yankee inventors who made New Haven an important manufacturing centre: Eli Whitney, who invented the cotton gin and the Winchester rifle and was among the first to experiment with interchangeable parts and assembly lines, Samuel F. B. Morse, who developed the first practical telegraph, and Charles Goodyear, who first patented the vulcanizing process for rubber. Much farther out along Prospect Street is Yale's startling new ice-hockey rink, designed by Eero Saarinen. The Yale Gallery of Fine Arts, two streets north-west of the green, on Chapel Street, has among other things the splendid Jarvis collection of Italian primitives and an interesting group of paintings by the late eighteenth-century Connecticut artist John Trumbull. In the summer, guided tours of the university begin at Phelps Gateway on College Street.

After New Haven you might leave the turnpike again at Guilford to see two attractive small New England towns, Guilford and Madison. Guilford has an unusually large number of colonial-period houses and a pretty green with tempting shops. The Guilford house most worth visiting is probably the Whitfield House (1639). But notice, just to the east of the First Congregational Church on the green at Guilford, the delightful Victorian house, and beyond it across the street an earlier house with exceptionally fine detail in its decorative mouldings.

The town next after Guilford is Madison, which has a fine Congregational Church on its peaceful green, and some charming houses. At the corner of Academy Street just beyond the green stands a dark unpainted wooden house, now rather neglected and almost hidden behind overgrown shrubbery; known as the Graves House, it is that rarity in America, a virtually unaltered seventeenth-century frame house.

After Madison, it is just as well to return to the turnpike unless you want to stop at Hammonasset, a fine state beach. The road from Guilford to Madison is part of the old U.S. Route 1, the Boston Post Road. For two hundred and fifty years it was the principal road from Boston to New York, but with the invention of the automobile it became a traveller's nightmare.

The turnpike skirts New London and ends at last at the Rhode Island border; to get from there to Boston, one must continue on ordinary roads. It is well to avoid Providence, because it is a large city, unless you are sufficiently interested in its past to want to stop there. The capitol of Rhode Island, it was founded in 1636 by Roger Williams, who had been banished from the Massachusetts Bay Colony because he would not acknowledge the church's authority in civil matters and he objected to land being forcibly taken from the Indians. With real religious freedom and good relations with the Rhode Island Indians, Providence flourished, and among its early settlers was a redoubtable family of Quakers called Brown.

The Browns are encountered everywhere in Providence: the most obvious trace is Brown University, where the library has the best Abraham Lincoln collection and the best general collection of Americana in the United States. In the eighteenth century, Providence was an important port; in that ironic manner so characteristic of New England, its kindly Quaker shipowners amassed considerable fortunes in the slave and rum trade. But Providence also nurtured craftsmen, and in the nineteenth century, when other New England seaports fell upon hard times, Providence shifted almost effortlessly from crafts to manufacturing, and remained prosperous. The Rhode Island School of Design in Providence has a fine collection of colonial Rhode Island wares and furniture as well as newer things. And the elegant John Brown house is now the headquarters of the Rhode Island Historical Association, and is open to the public.

For those who have two or three days to spare there is a longer route to Boston by way of Mystic and Newport. The Mystic Seaport and Marine Museum is a reconstruction of a section of the harbour as it was in the early nineteenth century; there are sailmakers' shops and ship's chandlers and several old sailing ships, including a splendid whaler. And there is a nautical museum, with a fine collection of navigational instruments and charts as well as such things as ships' figureheads, and another small museum full of clocks and chronometers. Five miles beyond Mystic is Stonington, one of the most attractive old sailing towns in Connecticut. In 1800, it was the largest city in the state, a bustling port; Nelson's Captain Hardy bombarded it in the war of 1812. Today it is quiet and unspoiled, and near the harbour are one or two pleasant inexpensive seafood restaurants.

Continuing on this alternative way to Boston, just east of Usquepaugh in Rhode Island along Route 138 is the site of the Great Swamp Fight, the most important battle in that bitter conflict between colonists and Indians which was known as King Philip's War. King Philip was the son of Massassoit, who had been one of the Pilgrim's first Indian friends, but Philip himself had come to realize that the white settlements meant eventual disaster for his people, and when he succeeded his father as chief of the Narragansetts he tried to unite all the various New England Indian tribes in order to wipe out the colonists once and for all. The coastal Indians, from Virginia to Boston, were largely Algonquins, but within the Algonquin grouping there were many separate and warring tribes: the Mohicans and the Narragansetts and the Pequots, to name only three. From the beginning, all the New England settlements except those in Rhode Island had had trouble with the Indians, and the whites had usually retaliated by persuading one Indian tribe to help them attack the other; most frequently, Unca's Mohicans were the settlers' allies. But now Philip of the Narragansetts persuaded his fellow chiefs to make common cause, and from 1675 to 1677 the united Indians waged a kind of sustained warfare which they were never to repeat. In those two years about nine hundred men on each side were killed, and that meant one out of every ten men among the colonists. Many whites were taken prisoner, too, and many Indians captured and sold as slaves. More than half of all the towns in New England were destroyed; even Providence was burned. But in the end Philip himself was betrayed by another Indian and killed, and a pathetic remnant of the Algonquins made their way to the Ohio territory, forced to evade en route the enemy Iroquois tribes in New York and Pennsylvania.

Route 138 leads through Kingston, a pretty little town, and then on over the Jamestown bridge and across Conanicut Island to the Jamestown–Newport ferry, across Narragansett Bay. As one nears Newport, old Fort Adams, an eighteenth-century harbour defence, is on the right, and on the left a gleaming white building on a shaven lawn, the Naval War College. As you approach the dock at Newport you can, in fact, see evidence of all four reasons for visiting Newport: behind Fort Adams are some of the enormous summer 'cottages' built in the days before the First World War when Newport was the *ne plus ultra* of fashionable watering places. Straight ahead is the spire of Trinity Church, a particularly lovely colonial church. On the left is the naval base. And in the harbour there are sure to be sailing boats of every description, for this is great sailing country; it is here that the America's Cup races are held.

Newport is exceptionally rich in colonial-period buildings of considerable architectural interest, and the best way to see them is to get one of the free brochures at the Chamber of Commerce Visitors Information Bureau and then set off on foot. The Old Colony House, Touro Synagogue, and Trinity Church are all open without charge. The synagogue is the oldest synagogue in America, and one of Peter Harrison's finest buildings. Peter Harrison also designed the Redwood Library, up the hill from the synagogue, on Bellevue Avenue; it was the first private subscription library in America.

In the middle of the eighteenth century, Newport was the most sophisticated town in New England. Not hampered by any narrow Puritanism, it attracted a varied group of remarkable men, from Isaac Touro, an aristocratic Portuguese Jew, to Bishop Berkeley, the Anglo-Irish metaphysician, who lived here for three years while he tried to organize a missionary college in the New World. Berkeley's first two children were born here; the second is buried in Trinity Churchyard. His house, Whitehall, is still standing and open to the public, in the country just east of the town.

Whitehall is one of the two old Newport houses one really must see; the other is Hunter House, which is splendidly furnished with what is called block-front furniture, mostly the work of those renowned Newport cabinet-making families, the Goddards and the Townsends. You can buy combination tickets, at a considerable saving, which will admit you to Whitehall and the Hunter House and also to the Breakers, that incredible

Vanderbilt house which is the most palatial of all the late-nineteenth-century 'summer cottages'.

At the Hunter House you are sure to hear how five thousand French troops under Rochambeau landed at Newport to aid the American cause during the Revolution; this army, which included among its officers Marie Antoinette's Count Fersen, stayed in and near Newport for nearly a year. But despite the French, Newport was ruined during the war. For three years it was occupied by British troops; trade collapsed and never recovered. Those who could, fled, never to return, and Newport lay neglected and poor. It revived, however, in the middle of the nineteenth century. First, wealthy Southerners discovered it as a pleasant summer resort they could easily reach on coastal steamers from Charleston or Savannah. Then after the Civil War the new Northern millionaires took it over and it became a byword in America for extravagant splendour and social distinction. Today, crowds file through the Breakers and gasp as the guides reel off the cost of every doorknob; it is fun to make the tour. The Breakers stables are delightful in quite a different way, with the mahogany horse-boxes still sanded and ready, the tack all oiled, and some twenty-five sorts of carriages lined up waiting to be driven.

The most elaborate houses are along Bellevue Avenue near the Breakers, but everyone should also go the nine miles around Ocean Drive, not only to see more houses, but also to see the surf pounding on the rocks and, in June, the wild roses blooming all along the way.

The smartest beach club is Bailey's Beach, on Ocean Drive. The public beaches are east of the town, and are called simply First Beach and Second Beach. Of First Beach, our invaluable 1885 Englishman's *Guide to the United States* says: 'The surf bathing here is exceedingly fine and quite safe. When the white flag is raised, bathing costumes must be worn. When the red flag is up, gentlemen are permitted to bathe without costume. Purgatory is a wonderful narrow chasm, 160 feet long and 40 feet deep.' Our own research indicates that Purgatory is still 160 feet long and 40 feet deep, but today the red flag merely means dangerous surf.

The Casino block along Bellevue has Newport's smartest shops, as well as the Casino itself, a tennis club with an annual grass-court tournament which serves as a prelude to the big matches at Forest Hills. Just to the rear of the Casino is the park where the

Newport Jazz Festival is held during the first week in July; some years the jazz here is so good it can even overshadow the bacchanalian orgy which takes place on the fringes.

East of Newport is New Bedford, of *Moby Dick* fame (the Seaman's Bethel is still there), and Plymouth and Cape Cod. About ten miles north of the centre of Newport, along Route 114, there is a sign pointing left to the Portsmouth Priory. This is a Roman Catholic boys' school and it has a chapel designed by Pietro Belluschi which is one of the most beautiful contemporary church buildings in the United States. Particularly in the summer when the school is on holiday, there seems to be no objection to well-behaved visitors driving into the school grounds and going into the chapel.

The only large town before Boston is Fall River, which is a mill town. The great grim old mill buildings with their high narrow windows give Fall River a certain distinction, but in 1892 the town acquired a different sort of fame when the daughter of one of its wealthiest citizens was accused of chopping up her father and step-mother.

> *Lizzie Borden took an axe*
> *And gave her mother forty whacks;*
> *When she saw what she had done*
> *She gave her father forty-one.*

Lizzie Borden was acquitted, rightly so according to the most recent student of the case, but it is hard to be sure either way and it remains America's most fascinating murder. The Borden house where the murders took place is still there, at what is now called 230 Second Street; it is somewhat altered, and not open to the public.

The easiest route from New York to Boston is by way of the Merritt Parkway, the Wilbur Cross Parkway, and finally the Massachusetts Turnpike. It goes through pretty, rolling country much of the way; for many miles you will not see even so much as a village in the distance. But one may leave the parkway for a while in Connecticut to look at an attractive small town such as Wethersfield where there are two fine colonial-period houses open to the public: the Buttolph-Williams House (1692) and the Webb House (1752). Or you could pause at Hartford, where Mark Twain's last house, at 351 Farmington Avenue, is open to the public, and where the Connecticut State Library has a fine collection of Colt guns, the Colt Firearms Company being one of Hartford's oldest industries.

Thirty or forty miles beyond Hartford is Sturbridge Village. After Williamsburg, this is the most elaborate reconstruction in the eastern United States. Sturbridge recreates a much simpler life than that of Williamsburg; New England after all was strongly Puritan. And Sturbridge is a more artificial reconstruction. The restored section of Williamsburg is an exact re-creation of what was once actually there, and an integral part of the modern town; Sturbridge, however, is a village that never was, with appropriate buildings brought from all over New England to be put into a village setting within an enclosure. But Sturbridge has considerable charm, and like Mystic it is well worth the entrance fee, provided that you can spend two or three hours there. It also has picturesque eating places to suit every purse.

The largest town between Sturbridge and Boston is Worcester, by-passed by the Turnpike but notable for its fine art gallery. This route also passes fairly close to the Fruitlands museum at Harvard, and Lexington and Concord.

Americans on holiday in New England go to many of the places already mentioned, but they also go to Cape Cod, and the islands of Martha's Vineyard and Nantucket, and the Berkshires, and the states of Vermont and New Hampshire and Maine.

Cape Cod still has several pleasant towns, and the more remote section of its south coast, once the delight of wreckers, has been made a new National Park area, but the Cape a casual visitor is most likely to see is now depressingly overcrowded in the summer. This is also true of Plymouth, on the way from Boston to the Cape, where there is an interesting reconstruction of the original Pilgrim settlement. The *Mayflower II* is also there. A replica of the original *Mayflower*, the ship was built in England and sailed over in 1957 during commemorative celebrations.

People who have gone for many years to Martha's Vineyard and Nantucket complain that these islands too are overcrowded now, but for a new-comer they still have great charm. Martha's Vineyard is closer to the mainland, larger, and more populous. It has several centres: Edgartown for the smart sailing crowd; Vineyard Haven, equally fashionable but quieter; Menemsha, a fishing village and artists' colony; and Oak Bluffs, characterized by the more conservative Vineyard people as full of penny arcades and people off the day-boats. Oak Bluffs is worth seeing, however, because it was once a thriving Methodist camp-meeting centre, and the camp-meeting ground is a delight with its hundreds of little cottages elaborately trimmed with fancy Victorian fretwork. At Gay Head on the Vineyard there still remain a few of the original Indians, whose forefathers often sailed with the newer settlers on whaling boats.

The island of Nantucket, like Martha's Vineyard, can be reached by boat from Wood's Hole on the Cape, or by plane from New York or Boston on days when the fog holds off. Like the Vineyard, Nantucket has fine sailing and swimming, but its particular charm is that it was once the most important whaling centre of them all. Nantucket ships, in fact, went everywhere, and not only after whales: the tea at the Boston Tea Party was thrown off a Nantucket boat, and the first ship to appear in English waters flying the new American colours after the Revolution was from there.

Today the whaling captains' houses with their silver door-knockers and the golden eagles over the fanlights are still ranged along the cobblestoned Main Street, and the memory of whale is everywhere. Two or three people still do and sell scrimshaw work, that intricate decorative carving on whalebone which whalers used to do to while away the long months at sea. Nantucket has capitalized on its past with more than usual grace. Almost every-one on the island in the summer either owns or hires a bicycle, to ride to the beach, or out across the moors to the wild south coast, or to Siasconset, a village on the east coast with tiny old fisher-men's houses called 'warted cottages'. It takes time to get to Nan-tucket, but there are few pleasanter spots for a New England holiday.

The Berkshires, those sparsely settled wooded hills of western Massachusetts, have a nostalgic nineteenth-century air about them. The views are lovely; particularly in the autumn when the leaves have just turned, there are few drives in America more exhilarating than the Berkshire Trail, Route 9 from Northampton to Pittsfield, or the old Mohawk Trail, Route 2 from Williams-town to Greenfield and on towards Boston. Tanglewood, the most famous summer music festival in the United States, is in the Berkshires near Lenox. Koussevitsky began it in his first years with the Boston Symphony, and the Boston Symphony is still its cornerstone, but there is also chamber music and opera and the season now extends through most of July and August. You need not book seats if you are willing to sit on the grass, as hundreds of people do; it takes place out of doors. Accommodation, however, can present a more serious problem at the height of the season.

Lenox is eclectic: the Berkshire Music Barn there has jazz concerts and folk-singing throughout July and August too. And in near-by Lee there is the Jacob's Pillow Dance Festival which includes both classic ballet and modern dance.

In this same part of Massachusetts is Amherst, a college town where Emily Dickinson, that remarkable nineteenth-century poet, spent her secluded life, and where Robert Frost, equally remarkable in twentieth-century American poetry, lived for many years. Williamstown has Williams College and a new gallery, the Clark Art Institute, which is one of those treasures one does not expect to find in so remote a place. And then there is Deerfield, with one entire street a virtual open-air museum. Ten houses here are open to the public; the Frary House is one of the best. In 1704 Deerfield suffered the worst Indian raid in New England history; the town was completely razed, forty-nine people were killed and one hundred and eleven carried off, many of them never to be seen again. Amazingly, it was rebuilt and resettled almost immediately, and today it is a nearly perfect little eighteenth-century town.

There is also a newly-restored Shaker colony in the Berkshires, Hancock Shaker Village, on Route 20 a few miles west of Pittsfield. It is worth the trip simply to see the ingenious round barn, but in addition one can sense here better than at any other Shaker centre the peculiar charm of the Shaker world.

North and north-east of the Berkshires lie Vermont and New Hampshire: ski-ing country, because they are mountainous, but equally popular in summer, and delightful and less crowded in the autumn. In New Hampshire, the attraction is the White Mountains, in Vermont the Green Mountains. Both areas have any number of large and small hotels and resorts. The White Mountains are particularly good for hiking; at intervals along the trails there are excellent hostels maintained by the Appalachian Mountain Club. At the centre of the region is Mount Washington,

only 6000 feet high but one of the most treacherous climbing
mountains in the world; the weather station there once recorded
winds at 231 miles an hour.

Route 119 is a pleasant road to take north-west from the Boston
area through southern New Hampshire into Vermont. Route 7
goes through unspoiled rolling country all the way from New
Haven, Connecticut, across the Berkshires, and on up through
Bennington and Manchester, Vermont, where countless people
in the arts have come through the years to settle, for reasons
readily apparent as one drives through. Almost all of Vermont is
tremendously picturesque. After Middlebury, another attractive
college town with a renowned modern-languages school and a
writer's conference in the summer, you come to Shelburne. Here
there is an early-American reconstruction less harmonious than
Sturbridge, but perhaps more rewarding. Among its countless
varied delights is the finest possible collection of old patchwork
quilts, some of them exquisitely worked and others simply a blaze
of colour.

'Down east' from Boston is Maine, and any sailor who has had
to beat his way back to Boston after skimming up the Maine coast
can tell you why what looks 'up' should be called 'down'; the prevailing winds blow relentlessly towards Nova Scotia. But any
sailor will also tell you that there is no lovelier coast in the United
States than the pine-fringed, rock-bound coast of Maine with its
profusion of bays and inlets.

No section of the United States is more nautical than New
England, and Maine stayed devoted to the sea long after some
other parts of New England had turned to manufacturing. It is
appropriate, therefore, that several enterprising people should
now have fitted out old coastal cargo schooners, 'wind-jammers',
to carry passengers on week-long sailing trips up the Maine coast.
On a well-run boat these trips can be great fun; cruising along the
pretty coast during the day, and then anchoring every night in a
different harbour, for lobster broils on the beach and other New
England jollities.

Inland Maine, rugged, heavily wooded, dotted with lakes, is
fine fishing and shooting country, very like parts of Canada. There
are even sizable French-Canadian settlements, where the children
go to Roman Catholic church schools conducted in French.

But coastal Maine, some people think, bears here and there a startling resemblance to the coast of Japan with its dark pines and deep bays. Not that part which is near Boston, where the roads and the waterfronts are lined with hamburger stands and souvenir shops and ugly motels, and all the other excrescences of over-popular holiday areas. But at Brunswick things begin to improve: Bowdoin College there has a delightful small art gallery and the town itself has many attractive streets. The charm of Maine begins to become apparent, and Wiscasset, just beyond, is very pleasant; like all proper New England towns it has a good Federal-period house open to the public, the Nickels-Stortwell House on Main Street. Seventy-five miles farther on, the Penobscot Nautical Museum in Searsport is also worth seeing. But the very finest sight in Maine is Mount Desert Island and Frenchman's Bay at Bar Harbor. Acadia National Park is there, and Northeast Harbor, on the far side of the park area, is a real fjord. Ferries run to the islands in the bay and there are good inns and eating places, but the holiday developments have been kept within bounds. Both Bar Harbor and Northeast are immensely fashionable but quietly so. East of this area, Maine becomes even more sparsely populated, the coast wilder, the water colder, the fog thicker. But its very remoteness is part of its attraction.

SPECIAL KNOWLEDGE

The best **map** we know of Boston and its vicinity is one issued by the A.A.A.

New England is cold and often snow-bound in the winter, and it expects tourists then only in the ski-ing areas. Therefore many places in the country are shut from 1 November to 19 April, the anniversary of the first skirmish of the Revolution. Still other places have an even shorter **season,** from the beginning of June to the end of September. Boston of course is an exception; the historic buildings there are open all the year round. One of the great advantages of such large-scale reconstructions as Sturbridge and Mystic is that they almost never shut their doors. But summer or winter, beware the possibility of a 4 p.m. closing in New England.

The **Freedom Trail** in Boston is not as clearly signposted as it should be. If you follow it all the way along, you must be particularly careful not to get lost at the point at which it weaves across the path of the Sumner Tunnel traffic on the way to Paul Revere's house.

We have mentioned a great many **old houses,** but we do not for a moment think anyone should try to see them all. We have just tried to suggest some of the best ones in every part of New England.

Boston brown bread and baked beans, Rhode Island jonny cakes, lobsters and steamed clams, fish chowders, Indian pudding, maple sugar; all of these are splendid **gastronomic specialties** in New England, and more recently Italian sandwiches and *pizzas* have begun to add a pleasing variety to the fare at New England drive-ins. But the inventor of the ubiquitous fried clam should be condemned to eat them three times a day as a suitable punishment.

There are now various organizations which advertise **windjammer cruises,** and some are much less expensive than others. It is only fair to point out, however, that you get what you pay for; the inexpensive cruises often call for bringing one's own linen, and use less comfortable and colourful boats, with less experienced crews. Information about these cruises can be obtained from the Maine Publicity Bureau, Portland, Maine.

All of the most popular **holiday centres** in New England may be reached by public transport, which in most instances will mean bus. Once there, you can certainly manage without a car, and you would not by any means be the only one on foot or with a bicycle. But it is best to write ahead to the local or state Chamber of Commerce Visitor's Bureau to inquire about accommodation; there will be a considerable variation in price and style and one must book early at some of the places.

Tourist Information for all parts of New England:

THE NEW ENGLAND COUNCIL, Statler Office Building, Boston, Massachusetts, or Rockefeller Plaza, New York City.

Boston, Massachusetts

CONVENTION AND VISITORS BUREAU, 125 High Street, Boston 10.

ARNOLD ARBORETUM, Arborway, Jamaica Plain. Sunrise to sunset.

FANEUIL HALL, Market Street. Monday to Friday 9–5, Saturday 9–12, Sunday 1–5. Free.

ISABELLA STEWART GARDNER MUSEUM, 280 The Fenway. Tuesday, Thursday and Saturday 10–4, Sunday 2–5. Tour of collections Tuesday, Thursday and Saturday 11, Monday, Wednesday and Friday 11 and 2. Closed August and holidays. Free.

KING'S CHAPEL, Tremont Street and School Street. Daily 9–4.

MUSEUM OF FINE ARTS, 465 Huntington Avenue. Tuesday to Saturday 10–5, Sunday 1.30–5.30. Sometimes open until 10 on Tuesday. Closed Thanksgiving, 1 July, 25 December, 1 January. Free.

OLD NORTH CHURCH, 198 Salem Street. Daily 10–4.

OLD SOUTH MEETING HOUSE, Washington Street and Milk Street. 1 June to 30 September, Monday to Friday 9–5, Saturday 9–4. 1 October to 31 May, week-days 9–4.

OLD STATE HOUSE, Washington Street and State Street. 1 October to 30 April, week-days 9–4; 1 May to 30 September, Monday to Friday 9–4.30, Saturday 9–1. Free.

PARK STREET CHURCH, Park Street and Tremont Street. Monday to Friday 9–5, Saturday 9–12, Sunday 9–1 and 4.30–9. Services Sunday 10.30 and 7.30.

PAUL REVERE HOUSE, 19 North Square. Week-days 10–4. Closed holidays.

SOCIETY FOR THE PRESERVATION OF NEW ENGLAND ANTIQUITIES, Harrison-Gray Otis House, 141 Cambridge Street. Monday to Friday 10–4. Closed holidays.

STATE HOUSE, Beacon Street. Monday to Friday 8.45–5. Closed holidays. Free.

U.S.S. CONSTITUTION, U.S. Naval Shipyard, Charlestown. Daily 9.30–4.

Cambridge, Massachusetts

HARVARD UNIVERSITY

HARVARD VISITORS INFORMATION CENTER, 20 Dunster Street. During the summer there are tours starting at Harvard Yard, four times daily on week-days and twice daily on Sundays and holidays.

BOTANICAL MUSEUM (including Ware Collection of Glass Flowers), Agassiz Hall, Oxford Street. Week-days and holidays 9–4.30, Sunday 1–4.30. Closed 4 July, 25 December. Free.

BUSCH-REISINGER MUSEUM, Kirkland Street and Divinity Avenue. Week-days 9–5. Closed Saturday during summer months. Free.

FOGG ART MUSEUM, Quincy Street and Broadway. Week-days 9–5. July and August closed Saturday. Free.

PEABODY MUSEUM OF ARCHAEOLOGY AND ETHNOLOGY, 11 Divinity Avenue. Week-days 9–4.30, Sunday 1–4.30. Closed 4 July and 25 December. Free.

HENRY WADSWORTH LONGFELLOW HOUSE, 105 Brattle Street. Monday to Friday 10–5, Saturday 12–5, Sunday 1–5.

MASSACHUSETTS INSTITUTE OF TECHNOLOGY, Massachusetts Avenue and Memorial Drive. Week-days, guided tours at 10 and 2. The guides are Students. Tours start from admissions office, Room 3108, Main Building, 77 Massachusetts Avenue.

Concord, Massachusetts

RALPH WALDO EMERSON HOUSE, Cambridge Turnpike and State Route 2. 19 April to 11 November, Tuesday to Saturday 10–11.30 and 1.30–5.30. Sunday 2.30–5.30. Closed holidays.

ORCHARD HOUSE, Lexington Road, east of the town. 19 April to 11 November, week-days 10–5, Sunday 2–6; 15 September to 18 June, closed Monday.

Deerfield, Massachusetts

Most of its restored houses are open from April to November, week-days 9–12 and 1.30–5, Sunday 1.30–5. Some are closed Monday and some Tuesday.

Gloucester, Massachusetts

BEAUPORT, June to September, guided tours only, Monday to Friday, 2.30, 3.30, 4.30. Closed holidays.

Guilford, Connecticut

WHITFIELD HOUSE, Whitfield Street. Tuesday to Sunday 10–5; closed 12–1 in winter.

Hancock, Massachusetts

HANCOCK SHAKER VILLAGE, U.S. Route 20, five miles west of Pittsfield. 1 June to 15 October, daily 9.30–5.

Hartford, Connecticut

CONNECTICUT STATE LIBRARY, 231 Capitol Avenue. Monday to Friday 8.30–5, Saturday 9–1. Closed holidays. Free.

CONNECTICUT HISTORICAL SOCIETY, 1 Elizabeth Street. Week-days 9.30–5.30. June, July and August, closed Saturday at 12. Closed holidays. Free.

MARK TWAIN'S HOUSE, 351 Farmington Avenue. Labor Day to 31 May, Tuesday to Friday 2–5, Saturday 10–5, Sunday 2–5; 1 June to Labor Day, Tuesday to Saturday 10–5, Sunday 2–5.

Harvard, Massachusetts

FRUITLANDS, Prospect Hill Road. 30 May to 30 September, Tuesday to Sunday, 1–5. Open Monday when a holiday.

Ipswich, Massachusetts

JOHN WHIPPLE HOUSE, 53 Main Street. 1 April to 31 October, Tuesday to Saturday 10–5, Sunday 1–5.

Lee, Massachusetts

JACOB'S PILLOW DANCE FESTIVAL. For schedule, tickets and lists of accommodation: Jacob's Pillow Dance Festival Ticket Office, Lee, Massachusetts.

Lenox, Massachusetts

TANGLEWOOD MUSIC FESTIVAL. For schedule, tickets and lists of accommodation: Festival Ticket Office, Tanglewood, Lenox, Massachusetts.

Lexington, Massachusetts

BUCKMAN TAVERN, on the Green. 19 April to 12 October, week-days and holidays 10–5, Sunday 1–5.

HANCOCK-CLARKE HOUSE, 35 Hancock Street. 19 April to 12 October, week-days and holidays 10–5, Sunday 1–5.

Lincoln, Massachusetts

DE CORDOVA GALLERY, Sandypond Road. Tuesday to Saturday 10–5, Sunday 2–5. Free.

Marblehead, Massachusetts

JEREMIAH LEE HOUSE, 161 Washington Street. 1 May to 12 October, week-days 9.30–4.30.

New Haven, Connecticut

YALE UNIVERSITY

TOURS. During the summer there are guided tours, week-days 10.30, 1.30 and 3, Sunday 1.30 and 3. In term-time, Saturday 11, Sunday 1.30 and 3. Free.

ART GALLERY, Chapel Street and High Street. Tuesday to Saturday 10–5, Sunday 2–5. Closed Thanksgiving, 25 December, 1 January, 4 July. Free.

PEABODY MUSEUM OF NATURAL HISTORY, Sachem Street and Whitney Avenue. Week-days 9–4.30 (to 5 in summer). Sundays and holidays, 2–4.30. Closed 4 July, Thanksgiving, 25 December, 1 January. Free.

UNITED CHURCH, on the Green. May be seen on application to Parish House, 302 Temple Street.

CENTER CHURCH, on the Green. Tuesday to Friday 9–12 and 1–4.30, Saturday 9–12.

TRINITY CHURCH, on the Green. Week-days 9–6, Sunday 8–6.

Newport, Rhode Island

NEWPORT CHAMBER OF COMMERCE AND VISITORS BUREAU, Washington Square

THE BREAKERS. Along Shepard Avenue, one street east of Bellevue. 1 June to 1 November, daily 10–5; July and August, open Sunday until 9; May open only Saturday and Sunday 10–5.

THE BREAKERS STABLE Along Shepard Avenue, one street west of Bellevue. 1 July to 4 September, daily 10–5.

HUNTER HOUSE, 54 Washington Street. 1 June to 1 October, daily 10–5.

OLD COLONY HOUSE, Washington Square. Monday to Friday 9.30–12 and 1–4.30, Saturday 9–1.

TOURO SYNAGOGUE, 72 Touro Street. 1 July to 4 September, Sunday to Friday 10–5; Labor Day to 30 June, Sunday 2.30–4.

WHITEHALL. In the country about 2 miles east of Newport. 1 July to 4 September, daily 10–5.

Old Sturbridge Village, Massachusetts

At the junction of the Massachusetts Turnpike, U.S. Route 20 and State

H

Routes 15 and 131. 1 April to 30 November, daily 9.30–5.30; 1 December to 31 March, Monday to Friday only guided tours at 10 and 2; Saturday and Sunday 9.30–4.30.

Plymouth, Massachusetts

MAYFLOWER II, Plymouth Harbor. Same opening hours as Plimouth Plantation, except June, July and August when open until 8.

Providence, Rhode Island

JOHN BROWN HOUSE, 52 Power Street. Monday to Friday 9–5. September to May, Sunday 3–5. Closed holidays and holiday week-ends. Free.

RHODE ISLAND SCHOOL OF DESIGN (MUSEUM), 224 Benefit Street, Tuesday to Saturday 11–5, Sunday 2–5. Closed August and holidays. Free.

Salem, Massachusetts

CROWNINSHIELD–BENTLEY HOUSE, 126 Essex Street. June to September, Tuesday to Saturday 9–4.30, Sunday 2–4.30.

PINGREE HOUSE, 128 Essex Street. Tuesday to Saturday, guided tours 10, 11, 12, 2 and 3. June to September, Sunday 2, 3 and 4. Closed holidays.

Saugus, Massachusetts

SAUGUS IRONWORKS, 224 Central Street. 17 April to 30 November, Tuesday to Sunday 9–4. Waterwheel and Forge. Demonstrations Tuesday to Friday 11 and 3, Saturday, Sunday and holidays 11, 1.30, 2.30 and 4. Closed 4 July and Thanksgiving.

Searsport, Maine

PENOBSCOT MARINE MUSEUM, mid-June to mid-September, week-days and holidays 9–5, Sunday 1–5.

Sturbridge, Massachusetts

See Old Sturbridge.

Waltham, Massachusetts

GORE PLACE, on U.S. Route 20 at the Waltham-Watertown line. 15 April to 15 November, Tuesday to Saturday 10–5, Sunday 2–5. Closed holidays.

LYMAN HOUSE, Lyman Street and Beaver Street. 26 May to 2 September, Thursday to Saturday 11–5.

Wethersfield, Connecticut

BUTTOLPH-WILLIAMS HOUSE, Broad Street and Marsh Street. 15 May to 15 October, daily 12.30–4.30.

WEBB HOUSE, 211 Main Street. March to October, Monday to Saturday 10–5, Sunday 1–5. November to February, Monday to Saturday 10–3.

Williamstown Massachusetts

CLARK ART INSTITUE, South Street. Tuesday to Sunday 10–5. Free.

Windjammer Cruises, Maine

SCHOONER *Victory Chimes* (132 ft. overall). Sails from Rockland, Maine.
Maine Coast Cruises, Castine, Maine. $100 to $125 per week.

SCHOONER *Stephen Taber* (68 ft. overall). Sails from Camden, Maine.
Down East Cruises, East Blue Hill, Maine. $100 to $115 per week.

Wiscasset, Maine

NICKELS-SORTWELL HOUSE, Main Street and Federal Street. Mid-June to
mid-October, Tuesday to Saturday 11–5, Sunday 2–5.

5 · Washington

In the nineteenth century, foreign visitors to America were in perfect agreement on only one subject: the city of Washington was the most wretched national capital they had ever seen. Today a diplomat used to a European capital which is also the heart and soul of its country may well complain that Washington has no music, no theatre, no life to compare with London or Paris or Rome, but at least most visitors now find it pleasing to the eye.

The perfect entrance into Washington is by way of the Arlington Memorial Bridge from Virginia, on a night with a full moon. Crossing the bridge, you suddenly come upon the Lincoln Memorial, all ghostly glowing white marble in the park along the river's edge, and the city at first glance seems to consist entirely of mock-classic public buildings. At night the slums which fringe this noble expanse hardly show at all.

Washington began as a compromise. New York would have liked to be the capital, or Philadelphia. But Alexander Hamilton, the first Secretary of the Treasury, badly needed to curry favour with the Southern States in order to get their assent to his financial policies for the new republic in 1790. He hit upon offering the South the capital, and the city of Washington was born, to be built on neutral ground donated by Virginia and Maryland. The entire seventy-square-mile-area is known as the District of Columbia; it is governed by a committee of Congress, to the considerable frustration of many of its residents, who want self-government.

A young French architect named Pierre l'Enfant was hired to survey the land and plan the city; central Washington today is substantially as l'Enfant conceived it, and the circles and broad avenues are reminiscent of Napoleonic Paris. But the public buildings rose slowly; there were endless disagreements, and there was never enough money. Meanwhile, with no industry other than government, Washington remained essentially a poor place in every sense of the word. The people who came there seldom thought of themselves as permanent residents, and the city suffered accordingly. Congress in those days was never in session

for more than a few months of the year; instead of building fine
houses, even the richer congressmen tended to leave their families
at home and stay themselves in boarding houses. Only in comparatively recent years has this situation changed, and central
Washington still bears the scars of a century of neglect.

Today there is no lack of splendid public buildings, but
Washington is still not a city in the sense that Boston or New
York are cities, varied and complex. The most prosperous
government people are likely to live outside the District of
Columbia, in Virginia or Maryland suburbs, where they can have
more space and a vote; naturally this drains wealth from the city.
Moreover, a sort of provincialism results from the fact that most
of the people who live in the Washington area work for the federal
government.

Because Washington was deliberately planned to look impressive, its chief public buildings are set at a considerable distance
apart, with malls and wide avenues between. However, anyone
can easily explore the capital on foot, perhaps taking a bus for
the longer jumps.

The visitor with only one day for sightseeing in Washington
might try to see the White House, the Capitol itself where Congress sits, one of the Smithsonian Institution museums, and the
Lincoln Memorial. Then in the evening it would be pleasant to
finish with a leisurely stroll through Georgetown, the most
interesting residential section of the city, and one which also
boasts several attractive restaurants.

In this chapter we go through central Washington quite
methodically, up one broad avenue and down the next, and only
after this do we discuss those other Washington attractions which
are not so conveniently grouped together. The order in which
things are mentioned must not be taken as one of importance; it
is merely a geographical arrangement.

The White House is the appropriate place to begin any tour of
Washington, since it is where the President lives. It is also the
right place to start from a practical point of view, because it is
only open to the public from ten to twelve in the morning, Tuesday to Saturday.

Purists sometimes dismiss the White House as an architectural
hodge-podge, but no one denies the charm of the rambling white
building, all wings and porticoes, comfortably ensconced in its

green park in the heart of the city. It was begun in 1792, burnt by the British troops in the war of 1812, and then rebuilt. It has been altered and added on to ever since, most notably in President Truman's administration; the Trumans moved to Blair House for three years so that the entire structure of the building could be strengthened, every inch gone over, without it being visibly changed inside or out. The public tour of the White House is a short one; you see only those state apartments which are used for official entertaining, and you are usually out again in less than twenty minutes. Yet it is a tour well worth taking. Like so many of the public attractions in Washington the White House has no admission charge.

Lafayette Square, facing the White House, has two particularly fine Federal-period houses at its western edge: Blair House, where the government lodges visiting heads of state, and, on the next corner to the north, Decatur House, now owned by the National Trust for Historic Preservation. St John's Church, facing the White House across the Square, is one of Washington's nicest old churches. When the President happens to be an Episcopalian, this is the President's church. The equestrian statue in the Square is of General Andrew Jackson, who first won fame as the victorious American leader in the Battle of New Orleans in the war of 1812, that abortive renewal of hostilities with Great Britain when the United States found herself caught in the backwash of the Napoleonic Wars. Jackson, a great frontier figure, later became President. More than any other man, he was responsible for changing the pattern of American democracy, from a sort of Athenian government-by-the-few to a popular government-by-the-many.

Leaving the White House, and going up Pennsylvania Avenue towards the Capitol itself, one passes buildings housing various government departments, all of them part of the executive branch, which means under the jurisdiction of the President and one of his cabinet ministers or department heads. For with the tri-partite balance-of-powers of the American political system, the President and the cabinet ministers are first of all administrators. Of course the President, as the leader of his party, can also ask Congress to pass bills, to make changes in existing laws, and to appropriate money, but Congress may or may not prove agreeable. A strong President, exercising every bit of power the Constitution permits and every scrap of influence he has, can sometimes dominate

Congress; a weak President may become merely the tool of Congress. Meanwhile, watching over both the legislative and the executive branches of the government is the judicial branch, the Supreme Court and the lower federal courts, there to see that neither Congress nor the President oversteps constitutional bounds. As one explores Washington, it is helpful to keep in mind this marked division of powers and roles in the government of the United States.

One of the largest government buildings on the right-hand side of Pennsylvania Avenue on the way to the Capitol is the Department of Justice, where any devotee of cops-and-robbers can tour the Federal Bureau of Investigation headquarters and be shown all the intricacies of their detection methods; the tour takes about an hour. Just beyond the Department of Justice is the National Archives building, where the Declaration of Independence and the Constitution repose in glass cases. Beyond the National Archives building, Pennsylvania Avenue slices across Constitution Avenue, and here, back a few steps to the west along Constitution, is the National Gallery of Art. The nucleus of the collection here was amassed by the financier Andrew Mellon under the tutelage of Duveen, that flamboyant art dealer who was responsible for so many American acquisitions in the first half of this century. Following Mr Mellon's example, many other rich collectors who had also come under Duveen's influence left their pictures to the new National Gallery, and thus today the Gallery is particularly rich in bright, glossy, freshly cleaned works of the Italian Renaissance, including some magnificent ones. There is also an excellent group of early American primitive paintings here. The National Gallery is one of the show-places of Washington, not to be missed.

Begun in 1793, the unfortunate Capitol itself took seventy years to complete; meanwhile any architect in Europe or America with time on his hands would seem to have drifted to Washington to amuse himself changing the designs for the building. Only recently it has again been altered, the east front pushed forward to make room for more offices. But one of the building's first authentically American details can still be seen in the north wing: the architect Benjamin Latrobe's columns, some crowned with a design of tobacco leaves and others with capitals of Indian corn. There are guided tours of the Capitol, starting every few minutes all day long. They include a glance into the House and Senate chambers; if either of these are sitting you may even watch for a few moments. You can also get passes to the gallery of the Senate by applying to the office of the Senate Sergeant-at-Arms; passes for the House gallery are available from the Doorkeeper's office on the House side of the Capitol. Except for a large group, it is usually not necessary to apply beforehand. However, it is best to be prepared for disillusion. Only rarely does one hear the kind of challenging debate one might hope for in the parliament of so powerful a country, and there is nothing which corresponds to Question Time in the House of Commons. The Congressmen no longer horrify lady visitors from abroad by chewing tobacco and spitting, but this improvement aside, one is not likely to be much more favorably impressed than Mrs Trollope long ago. And yet things really have improved since Mrs Trollope's day; the manner in which Congress conducts its business has undergone in-numerable subtle changes, and if the casual visitor only under-stood the inner workings of Congress, he might not be so sadly disappointed by what he sees on the House or Senate floor.

The Congress of the United States is divided into two parts, the House of Representatives and the Senate. The House of Repre-sentatives today has 435 members, elected every two years, and properly known as 'Congressmen'. According to the Constitution the Congressmen are apportioned according to population, one Congressman for every so many people, who may of course be widely scattered in a geographically vast rural district, or packed tight together in a geographically tiny city district. Nevada, for instance, has one Congressman for its 110,000 square miles, and yet the state of Massachusetts has twelve Congressmen with an area less than one-twelfth the size of Nevada. There are, however, two Senators for every state, large or small, and therefore the Senate now has an even one hundred Senators. When the republic was young and relatively small and there were far fewer Congress-men in the House of Representatives, a Congressman was every bit as eminent as a Senator. In fact many an idealistic democrat thought that being a Congressman was to be preferred, because Congressmen were directly elected by, and responsible to, the people, while Senators were loftier beings, elected in those days by the legislatures of the separate states. Today, however, almost all Congressmen secretly yearn to be Senators. Now directly elected by the people of their states every six years, Senators have a longer term of office, and since there are only one hundred of them, each Senator is far better known than any Congressman can hope to be.

However, this still does not mean that even the Senate looks impressive when in session. The chamber itself is handsome, but there never seem to be many members there unless they are actually about to vote on a bill. Someone will be presiding, but it is more likely to be a Senator deputizing for the Vice-President than the Vice-President himself. And someone will be speaking, but he is very likely to be speaking merely 'for the record', quite literally *The Congressional Record*, the American *Hansard*, and in that event he will not mind that few of his colleagues are listening to him. He simply wants to be recorded as having supported or opposed some bill, so that in the next election campaign he can point to this support or opposition. In the United States, party discipline is not nearly so strong as it is in most democracies. This looser system seems to suit well enough the size and complexity of America, but it does mean that each member of Congress must build his own individual record; he may well be elected quite irrespective of whether he is a Democrat or a Republican. (One must here always except the South; still nursing the wounds of the Republican Reconstruction period after the Civil War, the Deep South seldom elects anyone not labelled a Democrat. The result is that in the southern states both arch-conservatives and liberals belong to the Democrat party, which leads to anguish and considerable confusion in the halls of Congress.) Moreover, in America each member of Congress is considered in a very real sense to be the representative of his constituency. He must live in the area he represents in order to stand for election there, and he is regarded as a sort of delegate from, say, Iowa to the Congress of the States United. It is, after all, a federal system. All of this makes it difficult for him to speak freely on the House or Senate floor.

An increasing amount of the serious business of Congress has come to be transacted more privately, in the meetings of one congressional committee or another. There are committees concerned with every aspect of government, from a Foreign Relations Committee to a Committee on Fisheries. The chairmanship of an important committee is a coveted office, which usually goes to that member of the current majority party who has served longest on that committee. Committee hearings are often open to the public. They may be held in the Capitol itself, or in one of the old or new Senate or House office buildings which are ranged around the Capitol. The morning newspaper, *The Washington Post*, lists 'today's Congressional hearings', giving the time and the place and indicating whether or not the meeting is open to the public. So long as it is not 'closed' or 'in executive session', you need only go to the right place, open the door, walk in and find a seat. It will seem rather like going to a courtroom trial.

There is a cafeteria in the Capitol open to the public. There is also a little underground train which runs between the Capitol and the Senate Office Building; anyone may take it but it is particularly worth sampling when Congress is in session and the Senators themselves are hurrying back and forth.

Opposite to the east entrance of the Capitol is the Library of Congress, with the Folger Library directly behind it. The Folger Library is a scholars' library, housing America's finest Shakespearean collection, a great amount of related rare sixteenth- and seventeenth-century material, and a reconstruction of an Elizabethan theatre. The Library of Congress is a reference library for members of Congress; it is also the chief depository in the United States for books and printed matter, comparable in that respect to the British Museum, and it has many rare books and manuscripts of historical importance. One thing the casual visitor may find particularly interesting is the Library of Congress folk music collection, probably the most comprehensive in the world. Over the past twenty-five years, the Library itself has sponsored and supervised countless recordings of folk music, not only American but also Asian, European, and African. One can listen to the records there, and some of the most popular, particularly American folk ballads, have now been recorded in quantity and are for sale at the Library.

To the north, across East Capitol Street from the Library of Congress, is the Supreme Court Building. Visitors are admitted to the public gallery of the Court but one must not go there expecting pyrotechnics. It is lawyer's law, with intricate and quiet pleading and no jury.

Stretching from the Capitol west to the Washington Monument is the Mall, with the buildings of the Smithsonian Institution on either side. Constitution Avenue borders the north side of the Mall, Independence Avenue the south. If one goes west through the centre of the Mall, the first Smithsonian building on the right is the National Gallery. When people talk of the Smithsonian, they are usually thinking of the science museums and the historical collections, but the National Gallery is also administered by the Smithsonian Institution board of directors, and so is the zoo in Rock Creek Park.

After the National Gallery comes the Natural History Museum and beyond it the brand new Museum of History and Technology. On the opposite side of the Mall, along Independence Avenue, are the Arts and Industries Building, the Aircraft Building, the Freer Gallery, and the headquarters building; a new Air Museum is also to be built here, directly opposite the National Gallery. As the Smithsonian expands into its new buildings, the collections will be rearranged. Therefore if you are in search of some one particular exhibit, it would be wise to make inquiries before plunging into any one of the buildings. Naturally a museum-complex so vast has important collections in many fields, but the non-specialist from overseas is likely to find most interesting the American Indian section; the old cars; the early aeroplanes, including the Wright brothers' plane and Lindbergh's 'Spirit of St Louis'; the reconstructed early American rooms, and the gallery of President's wives in their inaugural ball dresses.

All of this splendid display is the result of a gift from an Englishman who had never seen the United States. In 1829, one James Smithson died and left his entire fortune, £120,000, for the founding at Washington of 'an establishment for the increase and diffusion of knowledge among men'. He was the natural son of the first Duke of Northumberland and Elizabeth Hungerford Keate Macie, whom Smithson later described as 'niece to the proud Duke of Somerset'. He himself never married. Educated at Pembroke College, Oxford, he became a considerable amateur chemist, and his bequest was clearly designed both to lend honour to his clouded name and to aid science. Moreover, although Smithson apparently knew little about the United States, he was a man of marked republican sympathies. In a letter to a friend at the time of the French Revolution, he observed that a country with a king was 'like a man who takes a lion as his guard-dog – if he knocks out his teeth he renders him useless, while if he leaves the lion his teeth the lion eats him'.

Many years ago the Smithsonian assembled all the accounts of its own founding, and one can spend a diverting afternoon looking through them. First there was a Dickensian three-year struggle in Chancery Court actually to get the money; we heave a great sigh of relief as Mr Richard Rush, the American emissary, finally boards the packet-boat at the London docks with his eleven cases of gold sovereigns. And then of course there was a nationwide debate on exactly how the money should be used: for a university, or a library, or an art gallery, or an observatory, for agricultural experimentation or a zoological collection, to establish lectures on moral philosophy or to subsidize geographical exploration. In the end almost everyone won except those who wanted a university; the Smithsonian is a little of everything. But there is no doubt that it has accomplished precisely what James Smithson hoped: it has increased and diffused knowledge among men.

At the western end of the Mall is the Washington Monument; visitors can have a splendid panorama of central Washington from the top of its slim shaft. The ornamental lake to the south-west of the Monument is ringed by Japanese cherry trees, a lovely mass of pink bloom in the spring and one of the famous sights of Washington. The Jefferson Memorial stands at the far side of this Tidal Basin. It is a particularly apt monument because it so perfectly captures Thomas Jefferson's own architectural style.

The Bureau of Engraving and Printing, where you can watch them make money and print postage stamps, is in the large building immediately to the south-east of the Washington Monument.

On to the west again, across 17th Street from the Washington Monument, is another park with a reflecting pool which forms the foreground for the Lincoln Memorial. Just as Lincoln's memorial dominates one entire section of Washington, so do his name and his political spirit dominate Washington and American history. One Captain Hamilton, a perceptive British visitor, wrote in 1833, 'Should a period of strong political excitement arrive, when men shall be arrayed, not in demonstration of mere personal partialities, but in support of conflicting principles connected with their immediate interests, I confess that I at least can find nothing in the American constitution on which to rest a hope for its permance.' And Captain Hamilton was not alone in his pessimism. Once the first flush of victory in the Revolution was over, once the leaders of the Revolutionary period were gone, the several states seemed to drift apart. Secession was talked of more than once, and not only by southerners. The Civil War, when it came, was more than a struggle over slavery, and more than a contest between federal power and states' rights within the Union. It was as Lincoln himself said many times, a battle to the death over the survival of the American system. Washington today might be only an unimportant town on the border between two separate and not particularly powerful countries had it not been for Abraham Lincoln.

There are four noteworthy public galleries in Washington in addition to the National Gallery. One, the Freer, is a part of the Smithsonian group. The Freer specializes; it has a remarkable collection of Oriental art, and on the other hand it has some good examples of the work of American painters of the late nineteenth century, Whistler and Sargent and Winslow Homer in particular. At 1600 21st Street, N.W., is the Phillips Gallery, in what used to be the Duncan Phillips's town house. This is Washington's modern art gallery; it is particularly strong in French paintings, post-impressionist and cubist. The Corcoran Gallery, New York Avenue at 17th Street, N.W., just west of the White House, has a good American collection, both traditional and contemporary, as well as a cross-section of European painting. And at Dumbarton Oaks, in Georgetown, in an attractive Federal-period house surrounded by a handsome formal garden, you can see the Bliss collection of Byzantine treasures. The Bliss family gave Dumbarton Oaks to Harvard University as a centre for Byzantine studies; the public is admitted to the museum section of it every afternoon but Monday except in July and August. Dumbarton Oaks Park, just beyond, is rustic and peaceful.

Dumbarton Oaks can also be treated as the starting point for an exploration of Georgetown. The Georgetown district is roughly bounded by Dumbarton Oaks Park at the north, Rock Creek on the east, the Potomac River to the south, and the precincts of Georgetown University on the west; the latter is a distinguished Jesuit institution. While the central part of Washington was still a marsh, the nation's capital still not finally designated, Georgetown was already a small but pleasant town. It remained independent until 1871, when it was officially joined to Washington and then seemed to slide downhill, engulfed by the capital, the small Georgetown houses mostly abandoned in favour of more lavish ones in newer parts of the city. Then, happily, Georgetown was rediscovered in the years between the two World Wars, and today houses there are the most sought-after in Washington.

No one can agree on any one 'best street' to see in Georgetown; you must simply wander. One of the most elegant eighteenth-century houses is Tudor Place, at Q Street and 31st Street, very near Dumbarton Oaks; it is still lived in by descendants of the family who built it, unusual continuity for America. Wisconsin Avenue is Georgetown's main street, and most of the antique shops and restaurants are along there or on M Street. The 3300 block of N Street is known as Cox's Row, and is reputed to be the finest row of Federal-period houses in America.

One of the newer attractions is a canal boat which does trips on the old Chesapeake and Ohio canal in the summer, starting from a dock at the foot of 30th Street at week-ends, and on Wednesday evenings. The trips take four hours, going through several locks, and there are sprightly but learned discussions of the flora and fauna *en route* to the turn-around in Maryland.

In the spring, many of the houses and gardens in Georgetown are open from time to time for the benefit of various charities; there are also other tours for charity which include several of the Washington embassies. Anyone who is in Washington in the spring should make inquiries.

Many of the government departments have sections open to the public: one of the most interesting is the Department of the Interior, south-west of the White House, which has an excellent small museum, devoted to American Indian arts and crafts of both past and present.

A delightful place for a drink on a summer evening is the roof-top of the Hotel Washington on Fifteenth Street at Pennsylvania Avenue; it has a splendid view of the city.

The most deservedly popular trip out of the city is that to Mount Vernon, George Washington's house in Virginia. Built high on a bluff overlooking the Potomac River, it is a fine example of a colonial manor house, with the pillared front one always asso-ciates with Southern American plantation houses. For of course it was a plantation, not simply a house; this was once an enormous and profitable estate, and many of the outbuildings can still be seen, together with a handsome formal garden.

The Virginia Revolutionary leaders were by and large aristocrats. They imported their furniture, their wines, and their books
from Europe, and frequently sent their sons back to England to be
educated. Next to New England, Virginia was the most British in
population of all the colonies, and Virginia had not even a religious difference to separate her from the mother country; the
Church of England was the established and accepted church in
Virginia. One can trace the American Revolution in New England back to the staunchly independent Puritan tradition, but in
Virginia it is easier to trace it to Locke and Hume and Montes-
quieu, and all the other authors a well-read English gentleman
might have been expected to know. George Washington was part
of this aristocratic Virginia tradition, and Mount Vernon illustrates this.

Mount Vernon is open all the year round. In the summer it is
possible to get there by boat; the trip takes about an hour each
way. There are also several ways of reaching Mount Vernon by
bus, with or without a tour.

Driving to Mount Vernon by car, it is easy to encompass more
of eighteenth-century Virginia. Woodlawn plantation, for
instance, is only three or four miles away; originally part of the
Mount Vernon estate, it belonged to Martha Washington's
daughter and her husband. It is a handsome place too: red brick,
and not painted over, which makes it more truly typical of Virginia colonial building than Mount Vernon. And then there is the
Pohick Church, a charming colonial church with box pews. And
Gunston Hall, another plantation house, this one designed by
William Buckland, who was one of the most gifted American
colonial craftsmen-architects.

To reach any of these plantations, one goes through or near
Alexandria, an old town now largely dormitory for Washington.
Both the Presbyterian Meeting House and Christ Church in
Alexandria are interesting colonial churches, and anyone with
the time to wander about in Alexandria may also see a great many
handsome old houses, particularly in the area squared by the
Potomac River and Queen, Washington, and Duke Streets.

Robert E. Lee's house, which he left, never to return, at the
start of the Civil War, is within the grounds of the Arlington
Memorial Cemetery, only a city bus ride from the centre of
Washington. Formally known as the Custis-Lee House, it is open

all the year round; in the winter there are frequent Sunday afternoon concerts there. The Pentagon, the mammoth War Department building, is also on the west bank of the Potomac near
Arlington Cemetery.

In the nineteenth century, when Washington was still raw and
unfinished, visitors in search of more charm and polish used to
flee to Baltimore, forty miles to the north-east in Maryland. Baltimore was much admired as a handsome city with an air of almost
European culture tinged with just enough Southern American
exoticism to make it even more attractive. As the years passed,
Washington improved, and time, traffic, and industry rather
choked Baltimore. Today the super-highway to the North avoids
Baltimore entirely by means of a long tunnel. But Baltimore still
has many charms: streets of elegant houses with the spotless
white marble steps for which the city was always famous, exceptionally good sea-food, and the remarkable Cone collection of
modern art in the Baltimore Art Museum. The Pimlico Racetrack
is also at Baltimore; several important racing events take place
there during the spring and autumn meetings.

Annapolis is an interesting Maryland city, too, the state capital
and the site of the United States Naval Academy. One can visit the
Academy virtually every day of the year, and the Hammond
Harwood House in Annapolis is another splendid example of
William Buckland's craftsmanship, open to the public and beauti-
fully furnished. October is a good month to visit Annapolis, for
there are special open-house tours then, sponsored by Historic
Annapolis, Inc.

Maryland was settled mostly by English Catholics under a proprietary charter granted to the first Lord Baltimore. His family,
the Calverts, and a few related families, controlled Maryland as
royal governors and as the leading landowners throughout the
colonial period. Something of this feudal tradition still seems to
linger on in that rather isolated part of Maryland known as the
Eastern Shore, on the other side of Chesapeake Bay; there are
several seaside resorts there, but otherwise it is very rural and
quiet.

Fifty miles or so north-west of Washington is Harper's Ferry:
here in 1859 a raid led by the abolitionist John Brown anticipated

I

the Civil War in ironic fashion, for Robert E. Lee, then a colonel in the army of the United States, was the officer sent to capture Brown, who was attempting to free a group of slaves in defiance of what was then still the law of the land. Harper's Ferry is only the first of countless Civil War landmarks in Virginia; no other state saw so much of the fighting. Time and again the Confederates threatened Washington itself, where a large share of the population was undoubtedly pro-Southern. In their most successful year, 1863, the Southern forces surged well to the north of Washington, until they crossed the Virginia line into Pennsylvania and suffered that decisive defeat at Gettysburg. But most of the famous battles were fought in Virginia. Bull Run, for example, is along the main road from Washington to the west; on the way to Charlottesville one sees the signs, 'Manassas National Battlefield Park', and a war which has been so often refought in novels and films that it no longer seems quite real suddenly becomes very real indeed. This is Manassas, the scene of two of the grimmest battles of the Civil War, where the river called Bull Run ran red with blood for days. Chancellorsville, and Spottsylvania, and Wilderness are close together thirty-five miles or so south of Washington, west of the main Washington–Richmond road at Fredericksburg. Appomattox Court House, where it all ended, is only a little farther away, in south-western Virginia. At Appomattox Court House, the blunt, dogged Grant accepted the surrender of the main body of the Confederate army from Lee, that noble, doomed knight of the Virginia aristocracy. Lee preferred his sword; Grant refused it. The Confederate officers, he said, could keep their side-arms, and the men their horses or mules, for the ploughing back home. He ordered rations distributed immediately to the starving Southern forces. For a moment it seemed that the ugliness of five years of civil war might heal over almost decently, and then five days later the mad Southern fanatic John Wilkes Booth shot and killed Lincoln, and the bitterness of the Reconstruction period began.

Military historians delight in the Civil War. The issues were dramatic, the leading figures endlessly fascinating, the odds at the beginning seemingly almost even, the strategy and counter-strategy as engrossing as that of a chess game. Thus it is not only Americans who tour Virginia to see the battlefields. But Virginia was important long before the Civil War, and for her earlier his-

tory one goes to Williamsburg, and to Monticello at Charlottesville.

One can drive to Williamsburg, either taking U.S. 1 through
Richmond, which is the usual way, or taking U.S. 17 beyond
Fredericksburg, which leads in a leisurely fashion through a much
less frequented part of the state, the old flat plantation country
along the Rappahannock. On either route, one can make side
trips in search of old churches and old houses, but it is as well to
take along a fairly detailed guide to Virginia.

Buses go to Williamsburg too, from Washington by way of
Richmond, a handsome town with many fine colonial and Federal-
period houses and a state capitol designed by Thomas Jefferson.
Its air of settled dignity notwithstanding, Richmond has had a
fiery past. It was here, at a meeting in St John's Church, that
Patrick Henry made the most inflammatory speech heard in the
colonies before the Revolution, finishing with the words 'Give
me Liberty or give me death!' And some eighty-five years later,
during the Civil War, Richmond became the capital of the Confederate States of America. There are now two Civil War museums
in the town.

Williamsburg, the most famous American effort to recapture
the past, and the oldest and still the best, is one of those places
which one should not try to see in a hurry. To those who glance
cursorily about for an hour or two, it may well seem disappointing. Admittedly it is in part a reconstruction, which sounds rather
ominous; one expects a sort of film set, with local girls in cambric
costumes selling Williamsburg rock. And indeed there are people
in the restored sections of Williamsburg in costume, but somehow after a few hours it is as if you and they were together
engaged in a cheerful conspiracy to step backward in time.

Ideally, one should be housed in one of the restored buildings,
and there are a few rooms available in the Brick House Tavern, on
Duke of Gloucester Street, bookable through the Williamsburg
Lodge. The Lodge itself is an alternative choice; it is less expen-
sive than the Williamsburg Inn and much more central than the
Motor House, an elaborate motel on the outskirts.

The first thing all visitors to Williamsburg should do once they
are housed is to go to the Information Center, taking one of the
free buses which roam the streets of the restored part of the town.

At the Information Center one can obtain pamphlets listing the special attractions scheduled each day, and find out about such things as the children's tours, and the near-by James River plantations. But most important, at the Information Center there are continuous showings of the film about Williamsburg which no visitor should miss. It is a brief history very pleasantly done; without it, half the sights may be virtually meaningless.

Afterwards one can simply wander in and out of the various buildings watching the wigmaker make wigs and the shoemaker make shoes. The restored area is particularly charming at night, when there is only dim lighting along the streets; then you can sample real Virginia ham and other local delicacies in one of the eating places and stroll back to your rooms feeling very eighteenth-century indeed.

Since Williamsburg was the capital of Virginia before the Revolution, the Governor's Palace and the old Capitol are the most important buildings in the reconstructed section. At the other end of the town is the College of William and Mary, the oldest university in America except Harvard. Before the reconstruction of Williamsburg's other past, William and Mary provided the only excuse for the town's continued existence; now it is all but overshadowed.

No one who likes classic murders should miss the Wythe House. It is in any case one of the most charming houses in Williamsburg, and George Wythe was a towering figure in colonial Virginia. He was fifty when the Revolution began, and a delegate to the Continental Congress; later he became the first professor of law at the College of William and Mary. But as friend and mentor over the years he had already strongly influenced such Revolutionary leaders as Patrick Henry, George Mason, Thomas Jefferson, and the future first Chief Justice, John Marshall. When he was over eighty, but still vigorous, still influential, and always much loved, Wythe was murdered, with arsenic in his breakfast coffee. For a year Virginia talked of little else. Surely his ne'er-do-well nephew must really have done it, although he was acquitted at the trial. But even more fascinating than the identity of the murderer was the mystery surrounding the motive. Did the nephew kill him in panic, to protect himself, or for gain? Was Michael Brown, the young freed slave, an accidental co-victim, or was he in fact the chief target? Or was it all even more complex, and was the trial in fact something of a sham? They sell a scholarly pamphlet at the Wythe House which discusses the murder in tantalizing detail.

There is one building in the restored section which seems almost an anomaly in the elegant capital of the Dominion of Virginia: the Abby Aldrich Rockefeller Folk Art Museum. Yet it is a charming collection, charmingly displayed, and since it is open in the evenings one can spend a pleasant hour or so there after supper.

From Williamsburg it is only a short drive to Jamestown, the scene of the first permanent settlement in Virginia, in 1607. Today there is a small museum, and some of the original buildings have been reconstructed, along with the three appallingly small ships in which the settlers sailed across the Atlantic. This was a 'planted' colony, never as autonomous as those of Plymouth and Massachusetts Bay, and therefore not as interesting to many people. But everyone is familiar with one Jamestown legend: it was here that Captain John Smith went reconnoitering in the forest, only to be captured by Powhatan's Indian braves and then saved at the last moment from death at the stake through the intercession of the gentle Pocohontas, Powhatan's daughter. Pocohontas later married another of the settlers, John Rolfe, and returned to England with him to live for many years near Hunstanton, a source of constant wonder to the noble savages of Norfolk.

In the opposite direction from Williamsburg, but just as near, is Yorktown. Here it was that the British General Cornwallis surrendered to the American forces under Washington and their French allies led by Lafayette and Rochambeau. Although a peace treaty was not signed until two years later, Yorktown was to all intents and purposes the end of the Revolution. The battlefield with its redoubts and ridges is well-marked; it seems intimate and peaceful today.

It is a longer trip from Williamsburg to the James River plantations, but anyone who will have no other opportunity to see a fine example of an old Southern plantation may well decide quite rightly to fit it in somehow. Williamsburg was, after all, the capital of the Virginia colony because it was at the centre of the richest colonial development, and such plantations as Berkeley and Shirley make one realize just how rich it was. These two, the best known, handsomely furnished and open to the public, lie along State Route 5, a minor road between Richmond and Williamsburg. One can hire a car with a driver, $10 for two people, to go to see them from Williamsburg, and of course one can, alternatively, hire a drive-yourself car. Unfortunately there is no public transport. The Colonial Williamsburg Information Center can supply exact information, and will also give advice about other plantations not far away.

On beyond Williamsburg to the south is the big naval centre of Norfolk and Newport News. In Hampton Roads, the waters off-shore, the battle between the *Monitor* and the *Merrimac* took place during the Civil War: the first naval encounter involving ironclad ships. Visitors driving in this area should take note that the Hampton Roads Tunnel is a triumph of engineering, but the toll charged is extremely high.

Below Norfolk, at the North Carolina border, lies the Great Dismal Swamp. The South, with its heat and heavy rainfall, has several remarkable swamps: the Everglades, in Florida, is the most famous, and there is also the Okefenokee in Georgia. But the Great Dismal is a good swamp, as swamps go, and boats can be hired to take you through it into Lake Drummond in the centre. Few people seem to go there, and it is solitary and ghostly. They say that sounds are simply swallowed up in the Great Dismal, that one cannot hear someone fifty yards away should he shout for help. The most obvious difficulty for tourists at the Great Dismal, however, is not getting help in the swamp, but finding Wallaceton, the village where the boat can be hired. It consists of nothing more than two or three houses along the road, U.S. Route 17, and you are likely to cross the North Carolina border two or three times before you finally realize that that hamlet you passed was the metropolis marked so prominently on the map. It is necessary to allow the better part of a day for the Dismal Swamp venture. It can take time to arrange for the boat, and then the trip itself, which cannot be hurried, must be started early enough so that one comes back through the waterway before the locks suspend operations for the night.

Thomas Jefferson's name occurs over and over again, both in Washington and in Williamsburg. To see Monticello, his remarkable house, and the University of Virginia whose buildings he designed, you go west from Washington to Charlottesville.

The main road from Washington, which passes Bull Run, runs for
the first half of the distance along the southern fringe of the Virginia hunting country, whose centres are Middleburg and Lees-
burg. Charlottesville, farther on, is in the foothills of the Blue
Ridge Mountains; the University of Virginia was founded there
in 1819 as a recognition of the growing importance of western
Virginia, with its Scotch-Irish and German settlers so unlike the
wealthy aristocrats of the coastal region. And yet the University
of Virginia today seems the epitome of the pre-war South, with all
the flaws as well as the virtues which that implies.

The main buildings, which Jefferson planned, are unique:
typically Jeffersonian-Palladian-colonial. No university in America
is more interesting architecturally. The complete eighteenth-
century man, continually experimenting, inventing, talking, writing, Jefferson was the third President of the United States as well
as Secretary of State in Washington's cabinet, but he asked that his
epitaph include only two things: that he was the author of the
Declaration of Independence, and that he was the architect of the
University of Virginia. One must certainly see the University of
Virginia, but even more memorable, perhaps because it is more
personal, is Monticello.

This was Jefferson's own house, on a hill overlooking Charlottesville. The house is full of his labour-saving inventions, the
garden is a record of his experiments, the whole estate reflects his
interests and enthusiasms. Jefferson is the most attractive figure
of the American Revolution, and certainly one of America's most
brilliant Presidents. Like most thinking Virginians of his day, he
deplored slavery and tried to write its end into the Constitution.
Ironically, his efforts failed not only because the rice planters of
the Carolinas were opposed, but also because the pious New
England shipowners were reluctant to give up their slave-trade
profits. In almost every other respect, however, Jefferson's
opinions eventually prevailed, and he did more to shape the
course of American government than any other leader except
Lincoln. His deftly-managed Louisiana Purchase opened the Mississippi Valley to American settlement, and the Lewis and Clark
expedition, which he sponsored, presaged the extension of the
United States all the way across the continent. Yet even more
important for the future was his faith in a genuine democracy at a
time when many Americans were not at all sure the people could

really be trusted with such vast power. See Monticello, and delight in the flavour of the man.

Beyond Charlottesville are the Blue Ridge Mountains, and on the other side of the mountains is the Shenandoah Valley, as lovely as its name when the apple trees blossom in the spring. There is a splendid road, the Skyline Drive, which goes along the crest of the Blue Ridge through the Shenandoah National Park. In the spring people drive hundreds of miles to see the wild rhododendrons and azaleas in bloom along the Skyline Drive, and in the autumn the colours are exciting too. Bus tours come here from Washington. But like all National Parks, this area is kept in its natural state, with no houses or commercial enterprises allowed to intrude. There are picnic stops and camping places here, and you can see bears, and deer, and get some feeling of what the wilderness must have been like when the Virginia colonists first began working their way west through the mountains. 'Fruitfull Virginia', the Elizabethans called this land, and so she is, as fruitful today for tourists as ever she was for settlers.

SPECIAL KNOWLEDGE

Washington is accustomed to foreign visitors and foreign likes and dislikes and there is no need for much in the way of special strictures here. We might, however, call your attention to the fact that the **government buildings** in Washington close to the public at a comparatively early hour in the day. This applies particularly to such places as the F.B.I. headquarters and the Mint, but even the Smithsonian Institution buildings close early by European standards, at 4.30 p.m.

In the **summer** Washington can be terribly hot, with the heavy, humid heat typical of the South as a whole. There is a great deal of air conditioning, of course, but equally helpful is the fact that the government buildings tend to open as early as they close.

In the **spring,** late March and April, when Washington is at its loveliest, it is also very crowded. It is a custom in the United States for groups of high-school students to spend part of their spring holiday on a trip to the capital, and since everyone else also knows that Washington is particularly nice at that time of year, it can be almost impossible to get a room at short notice.

Washington, D.C.

THE CONVENTION AND VISITORS BUREAU, 1616 K Street, N.W.
A.A.A. OFFICE, 1712 G Street, N.W.

BUREAU OF ENGRAVING AND PRINTING, 14th and C Streets. Monday to Friday 8–11 and 12.30–2. Closed holidays. Free.

CANAL BOAT TRIP, Lock 3, 30th Street and M Street, N.W., Georgetown. 6 May to 29 October, Saturday and holidays 9 and 2, Sunday 2. 31 May to 6 October, additional trip 6.30 p.m.

THE CAPITOL, Centre of North, South, East Capitol Streets and The Mall on Capitol Hill. Daily 9–4.30, also after 4.30 if Congress is in session. Frequent tours 9–3.55. Closed 4 July, 25 December, 1 January.

THE CORCORAN GALLERY, 17th and New York Avenue. Tuesday to Friday 10–4.30, Saturday 9–4.30. Sunday and holidays 2–5. Closed 4 July, 25 December, 1 January. Free.

DECATUR HOUSE, 748 Jackson Place. Monday to Saturday 12–5. Closed holidays.

DEPARTMENT OF THE INTERIOR MUSEUM, C to E Streets and 18th and 19th Streets. Monday to Friday 8–4. Free.

DEPARTMENT OF JUSTICE, Pennsylvania Avenue and 9th Street. Monday to Friday 9.30–4. Tours. Closed holidays. Free.

DUMBARTON OAKS, 1703 32nd Street, N.W. Tuesday to Sunday 2–5. Closed July and August. Gardens open Monday to Saturday 10–4, Sunday 1–4. Closed July to Labor Day.

DUMBARTON OAKS PARK. Entrance off Massachusetts Avenue below Whitehaven Street. 1 April to 31 October, Saturday, Sunday and holidays 9–5. Free.

FOLGER LIBRARY, 201 East Capitol Street. Monday to Saturday 11–4.30. Closed holidays. Free.

FREER GALLERY, 12th Street and Independence Avenue, S.W. Daily 9–4.30. Free.

LIBRARY OF CONGRESS, 1st Street and Independence Avenue, S.E. Monday to Friday, 9–10, Saturday 9–6, Sunday 2–6. Conducted tours, Monday to Friday at 9.15, 10, 11, 12, 3, 4, starting from the Office of the Captain of the Guard. Free.

NATIONAL ARCHIVES BUILDING, Constitution Avenue between 7th and 9th Streets, N.W. Monday to Saturday 9–10, Sunday and holidays 1–10.

NATIONAL GALLERY, Constitution Avenue, at 6th Street, N.W. Monday to Saturday 10–5, Sunday 2–10.

PHILLIPS GALLERY, 1612 21st Street, at Q Street, N.W. Monday 11–10, Tuesday to Saturday 11–6, Sunday 2–7. Guided tours Saturday at 3. Free.

ROCK CREEK ZOOLOGICAL PARK, 3000 Connecticut Avenue, N.W. Buildings November to April 9–4.30, May to October 9.30–5. Grounds open daily, daylight to dark. Free.

ST. JOHN'S IN GEORGETOWN, Potomac Street and O Street, N.W. Services Sunday 8 and 11. Other visits by arrangement.

SMITHSONIAN INSTITUTION BUILDINGS, Jefferson Drive, between 9th and 12th Streets, N.W. Daily 9–4.30. Free.

SUPREME COURT, 1st and Maryland Avenue, N.E. Monday to Friday 9–4.30, Saturday 9–12. Conducted tours, except when court is in session, every 15 minutes up to half an hour before closing time. Closed holidays.

WASHINGTON MONUMENT, The Mall at 15th Street. 15 March to Labor Day daily 9–11 p.m. Student tours available 8–9 a.m. Labor Day to 14 March, daily 9–5. Tours by appointment 6–9.

THE WHITE HOUSE, 1600 Pennsylvania Avenue. Tuesday to Saturday 10–12. Free.

Near Washington

CUSTIS LEE HOUSE, Arlington. October to March, daily 9.30–4.30, April to September 9.30–6.

CHRIST CHURCH, Cameron and Washington Streets, Alexandria. Weekdays 9–5, Sundays 2–5. Closed Thanksgiving, 25 December, 1 January.

GUNSTON HALL, State Route 242, north of Woodbridge. Daily 9.30–5.

MOUNT VERNON, George Washington Memorial Parkway, south of Alexandria. March to September daily 9–5, October to February daily 9–4. Boat trip leaves Washington daily 2, summer also 10.

POHICK CHURCH, 2 miles south-west of Accotink on U.S. Route 1. Open daily.

PRESBYTERIAN MEETING HOUSE, Fairfax Street, between Wolfe and Duke Streets, Alexandria. Monday to Friday 9–5, Saturday 9–12.

WOODLAWN, U.S. Route 1, south of Alexandria. Tuesday to Sunday, summer 10–5, winter 10–4.30. Closed Thanksgiving, 25 December, 1 January.

Neighbouring States

Annapolis, Maryland

HAMMOND HARWOOD HOUSE, Maryland Avenue and King George Street. 1 March to 31 October, Monday to Saturday 10–5, Sunday 2–5. 1 November to 28 February, Monday to Saturday 10–4, Sunday 1–4.

UNITED STATES NAVAL ACADEMY, Sands Road. Daily 9–5. Spring and autumn, dress parades 3.30 on Worden Field.

HISTORIC ANNAPOLIS, INC., Old Treasury Building, State Circle.

Baltimore, Maryland

MUSEUM OF ART, Charles Street at 31st Street. 1 June to 30 September, Tuesday to Saturday 11–5, Sunday 2–6. 1 October to 31 May, Tuesday 2–5 and 8–11 p.m., Wednesday to Saturday 10–5, Sunday 2–6. Free.

Berkely Plantation, Virginia

On State Route 5, 6½ miles west of Charles City. Daily 9–5.

Charlottesville, Virginia

MONTICELLO, 3 miles south-east on State Route 53. Daily 8–5.

UNIVERSITY OF VIRGINIA, on West Main Street and Park Road. Guided
tours may be arranged by writing to the Hostess, The Rotunda, University
of Virginia (office hours: Monday to Friday 9–1 and 2–5. Saturday and
Sunday 9–1.)

Jamestown, Virginia

VISITOR CENTER, terminus of the Colonial Parkway. Open daily.

Shirley Plantation, Virginia

On State Route 5, 9 miles west of Charles City. Daily 9–5.

Williamsburg, Virginia

INFORMATION CENTER, Route 132 near Colonial Parkway junction. 1
April to 31 October daily 8.30–10 p.m. 1 November to 31 March, daily
9–10. Tickets for exhibition buildings sold from 9–5. For reservations or
information write: Colonial Williamsburg Inc., Williamsburg, Virginia.

EXHIBITION BUILDINGS OF COLONIAL WILLIAMSBURG. Open daily.

ABBY ALDRICH ROCKEFELLER FOLK ART COLLECTION, off South
England Street, near Williamsburg Inn. Tuesday to Sunday 12–9.

6 · The South

It is sad that the South, one of the loveliest regions of the United States, today means only Little Rock and segregation to most of the world. Clearly anyone who feels uncomfortable when confronted by obvious segregation will not enjoy being there for long. The resort areas most heavily patronized by Northerners tend to be an exception: New Orleans, Williamsburg, and most of Florida. There is still segregation there, but there is less of it and the tone is different; this is also true of the border states nearest the North, and the booming industrial cities of the south-eastern region. Of course even in rural Mississippi or rural South Carolina a visitor need not expect naked violence; you are very unlikely to encounter unpleasant incidents. But the integration upheaval is in the air, and if nothing else, a visitor is likely to find himself in continual arguments with segregationist Southerners. Of course, conditions are hardly perfect in the North for the American Negro either. But at least in the states outside the South, segregation is not written into the laws.

Actually the current unhappy image of the South is no more than the continuation of an old story; before the Civil War, foreign visitors found the South beautiful but unpleasant because of slavery. Then after the war, in the late nineteenth century, tourists did begin to go there, to delight in the fine winter climate, the exotic subtropical luxuriance, and the soothing gentility of the best of the South. For the best of the South was very good indeed. Southerners who boast of their glorious traditions have every right to be proud. The old aristocratic South nurtured a concept of the gentleman and the gentleman's life which at its best was both rational and chivalric. Those three noble Virginians, George Washington, Robert E. Lee, and Woodrow Wilson, were all products of this tradition; the Southern ideal reached its apogee in Virginia, where slavery seemed at least no worse than it had been in democratic Greece, and where many leaders openly disapproved of the slave-system.

The Atlantic coastal states were the heart of the old South.

Virginia represents one aspect; in South Carolina and in Georgia and in Mississippi and Alabama the Virginia traditions existed, but exaggerated, grown extreme. As the oldest Southern state, the first settled, Virginia continued dominant until a few years before the Civil War, and on the whole Virginians stood for moderation. However, as the argument over slavery and states' rights grew hotter, the fire-eaters from the Carolina and Mississippi plantations gradually won over popular opinion, until, like Athens, the old South was destroyed from within by demogoguery.

It is important to remember that aristocratic tradition stemmed only from a smallish part of the South, the rich slave-owning plantation country of the coastal regions and the Mississippi delta. There is another South, much less often rhapsodized, and yet equally interesting. The mountain settlers and the people who lived along the plateau country known as the Piedmont were totally different, and yet numerically they were and are today more significant.

The South, as tourist country, is by no means one homogeneous whole. We will divide it into five parts, describing a great circle beginning in southern Virginia, going down the Atlantic coast to Florida, across to New Orleans, up the Mississippi to Kentucky, and then across Kentucky through the mountains, back to the starting point.

The coastline all the way from the southern border of Virginia to Florida is swamp and marsh and sandy islands. This is most noticeable in North Carolina, where the upper coast is sparsely populated even today. Here lie the treacherous Outer Banks and Cape Hatteras, 'the graveyard of the Atlantic'. Over the years, the few people who settled along these sandy shoals acquired an evil reputation as wreckers, but this section had earned a bad name as early as 1590. In that year a ship arrived at Roanoke Island from England to provision a small colony planted by Sir Walter Raleigh in 1587, which had been the first English colony in America. To their distress the men off the ship could find no trace of any of the colonists they had last seen three years before. There was no sign of violence or hasty departure; there was simply nothing at all, except for the word 'croatoan' carved on a tree. Croatoan was the name given on some maps to a neighbouring

island, and also to a local tribe of Indians. But the island yielded
no clue, and the Indians were friendly but seemed not to understand the inquiries. To this day no more has ever been learned
about the fate of those men, women, and children, including the
first white child known to have been born in America, the little
Virginia Dare.

In 1903, on a deserted flat stretch near a place called Kitty
Hawk, itself very near the site of Raleigh's ill-fated settlement, the
Wright Brothers launched their first successful flight. More
recently these islands have been recognized as magnificent natural
bathing beaches, roads and bridges have been built, and resort
towns such as Nag's Head have become popular.

Before the Civil War, much of the low country of the Carolinas
and Georgia, farther south along the coast, was given over to rice
and indigo. As long as there was an ample supply of free labour,
slaves, these rice plantations were immensely profitable. But it was
a miserable existence for the slaves; even the sugar plantations of
Louisiana and the West Indies were less dreaded. A slave in
Virginia or Maryland regarded it as a sure sentence of death if he
were 'sold south' to the rice fields. Mrs Trollope wrote of staying
with a Virginia family who in her presence told a slave that he was
to be sent to South Carolina. The man ran to the woodshed and
hacked off his right hand with a hatchet; that way he could not be
sold profitably anywhere.

This was one side of the coin, and it cannot be forgotten. But
there was of course the other side as well: the culture which
flourished as a result of all this wealth. Half-forgotten towns all
up and down the coast bear witness to the elegance this region
once knew; one of the most charming examples is New Bern, in
North Carolina, with its splendid Tryon Palace, and the many fine
smaller houses along its quiet streets. The Carolinas were organized in a feudal manner. The lands had been given by King Charles
I to a group of his courtiers, which meant a 'proprietary' government with immensely large land-holdings not unlike the original
Dutch pattern in the state of New York. Moreover, the culture of
the Carolinas had a special flavour all its own because of French
influence. Before any English settlers at all had arrived, there had
been an abortive attempt by French Protestants to found an
independent colony on the South Carolina coast just below
present-day Beaufort. Despite their failure there, the French

continued to be strongly drawn to this country, and after the English came, many French Protestants settled down amongst them, giving such towns as Charleston a cosmopolitan air from the very beginning. French names are commonplace in this region, and there is still an active Huguenot church in Charleston.

Charleston (South Carolina) and Savannah (Georgia) were the chief towns of this low country then, and they still are, each quite distinctive, each with its own partisans. Charleston is much the more renowned as a tourist attraction. Moreover, Charleston is proud and wants tourists to be suitably impressed with its past as the most sophisticated and aristocratic city in the South. You may remember that Rhett Butler in *Gone With The Wind* had particular fascination for the ladies of Atlanta because he was not only a black sheep, but the black sheep of a Charleston family.

Charleston was originally a walled city, one of the few in America, and it is therefore compact, with most of its finest houses close together on a few streets near the waterfront. The houses are delightful. Some of them, the town houses of the wealthy planters, are large and elegant, here pure English Georgian and there French, or romanticized with curves and ironwork. Still others are small row houses or converted carriage houses, painted every colour of the rainbow. Among the most unique are the long thin houses which seem to sit sidewise, one end on the street and the wide front facing the enclosed garden; typically this sort of house has a two-story veranda the length of the front, and the street door leads first on to this veranda. Another of the charms of Charleston is the profusion of mews and alleys and hidden courtyards: Stoll's Alley is a good example. But what makes it all particularly lovely is the tropical luxuriance, the flowering vines, the enchanting colours and scents everywhere: bougainvillea and jasmine and oleander and gardenia. And the mellow brick; Charleston is rich in lovely old brick and tile, much of it brought over as ship's ballast in the early days.

The best way to see Charleston is to walk, up Meeting Street and down Church Street, back and forth on Tradd Street, along East Bay. From Battery Park on the waterfront you can just glimpse the flag flying over Fort Sumter out at the mouth of the harbour. In 1860 the Civil War began when a detachment of South Carolinians fired on the federal garrison at Fort Sumter. Today the Fort is being restored to its pre-Civil War condition, and you can take a boat trip in the harbour which goes out to it. On the way back, the view of Charleston from the sea is particularly attractive.

There are a great many churches in Charleston which make some claim on the visitor's attention. For example, there are two Episcopalian churches, both of which suffer from the St Martin-in-the-Fields syndrome. The first time in America you encounter a church which claims to be descended architecturally from London's St Martin-in-the-Fields, you accept the information solemnly and in good faith. But eventually it becomes a joke, and we are guilty of heresy in feeling not only that the two famous Charleston Episcopalian churches are not particularly exciting but also that they remind us scarcely at all of St Martin-in-the-Fields. It may be perverse, but our favourite Charleston churches are the First Baptist Church (1822), four-square and solid, with fat white pillars and box pews, and one known as the Circular Congregational Church (1892), a strange but winning dark brown mock-Romanesque structure with an unusual arena-style seating plan that seems to pre-figure the most *avant-garde* church designs of today.

Charleston still has its public market, housed in a handsome old open market building. Every morning Negroes from the country come into town with vegetables and eggs and berries and melons, and set up stalls in this public market; many of the women also sell flowers along the streets. The Negro traditions of the Charleston area are one of the main tourist attractions: George Gershwin's *Porgy and Bess*, that splendid American folk opera, was based on stories by a Charleston writer, Dubose Heyward, and what was once the prototype of Catfish Row is now one of the newly smart sections of the town.

In the nineteenth century many Carolina Negroes made their way to the deserted marshes of the coastal islands. Some of those who settled there were escaped slaves; others were Negroes who wanted to make their own way after emancipation and probably felt that life would be simpler well away from their former masters. Much of the land on these coastal islands is still owned and farmed by Negroes, and the dialect they speak is called 'gullah'. Some of the Negro churches on the islands do not object if polite visitors come to hear the gullah spirituals on a Sunday morning.

5 An early nineteenth century house in the Garden District of New Orleans

6a Belle Grove, Louisiana. A decayed plantation house with Spanish moss
hanging from the trees

6b A plantation house in Louisiana, with garconnières built for the sons of th
family

The very best time to go to Charleston is between mid-March and mid-April, when there are special house and garden tours which make it possible to see places normally closed to the public. Two of the three most famous Charleston gardens are then at their very best: Magnolia Gardens and Cypress Gardens. Despite their names, both of these gardens are loveliest in the azalea season, for this is superb azalea country, with the ideal climate and soil. Cypress Gardens is particularly exciting because it is really a swamp, with ink-black water and the dark cypress trees all hung with soft grey Spanish moss; you go through in a boat. When the brilliant colours of the azaleas are splashed against the sombre background, it is a sight one does not soon forget. The third of the famous gardens is Middleton Place, said to be the first elaborate formal garden in America. Like many eighteenth-century formal gardens, Middleton Place lacks flowers, but it does have flowering shrubs. Its chief glory is camellias, hundreds of camellias of every possible variety, old and new. These are at their best from Christmas to early February, but even at other times of the year Middleton Place is handsome because of its situation and the charm of its carefully contrived vistas. Unhappily, while each of these gardens is actually part of an old plantation, the houses there are neither particularly interesting nor open to the public. In fact, there are no pre-Civil War plantation houses one can normally go to see in this area. Many of them were destroyed during the last grim year of the Civil War, and afterwards, when the once-proud planters were reduced to poverty, many other houses were simply abandoned to rot away. The few really old plantation houses left in South Carolina and Georgia are hard to find and seldom open to tourists.

Many of the oldest public buildings in the town of Charleston itself were destroyed not in any war but in the course of a severe earthquake in 1886. The Dock Street Theater, however, has supposedly been used for theatrical performances longer than any other in the United States, and it is amusing to go there to a play. Three or four private houses in Charleston are regularly open to the public; one of them, the Nathaniel Russell House, with a particularly lovely oval sitting-room on the upper floor, is also the headquarters of the Preservation Society. The Brewton Inn and Tea Room on Church Street is a pleasant place to eat; in fine weather there are tables out of doors in its courtyard and at all

K

times it has excellent regional food. All through the old part of Charleston there are private houses which take paying guests; the Chamber of Commerce can supply lists of accommodation. Anyone who is in Charleston in warm weather but who has no car can nonetheless get to the beaches out on the islands; there are buses. And anyone who wants personal guiding in Charleston can get a list of approved guides from the Chamber of Commerce. Some of the guides are members of solid old Charleston families, some specialize in one particular aspect of this area; one of the guides drives his tourists about in a carriage, the others use cars. But all the properly-registered guides pride themselves on giving accurate Charleston history, not merely colourful legends. Moreover they whisk their tourists in and out of places they would not otherwise see, and they will drive to the outlying plantations as well as around the town, all for the standard $4 an hour. It is a vast improvement upon the usual sort of guided tour.

Moving southward along the coast, the next sizeable old town is Beaufort, pronounced 'Bewfert'. Once a busy port, Beaufort survives mainly as a winter resort for Northerners. Its quaint and quiet atmosphere has been somewhat altered by its nearness to Parris Island, now a Marine base, but there are still many handsome old houses near the waterfront, as well as a lovely Episcopalian church, St Helena's. Beaufort is actually on an inlet, with a group of flat coastal islands between it and the sea. These islands were one of the chief strongholds of the gullah Negroes, still the principal inhabitants. On the farthest island there is also a fine stretch of sandy beach, palm-fringed and peaceful.

Savannah, traditionally the aristocratic centre of Georgia, is only another fifty miles farther down the coast. In contrast to Charleston, which is very self-conscious, Savannah is seemingly quite heedless of its reputation. This means that while Charleston works diligently to preserve its past, Savannah lets most of its magnificent old squares slowly crumble, and attracts far fewer visitors. Yet this very fact lends Savannah a certain distinction. For one thing, it remains purely Southern, for good or ill. In the De Soto Hotel in Savannah, one feels oneself in the heart of a completely insular society, totally unlike the more cosmopolitan world of Charleston. It is sad to see so many handsome houses neglected, slowly falling to bits, but so long as there is something left to see, one can take romantic pleasure in wandering through

Savannah's old squares, along the brick pavements, beneath the great live oak trees and the magnificent magnolias. All through the South one encounters this magnolia grandiflora, the huge sort with white scented flowers, intoxicating on a soft southern June evening, and especially intoxicating in Savannah.

Savannah's squares were symmetrically arranged, one every other street. In fact the whole town was carefully laid out by its founder, James Oglethorpe, who had established the colony of Georgia in 1733 as a refuge for English debtors and persecuted Continental Protestants. Like most such ideal schemes it was soon altered by circumstance, and the tone of the colony quickly came to resemble that of South Carolina.

There is not nearly as much for visitors to do in Savannah as in Charleston, yet it does have great charm. To explore the old section one might walk from Madison Square to Chippewa Square, where there is a handsome Presbyterian church very reminiscent of New England, then on to Wright Square and across to Oglethorpe Square. In this section, east of Drayton Street, one senses most poignantly the slow decay of Savannah, but somehow it is not quite depressing, any more than the tumbledown state of much of eighteenth-century Dublin is depressing. Moreover, there is one well-preserved house in Oglethorpe Square which is open to the public, the Owens-Thomas House. Designed by a young English architect in the early nineteenth century, its style is a sort of planter's Regency. It is maintained by the local Preservation Society in a pleasant lived-in manner, nicely furnished even to the kitchen and the wine cellar on the ground floor. Like so many of the houses in this part of the country, it has its principal rooms high up, well clear of the marshy ground and set to catch any passing breeze.

From the Owens-Thomas House one can walk to the waterfront to see the old business blocks along Factors Walk. These buildings are still used as offices; one cannot help thinking that in some other city they would all by now have been turned into smart little houses. Between Factors Walk and the Colonial Park Cemetery are several streets that once must have been elegant but are now fast disintegrating. In the cemetery itself is the grave of Nathaniel Greene, a Rhode Island Quaker who foreswore his upbringing to become one of America's most brilliant Revolutionary War generals. In a remarkable collaboration with such

Southern guerrilla leaders as Francis Marion, 'the swamp fox', he succeeded in crushing any British hope of holding the South loyal to the Crown and gave to the Southern campaigns real military style. There is another graveyard, Bonaventure, at the edge of Savannah, where the Spanish moss seems about to smother the live oak trees completely, but Southerners say that it actually does no harm at all to the host-tree and is not a parasite.

Along the Georgia coast near the Florida border are the Sea Islands, from whence came Sea Island cotton until the boll weevil wiped out the island cotton industry here. It is now popular with golfers in the winter; there are some well-known and expensive inns on St Simon's Island, and Jekyll Island, once privately owned, is now a State Park. John Wesley had a church on St Simon's Island as a young man; unfortunately the original building has since been replaced with something more elaborate.

Atlanta is a newer town than Savannah, inland and never as aristocratic. It first became important in the nineteenth century as the centre of the Southern railway network; that was one of the reasons why Sherman burned it. Today it is still a transport centre; anyone flying in the South is likely to find himself changing planes in Atlanta. Moreover, the federal government has many regional offices there. Atlanta is an attractive, modern, industrial city. Its most important business is Coca Cola, Georgia's gift to the world.

Atlanta does not spend nearly so much time looking back as such picturesque Southern towns as Charleston and Savannah. Nevertheless even in Atlanta, as everywhere in the South, the Civil War is remembered as if it were yesterday. Southerners would prefer you to call it the War between the States, and they sometimes make it sound entirely romantic, like a medieval tournament.

Most of Florida was settled after the Civil War. It is greatly influenced by its steady stream of Northern visitors and has little in common with the 'Old South'.

When the great Florida tourist boom began, at the end of the nineteenth century, it was almost entirely concentrated along the east coast, and the west coast was considered thoroughly uninteresting. Today the east coast is still delightful if one has money, and friends at Palm Beach, or if you have the funds and the inclination for one of the great big lavish Miami Beach hotels. Palm Beach has always been the most fashionable Florida resort, an American Cannes, expensive and discreet, with elegant shops. Miami Beach is much gaudier, Las Vegas without the gambling but with the same highly paid cabaret stars to make the nights as euphoric as the days. Between Palm Beach and Miami Beach there is Fort Lauderdale, where undergraduates flock like lemmings every spring.

However, quite recently the west coast of Florida has been 'discovered'. People who wearied of the standard charms of the east coast began to go farther afield. At first they tried the Keys, which stretch from Miami toward Cuba, but then the Keys in turn became too popular, and so the more adventurous sun-worshippers took to investigating the little off-shore islands along the west coast. Some of these islands can only be reached by infrequent ferries, which saves them from the trippers. They have good beaches, not yet too crowded. The best known are Sanibel and Captiva near Fort Meyers. They are called 'the Shell Islands' because of the endless variety of sea shells to be gathered there, but they also boast such attractions as pelicans which provide a splendid welcoming sight at the dock. And they are of course handily situated near the Everglades.

All of Florida is flat, covered with scrub pine and palm, tropical vines and shrubs. The climate and the tendency to marshiness make Florida tremendously attractive to birds, and so the Everglades Swamp in particular is fascinating to anyone with an interest in wild life. Here, once seen only by the Seminole Indians who live in the swamp, are ibis and white herons and egrets and the rare roseate spoonbill, bears, panthers, alligators and crocodiles, and lovely butterflies. One can take week-long boat trips through the Everglades, or go in for a few hours; the best centres for arranging trips are Miami, the towns of Everglades and Flamingo at the edge of the swamp, and Fort Myers on the north-western fringe. The Audubon Society, a non-commercial conservation group, runs the best boat trips, and anyone contemplating a proper trip into the Everglades should get in touch with them. There are not only boat trips; in the Corkscrew Swamp Sanctuary, farther north, the Society has also built a mile-long boardwalk, accessible by road, into one of the most interesting parts of the swamp. Part of the Everglades is a

National Park, and the Park Superintendent can supply additional information.

Elsewhere in Florida, there is Florida Southern University at Lakeland, noteworthy because its buildings were designed by Frank Lloyd Wright. The University of Miami has handsome contemporary buildings too. Sarasota, once the winter quarters of the great Ringling Brothers – Barnum and Bailey Circus, now has the Ringling Museums to attract visitors. These consist of an art gallery with an extravagant baroque collection of big bright fleshy canvases by Rubens and Franz Hals and Velasquez and Tiepolo and the like, a circus museum, and the mock-Venetian Ringling house. In addition, several towns in Florida have major league baseball teams there for two months every spring for pre-season practice, and one can watch the exhibition games. And at Cypress Gardens, near Winterhaven, there are spectacular water-skiing exhibitions.

At either end of Florida's east coast there is an elaborate aquarium complete with delightful performing porpoises: the Seaquarium at Miami and Marine Studios near St Augustine. The admission charges are high, but well worth while. The fish are all together in great communal tanks which simulate their ocean environment, and one walks around underneath, as it were, almost like a diver. It is more interesting than one perhaps expects it to be.

For fish from another angle, there are deep-sea-fishing trips from almost every seaside town in Florida. You can charter your own boat, or go with a group. In either case, given the usual hot sun and clear smooth tropical water, it is a very pleasant way to spend the day regardless of your success at pulling in a sailfish or a tarpon.

St Augustine is the only resort town in Florida with any real history. Founded in 1565, forty years before the first permanent English settlement in America, it was an important Spanish base during those three hundred years when Spain held most of the southernmost sections of what is now the United States. St Augustine talks a great deal too much about being 'the oldest town'; actually much of the old part is not very old at all. But the town has nonetheless preserved a Spanish air in a way no other American town east of Santa Fé has done. This may be partly due to the fact that long after the Spanish occupation had ended, many Minorcans arrived at St Augustine. But there is also the fact that fragments of the city wall are still to be seen, and the huge Spanish fort, el Castillo de San Marcos, still guards the harbour, and the central plaza still retains a languid Latin air. You can walk from the plaza south along narrow little Aviles Street to St Francis Street, where the Historical Society has the oldest house in St Augustine suitably furnished and open to the public; there is also a pretty little garden with marked specimens of native trees and shrubs, and a small museum. There are two amusing ways to see St Augustine without walking: one is to take the little trackless train that rumbles through the streets, and the other, the more traditional and delightful, is to hire a horse and carriage. The gaily decorated surreys with their be-plumed horses stand in the plaza and near the old fort; their drivers, elderly Negroes wearing battered top-hats, importune you as you pass.

Unfortunately, every place in Florida suffers from the blight of tasteless advertising and blatant commercialism. In St Augustine it goes to such comic extremes as brass studs in the pavement with advertisements on them. Everywhere in Florida everything is 'the biggest' or 'the oldest' or 'the only'. Of course this is a vice all over America, but it is at its worst in the Southwest and in Florida. In Florida you are frantically urged to see alligator-wrestling and girls under water dressed as mermaids and minia-ture cathedrals with organs which really play and da Vinci's Last Supper recreated full-size in mosaic. Even those attractions which are genuinely interesting are over-advertised, and nothing is left alone. One of the most unattractive parts of Florida now is the region around Cape Canaveral, where the United States tests missiles and rockets. Every imaginable sort of raucous enterprise has sprouted there, to profit from the curious crowds which gather whenever a launching is imminent.

With a few exceptions, therefore, it is best to concentrate wholly on the glorious beaches, looking only out to sea. After all, the beaches are Florida's greatest claim to fame. The high season is from Christmas to April, although only southern Florida is sure to be warm enough for bathing in mid-winter. Autumn and late spring are generally delightful and less crowded, with lower prices; summer is tropically hot.

Driving from Florida to New Orleans, one passes through Mobile, Alabama. Bellingrath Gardens there are famous for their magnificent azaleas and camellias. In the state of Mississippi, nearer New Orleans, the highway runs along the sea, through a string of resort towns with tempting motels right on the beach.

New Orleans is the most fascinating city in the American South, just as San Francisco is the most exciting city in the American West. San Francisco, perched on its steep hills over-looking the Pacific, is young and exhilarating, with just a whiff of Oriental spice in its fresh sea breezes. New Orleans, on the other hand, seems old and mellow and sensual, a Mediterranean town transposed to the marshy delta of the Mississippi River. Much of Louisiana is every bit as 'Southern' as that section of Arkansas which lies just above it, or as the state of Mississippi across the river. But New Orleans and the region to the south-west of the city are different, their Franco-Spanish heritage plainly visible. There is a tradition of sophistication in New Orleans, a certain *panache*. It is not surprising that jazz should first have flowered there.

Spanish explorers had been the first to penetrate the New Orleans region, but they had neglected to claim it for Spain, and so the French claimed it instead, coming to it down the Mississippi from their Canadian territories. The town itself was founded in 1717, prospering first as the centre of a private domain and later as the headquarters of the French colonial government in this area. Jesuits introduced the cultivation of sugar cane into Loui-siana, and New Orleans grew rapidly as a port and a gathering place for the rich French planters. With Spanish territory on either side, in Florida and Texas, there must always have been a good many Spaniards in and about New Orleans, too, even in the days when it belonged to France. In any case, as the French empire in Canada dissolved, France gave up Louisiana as well, ceding it to Spain in 1762. Naturally, many of the old French families were not pleased, and there was a revolt in 1768. This was put down by Spanish troops commanded by one Alexandro O'Reilly; the his-tory of New Orleans is nothing if not exotic. Years later, in the war of 1812, the decisive defeat of the British in the Battle of New Orleans gave Andrew Jackson his reputation as a general, but when the smoke cleared, the combatants made the ironic dis-covery that peace had really been signed fifteen days before the battle began.

In 1803 Napoleon artfully got back the Louisiana territory
from Spain, and then promptly sold it to the United States for
twenty-seven million dollars. Since the signs of Franco-Spanish
occupation linger on most vividly in Louisiana and the arrangement was called 'the Louisiana Purchase' one tends to think of it
as involving only that one state. However, the Louisiana territory
actually included not only Louisiana itself, but also the modern
states of Arkansas, Missouri, Oklahoma, Iowa, Nebraska, Minnesota, North Dakota, South Dakota, and most of Kansas, Colorado, Wyoming, and Montana: the whole great Missouri-Missis-
sippi River basin, in fact, at approximately fourpence an acre. It
doubled the area of the United States at that time, and represented
President Jefferson's greatest gamble.

The Louisiana Purchase opened up the territory to Anglo-
American settlers from other parts of the United States, but in
and around New Orleans the old French and Spanish families
continued in control. Americans pushed on towards the West and
many strange types drifted through New Orleans, but on the
whole the town changed them more than they changed the town.
Frontier gamblers learned subtlety here, and for those who craved
something more sophisticated than the usual shot of whisky, New
Orleans invented the cocktail. Then there was the irresistible New
Orleans praline, the result of sugar-coating the local pecan nut in
a French manner. And, equally irresistible in quite another way,
there were the lovely quadroons, who made the demi-monde in
New Orleans a thing of almost Parisian glitter. If these refinements
did not finish you off, there remained the bowie knife, the ingenious invention of New Orleans' own Jim Bowie.

All visitors to New Orleans today go first to the French
Quarter, the heart of the old Franco-Spanish town and New
Orleans' greatest tourist attraction. Some people are disillusioned
there. Half the romantic legends turn out to be false, and Bourbon
Street, once synonymous with jazz, is now principally devoted to
girls, girls, girls in various stages of deshabille. This can be amusing at night, but in the daytime it only seems tawdry. On the
whole, however, the French Quarter proves every bit as good as
advertised, as long as one exercises a sensible reserve and resists
the obvious tourist traps. For example, New Orleans is famous for
its food; even the lowliest cafeteria will offer delicious craw-
fish bisque, superb oyster sandwiches. And some of the best

restaurants are in the Quarter. One of them, Brennan's, even makes a specialty of distinctive New Orleans breakfasts, after which one may long to go back to the hotel and sleep until the lights go on along Bourbon Street. Then too, there is still good jazz to be heard in the Quarter, if one seeks it out. For example, there is Preservation Hall on St Peter Street, where one can simply wander in, sit on a bare bench and hear superb Dixieland for hours on end, all for the price of a modest contribution at the door. Jazz bands even play on the streets in the Quarter at Mardi Gras time, when New Orleans puts on its greatest spectacle.

The most obvious attraction of the French Quarter, however, is its architecture, the wrought-iron gates and balustrades, the tiled roofs, the enclosed patios. After the Civil War, people began to move away from this section of New Orleans and many of the old houses have slowly decayed, their lovely courtyards overgrown. All of this adds now to the Quarter's peculiar charm.

There are many pamphlets about the French Quarter which suggest specific routes for a walk through it, but it is pleasant enough just to wander about, looking up at the galleries, peering through the gates at the patios, going down any passages which look interesting. Bourbon Street and Royal Street and Chartres Street are the principal thoroughfares, parallel to each other. Unfortunately the streetcar named Desire no longer passes along them; it has become a prosaic bus. St Peter Street, which crosses these others to lead to Jackson Square, has some particularly attractive buildings. And at Jackson Square, formerly the Place des Armes, is the Cathedral, built in the late eighteenth century but greatly altered since, and the Cabildo building, seat of the French and Spanish governing councils. Beyond the Square, towards the wharves to the east, is the old French Market, where one can have delicious doughnuts at the coffee stalls. It is interesting too to go past the French Market all the way to Esplanade. In the area around the old Ursulines Convent, at Ursulines Street and Chartres, one feels much closer to the nineteenth-century French Quarter than in the more 'tourist' sections.

The French Quarter is not the only interesting section of the city, however. The Garden District is charming in quite a different way. In the nineteenth century, while the old French families tended to keep to themselves in the Quarter, wealthy

Anglo-American planters built houses on the opposite side of town, along the Mississippi. The French Quarter is now largely abandoned to tourists and artists, but the Garden District remains the most fashionable part of New Orleans, its handsome Greek Revival houses still beautifully cared for. The centre of the Garden District lies along Prytania and Chestnut Streets, between Washington Street and Jackson Avenue; the last of the New Orleans streetcars take one there, out along St Charles Avenue. It is pleasant simply to stroll through the Garden District and to eat perhaps at the Commanders Palace. In February it is also possible to go through some of the houses; the Louise McGehee School offers such tours as part of its fund-raising scheme.

Among New Orleans' more unusual attractions are the old burying grounds. These have only tombs, not graves, and many of the tombs are particularly lovely, now romantically overgrown with flowering tropical vines almost hiding the crumbling masonry. Two of these old French cemeteries are at the edge of the French Quarter, and one is in the Garden District, on Prytania Street between Conery and Sixth.

The Gulf of Mexico near New Orleans is rather uninteresting except for the giant oil rigs working away miles out at sea. But there are two fascinating trips to be made out of the city: to the old sugar plantations along the Mississippi River, or into the Cajun country. Since they lie in the same general direction, one can also combine the two, given two or three days for the trip.

At one time there were great plantations all along the Mississippi, and there still are minor roads which run close to the river on either side, west of New Orleans, past many of these plantation houses. Few of them are officially open to the public, but several can be seen from the road, and others, in ruins, can sometimes be explored. One of the most handsome, and also open to the public, is Oak Alley, just west of Vacherie on the south side of the Mississippi; the name derives from the magnificent allée of live oaks which leads to the house. On the way from New Orleans to Oak Alley, along the south bank of the Mississippi, five miles east of Edgard, one passes Evergreen, an exceptionally lovely, gleaming white plantation house which is unique in still possessing most of its out-buildings. In the same area but on the opposite bank, easily reached on the Donaldson-Darrow ferry, are several other splendid plantations. One, the magnificent Belle Hélène, five miles west of Darrow, is open to the public; it is beautifully furnished. East of Darrow, along the dusty State Route 942, are two other fine plantation houses, well worth driving past even though one cannot go in.

Many of the finest plantation houses in Louisiana were built in the first half of the nineteenth century, in a style called Greek Revival, with great white columns, often all the way round in the manner of the Parthenon. The houses were built high, the living quarters well clear of the ground; even so, malaria was rife all through Louisiana. The earlier houses had been simpler in design, usually constructed in a manner known as *briquette entre poteaux*, tough cypress timbers framing the soft peaty Louisiana bricks; only a few of these buildings have lasted. Later ones were often 'steamboat Gothic', mock-Gothic with carved wooden fretwork. A good example of Louisiana steamboat Gothic is the house called 'San Francisco' on the north side of the river, west of Reserve.

The Cajun country is French Louisiana again, but these French settlers were totally unlike the wealthy sugar-cane planters. This is the region west of New Orleans, along the bayous of the Mississippi flood plain. The word 'Cajun' is a corruption of 'Acadian'. The Acadians were French Canadian settlers driven out of New-foundland in 1755 by the British, and many of them found their way to New Orleans, where the French colony later helped to resettle them in Louisiana. The rather questionable help con-sisted of giving them 'the land of trembling prairies', low and marshy delta country where the unpredictable Mississippi floods made farming impossible, and so the Cajuns took to fur-trapping and fishing and hunting alligators for the hide. Much of their region was inaccessible except by boat, and for almost two hundred years they led a lonely and isolated life. Recently, the growth of the shrimp industry and the discovery of oil in these parts have brought about a considerable change in their world; there are better roads now, and real schools. But less than ten years ago, the man from whom you asked directions along the road would probably have spoken no English at all, only 'Cajun' French, which bears slight resemblance to the Parisian variety. Today the only way to see the Cajun country as it used to be is to go along the lesser bayous in a boat, which is hardly practicable for the average tourist. But this section of Louisiana still attracts visitors.

The town of Franklin has some beautiful old houses, as does St
Martinsville, where even the post office is in a handsome old
house. (American post offices are frequently worth noticing.
In many places, and St Augustine, Florida, and Santa Fé, New
Mexico, come immediately to mind, the postal service has preserved a fine building by taking it over to use as a post office.)
There are some plantation houses in this region, too, and one or
two take paying guests. Finally, one of the high points of any trip
into this part of Louisiana is a stop at Avery Island, which is
actually no more nor less an island than the rest of this swamp
country. Avery Island was known originally for its vast salt mines,
the most important in the South. Today this area specializes in
growing hot peppers to be turned into a famous Louisiana condi-
ment called Tabasco Sauce, but the real attraction at Avery Island
is its bird sanctuary, part of an estate called Jungle Gardens.
Particularly at dusk in the nesting season one can see thousands
of snowy egrets, and there are also beautiful flowering shrubs,
camellias and wisteria and azaleas.

The Mississippi River winds a tortuous course from the top to the
bottom of the United States. A hundred years ago it was the only
practicable road into the heavily wooded interior to the north, and
crowded with every imaginable sort of barge and boat. The young
Abe Lincoln, for example, took a load of hogs down the Mississippi on a flatboat; it was in New Orleans that he first saw slaves
sold. 'That sight was a continual torment to me,' he wrote to a
friend a few years later, 'a thing which has and continually exercises the power to make me miserable.'
    Mrs Trollope, writing in the 1830's, gives a dreadful picture of
her trip up the Mississippi. She was not enchanted by the colourful riverboat gamblers; nor was she pleased by anything else along
the way. The forests were far too densely grown, there was 'not
an inch of what painters call a second distance', the men were too
rough, the women too familiar, and, the last straw, 'there are no
castles crowning the heights'. It is too bad that Mark Twain was
not on the river in Mrs Trollope's day; she would have afforded
him vast pleasure. Twain was perhaps prouder of his early years
as a licensed Mississippi River pilot than of his writing success,
and with some justice, since the Mississippi is a treacherous river,
very shallow in places, with shifting underwater mud banks and

perverse currents and eddies. His pseudonym, Mark Twain, was itself a river pilot's sounding cry, and his work is a good source for a picture of the river in the 1850's.

Mrs Trollope had only a brief glimpse of Natchez and Vicksburg, then important river ports, with great houses and a 'season' when the rich planters of the interior came into town; she was, however, willing to grant Natchez more virtues than any other town along the Mississippi. Both Natchez and Vicksburg are pleasant to visit today, with near-by plantations open to the public. In March there is the added attraction of the Natchez Pilgrimage, when for a period of two or three weeks the local garden clubs sponsor tours of houses and gardens not ordinarily open, and the local ladies dress up in ante-bellum gowns. If one is driving, a stop in one of these towns provides almost the only opportunity actually to see the river; ordinarily the great levees, or embankments, are between the road and the water. Dams on tributary rivers have almost tamed the Mississippi now, but the levees continue to be an important additional protection. It is still possible to go down the Mississippi on an old-fashioned paddlewheel steamer, for there is one which runs as an excursion boat, making trips of varying length along the Ohio and the Mississippi rivers, starting from Cincinnati, Ohio. The fare for two people can be from about $34 a day all-in.

You get a sense of the remarkable flatness and richness of this vast Mississippi Valley if you continue along U.S. Route 61 north of Vicksburg. Here is the real cotton country, on both sides of the Mississippi from New Orleans almost to Cairo, Illinois. It is known locally as the Delta, despite its distance from the mouth of the Mississippi; it has rich black alluvial topsoil. Throughout this country there is a great gulf between rich and poor, and an even greater gulf between black and white. Here and there in the Delta you come upon perfect little Greek Revival towns, most of them now rather shabby, the paint peeling off the houses. This is the country of William Faulkner's novels; Jackson, Mississippi, is supposedly the Jefferson of Faulkner's stories, and he himself spent much of his life in Oxford, Mississippi, farther north, toward Memphis. Memphis, in Tennessee, is the most important city in these parts, the great cotton market centre.

For the first forty years of the nineteenth century, the frontier in

America meant the lands of the Ohio and Mississippi River valleys. The far West was then known only to trappers and hunters; Texas still belonged to Mexico until 1837, while California did not become part of the United States until 1848.

The earliest frontier settlements west of the Appalachian Mountains were along the rivers in Kentucky and Tennessee and Ohio. The hardy pioneers here were almost all descended from East Coast Anglo-American stock: English, Scotch, Scotch-Irish, Irish. On the frontier they lived an incredibly rough, primitive life, menaced by Indians and bears, floods and drought, disease and crippling accident, and, perhaps worst of all, loneliness. Out of this world there came prodigious frontier heroes like Daniel Boone and Davy Crockett, their exploits partly legend but partly true too. And there was another sort of hero moulded by the rigours of the frontier: Andrew Jackson and Abraham Lincoln were both examples of native genius tempered with the infinite hardships and presented with the limitless opportunities of this raw new land.

Andrew Jackson was the first President from the new lands of the West, and his two tempestuous terms had lasting effects on the United States government. The Hermitage, where he lived with his beloved wife, Rachel, whenever he was not in Washington, is still standing and open to the public, a few miles east of Nashville, Tennessee.

Abraham Lincoln, younger than Jackson, was born in a rough log cabin near Hodgenville, Kentucky; his father later moved the family to an even meaner existence in Indiana, and finally Illinois. The cabin in which Lincoln was born is still there, now part of a National Historic Site. Unhappily, the cabin itself is completely encased in a kind of mausoleum, as depressing a sight as ever was. But much of the country in this part of Kentucky has scarcely changed at all in the past hundred years, and if one disregards the artificialities at Hodgenville it is easy to imagine the Lincoln family here.

Mammoth Cave is about fifty miles south of Hodgenville; advertisements for it adorn every road in Kentucky. A series of limestone caverns, it is a great tourist attraction; Mammoth Cave and the Carlsbad Caverns in New Mexico are the two largest caves in the United States. The main part of Mammoth Cave system is now protected within a small National Park, but the rest of the area, including several other caves, is individually owned and hideously commercial.

Going north-east from Hodgenville, one passes several of the leading bourbon whisky distilleries, and then, after a stretch of poor hill country, one comes to the rolling blue-grass region around Lexington, Kentucky, where according to tradition the finest American racehorses are bred. Many of the big horse farms here allow visitors to see the stables and watch the horses being exercised. Lexington, like Louisville, along the Ohio River farther north, was an oasis of refinement in Kentucky's frontier days; these are both still attractive towns. Every spring Louisville has the Kentucky Derby, America's most important flat race.

Most of Kentucky and Tennessee was 'frontier' for only thirty or forty years, and then it was too populated to count as frontier any longer. But the eastern sections, hilly and not fertile enough for successful farming, have always retained some of the characteristics of frontier country. It is a gross over-simplification to discuss the western parts of the Carolinas and the eastern parts of Kentucky and Tennessee as if they were exactly alike, but there is a rough similarity. It is all mountain country, the southern end of the Appalachians, and the settlers here were mostly English and Scotch, and mostly very poor. The people in the more isolated parts of this region kept to themselves over the years, scratching a bare living from smallholdings. If there was one trait they all seemed to have in common, it was a devotion to the Bible. Lonely frontier life had few consolations other than religion; in the nineteenth century the bigger frontier towns were famous for their camp meetings, when people gathered from miles around to listen for a week or more to celebrated preachers. If sometimes there seemed to be an excess of emotion at these camp meetings, it was after all the only sort of outlet the frontier permitted. And for those who lived in the most remote parts, there was never even the treat of a camp meeting; they simply had the Bible. Those frontier settlers who were most isolated also clung through the years to several vestiges of their past: old ballads, and a form of English country dancing which evolved into square-dancing, and a degree of proficiency in weaving and quilting superior to that of more sophisticated regions. Until very recently this mountain country remained a fertile field for folk-song collectors and stu-

7 Cypress Gardens, near Winterhaven, Florida

8a Intersection at night

8b Sunshine Skyway, St Petersburg, Florida, crossing eleven miles of open water at the mouth of Tampa Bay

dents of old customs. Some scholars say that the English spoken
here was virtually Elizabethan.

These mountain people were proud and unpredictable, in the
manner of mountain people the world over. Hating the wealthy
aristocrats of the coastal regions, they were prepared to side with
the British during the Revolution, but British officials were tact-
less in dealing with them and so they shifted allegiance and proceeded to fight like tigers on the side of the rebels. Owning no
slaves, they seemed unlikely to support the Confederate cause in
the Civil War, but it turned out that their devotion to independence made them ardent supporters of the states' rights principle,
and countless numbers of them came down from the hills to enlist
in the Confederate armies. Today, in North Carolina, and at
Berea, Kentucky, there are centres devoted to the preservation of
this folk culture. Berea also has a celebrated college, with nursing,
agricultural, and technical courses for poorer students from the
mountain regions.

On the Kentucky and Tennessee side of the mountains, the
T.V.A. has made a tremendous difference to the life of the region.
Some sections, like the coal-mining areas of the Kentucky hills,
are still very poor, but on the whole this part of the country now
enjoys a modest prosperity undreamed of thirty years ago. There
are several big new lakes as a result of the dams, and people flock
to them in the summer, but the most important effect was the vast
increase of electric power for the area. Eighteen of the T.V.A.
dams and six of the steam plants are open to the public.

Oak Ridge, near Knoxville, is one of the four major atomic
research centres in the United States. The experiments begun at
the University of Chicago in the early days of the Second World
War were continued here; in 1942, when the project grew too big
and potentially too dangerous for a laboratory in the middle of a
city, all the equipment was transferred to Oak Ridge, then no
more than a crossroads in the Tennessee hills. Oak Ridge therefore has the oldest continually operating atomic generator in the
world. Research is now devoted to peaceful uses for atomic power
in such fields as medicine; the United States obviously does other
kinds of atomic research as well, but not at Oak Ridge. There is a
very good atomic museum there, run by the Atomic Energy
Commission.

North-east of Oak Ridge there is an almost deserted village

L

called Rugby. It was founded in the 1870's by Thomas Hughes, author of *Tom Brown's School Days*. Hughes had become deeply interested in Christian Socialism, and he had high hopes for a co-operative settlement in America for honest British working-men and young English gentlemen with enthusiasm and enter-prise but slight capital. He hoped that among other things his community could be a help and an inspiration to the poor moun-tain people near by; one of his first deeds was the establishment of a sizeable free library. A charming little 'carpenter's Gothic' church was built too, and a hotel for the throngs of visitors who were expected to come and breathe the pure mountain air. But the colony failed, and today most of the buildings stand empty. The church still holds occasional services, however, and the library is still open; it now functions as the Rugby historical museum as well.

Along the border between Tennessee and North Carolina, near Asheville, North Carolina, is the Great Smoky National Park, in the loveliest part of the Smoky Mountains. This region is parti-cularly beautiful in the spring: early, when the dogwood blooms, and later, when the mountain laurel is at its best. It is also magnifi-cent when the leaves turn in the autumn. The Smokies were already old when the Rockies first thrust up above the earth's crust; they are worn and mellow mountains with a rich, verdant, tranquil beauty all their own.

The Cherokee Indian Reservation is at the south-eastern edge of the Great Smoky Park. Here, at the village called Cherokee, the Cherokees themselves have re-created a pre-colonial Indian village, known as Oconaluftee. It is extremely well done, with the Indians dressed in their ancient tribal costumes, demonstrating the old crafts and way of life. Here, too, fine examples of Indian work are for sale at the Qualla Craft Center.

East of the Smokies, in the North Carolina tobacco country, are two of the finest universities in the South, Duke University at Durham and the University of North Carolina at Chapel Hill. In this same region too lies Winston-Salem, where the charming old Moravian-colonial section of the town has recently been restored.

Before we leave the hill country of the South, we must in all fairness admit that there are a few undesirable off-shoots of the highland traditions. Mountain music was not all quaint old-English ballads; there is also what is known as hillbilly music.

Nashville, Tennessee, has many legitimate claims to distinction, but for many years it has been the hillbilly music centre of the country as well, spewing out recordings of that questionable form of art. The local radio stations in America are always a source of wonder and amusement to foreign visitors, and in the South they can be quite incredible, emitting a ceaseless flow of hillbilly music and insistent, primitive religion. For a long time this music had only a limited, albeit devoted, following, until Elvis Presley, a Tennessee boy himself, made it known all over the world. Along with English common law, those first British settlers apparently brought the seeds of rock-and-roll.

SPECIAL KNOWLEDGE

The South is rich in contrasts: very rich and very poor, for example, and tremendously hospitable, yet always faintly suspicious of strangers. Lulled by the warmth and the scented air in the South, one can sometimes be brought up short by an act of real barbarism. One of the least controversial instances of this is the Southern **speed trap**. Many villages in the South have posted speed limits for cars which are wildly out of proportion. You can be bowling along the open road at a perfectly legal sixty miles an hour, and suddenly come upon a notice which proclaims 'town limits: 25 miles an hour speed enforced', or something of the sort. There will have been no warning, and unless you are constantly on guard, you will not be able to slow down in time to avoid breaking the law. Then, since the village probably lives on its traffic-fine revenues, you may be arrested, charged, convicted, and parted from a considerable sum of money almost before you realize what has happened. Every little village has the legal right to do this sort of thing, and the state and federal governments are powerless to interfere. Many Southern state governments are now trying to get rid of the worst speed traps by means of various subtle pressures, but for the time being drivers in the South must continue to be particularly alert.

For anyone interested in the **plantations,** we heartily recommend the brochures of the Tourist Bureau of the Louisiana Department of Commerce and Industry in Baton Rouge, Louisiana.

In connexion with the **T.V.A. scheme,** if a visiting specialist wishes to make some special sort of tour, this can be arranged through the office of the Director of Information, Tennessee Valley Authority, Knoxville, Tennessee.

Avery Island, Louisiana

JUNGLE GARDENS, 8 miles from New Iberia (nearest accomodation). One can enter the Gardens daily, 8–5 in winter, 8–6 in summer, staying until sunset, if one wishes, to see the birds return to settle for the night.

Charleston, South Carolina

CHAMBER OF COMMERCE, 50 Broad Street at Church Street. Monday to Friday 8.30–8.30, Saturday 9–12.

CIRCULAR CONGREGATIONAL CHURCH, 136 Meeting Street.

CYPRESS GARDENS, 20 miles north of Charleston, off U.S. Route 52. 15 February to 1 May, daily 8–6.

DOCK STREET THEATER, corner of Church Street and Queen Street. Daily 9–5.

FIRST BAPTIST CHURCH, 61–63 Church Street. Daily 8.30–12 and 1–5.

MAGNOLIA GARDENS, North off State Route 61. 2 January to 1 May, daily 8–6.

MIDDLETON PLACE, North, on State Route 61. Daily 8–6. Camellias bloom December to early March and the azaleas during March and April.

NATHANIEL RUSSELL HOUSE, 51 Meeting Street. Monday to Saturday 10–1 and 2–5, Sunday 2–5.

Cherokee, North Carolina

MUSEUM OF THE CHEROKEES, at junction of U.S. Routes 19 and 441. 1 May to 31 October, daily 8–6.

OCONALUFTEE INDIAN VILLAGE, Mid-May to Labor Day, daily 9–5.

Darrow, Louisiana

BELLE HELENE PLANTATION HOUSE, River Road, 5 miles west of Darrow. Daily 9–5.

The Everglades, Florida

EVERGLADES NATIONAL PARK, Box 279, Homestead, Florida.

AUDUBON SOCIETY, 143 North East 3rd Avenue, Miami. Tours 2 January to 29 April. Prices range from $30 for a 2-day combined boat and car trip (not including meals or lodging) to $4 for a 2-hour boat trip. Brochure sent on request.

EVERGLADES PARK CO., Flamingo, Florida. Daily tours. Accommodation. Write to The Everglades Park Co. Inc., 3660 Coral Way, Miami 45, Florida.

Hodgenville, Kentucky

ABRAHAM LINCOLN BIRTHPLACE, 3 miles south of Hodgenville. Daily 8–5. Free.

Mammoth Cave National Park, Kentucky

Prices and schedules of the various guided tours are available from The Superintendent, Mammoth Cave, National Park, Mammoth Cave, Kentucky. Mammoth Cave Hotel has overnight accommodation. There is also a free campsite.

Miami, Florida

THE SEAQUARIUM, on Rickenbacker Causeway. Daily 9–5.30. Divers feed fish hourly.

Mississippi River Trips

GREEN LINE STEAMERS INC., Main Street, Cincinnati 2, Ohio. 20-day cruise from Cincinnati to New Orleans and return operates twice in the spring and twice in the autumn.

Mobile, Alabama

BELLINGRATH GARDENS, 20 miles south-west of Mobile on U.S. Route 90. Gardens open daily 7 to sunset. House open daily 8–5.

Nashville, Tennessee

THE HERMITAGE, 13 miles east of Nashville off U.S. Route 70 N. 1 April to 30 September, 8.30–5; 1 October to 31 March, 8.30–4.

New Bern, North Carolina

TRYON PALACE, George Street, between Eden and Metcalf Streets. Tuesday to Saturday 9.30–4; Sunday 1.30–4.

New Orleans, Louisiana

THE CABILDO, Jackson Square. Daily 9–5.

GARDEN DISTRICT TOURS, Louise McGehee School for girls, 2343 Prytania Street. Walking tours to see four houses and gardens. February only, Tuesday and Friday 3. Tour price includes tea.

TOURIST INFORMATION OFFICE, 418 Royal Street.

Oak Ridge, Tennessee

AMERICAN MUSEUM OF ATOMIC ENERGY. Monday to Saturday 9.30–5; Sunday 12.30–6.30. Closed Thanksgiving, 25 December, 1 January. Free.

Reserve, Louisiana

SAN FRANCISCO PLANTATION HOUSE, West of Reserve, State Route 44. Daily 9–5.

Rugby, Tennessee

RUGBY HISTORICAL MUSEUM, Monday to Saturday 10–5, Sunday 10–4.

St. Augustine, Florida

CASTILLO DE SAN MARCOS. Just off Fort Marion Circle. Daily 8.30–5.30.

MARINE STUDIOS, 18 miles south on State Route A 1 A. Daily 8–6. Feeding times 9.30, 11, 12.30, 2, 3.30, 4.50.

OLDEST HOUSE, St Francis Street at Charlotte Street. Daily 9–6.

Sarasota, Florida

THE RINGLING MUSEUMS, on U.S. Route 41 north of town. Week-days 9– 4.30, Sunday 12.30–4.30. Closed Thanksgiving Day and 25 December.

Savannah, Georgia

BONAVENTURE CEMETERY. At the end of Bonaventure Avenue. Daily from sunrise to sunset.

THE INDEPENDENT PRESBYTERIAN CHURCH, Bull Street at Oglethorpe Avenue. Week-days 9–5. Sunday, services 11 and 7.30.

THE OWENS-THOMAS HOUSE, 124 Abercorn Street, on Oglethorpe Square. Tuesday to Saturday 10–5, Sunday 3–6, Monday 2–5. Closed Thanksgiving, 25 December, 1 January, 4 July.

Vacherie, Louisiana

OAK ALLEY, North on State Route 18. Daily 9–5.

7 · The Midwest

Visitors from abroad who find themselves obliged to spend a week
or a month or a year in the Midwest console themselves with the
thought that this is the true America. All of the American characteristics seem more pronounced there. The Midwest is the crucible
in which pioneers from the older states of the east coast and from
every country in Europe have been fused into the representative
American; it has brought forth Thomas Edison and Abraham
Lincoln, Mark Twain, Walt Disney, Ernest Hemingway, Carl
Sandburg, Henry Ford, Harry Truman, and General Eisenhower.

When you say 'Midwest' to an American, he sees a small town
in the middle of fertile farming country. The houses are made of
wood and painted white; they are plain but comfortable, with no
fences between the gardens, and there are big 'shade' trees in
front of each house. There is only one main street but there are
several churches: Baptist, Methodist, Episcopalian, Roman
Catholic, Lutheran, and perhaps churches for two or three less
familiar sects as well. Everyone is hearty and cheerful despite the
bitter cold in the winter and the extreme heat in the summer, and
everyone helps each other in time of trouble. It is both the idyllic
Midwest of Tom Sawyer, and the deadly provincial Midwest of
Sinclair Lewis's damning novels of the Twenties, *Main Street* and
Babbitt.

In reality this Midwest, with its rich farmlands and the small
towns each just like the other, is only a part of the picture today.
As farms grow bigger and more mechanized, the farming population dwindles and industry becomes more and more dominant.
This does not change the 'typicalness' of the Midwest, however,
for despite the obvious superficial differences, the industrial
Midwest is just as much the essence of America as the rural Midwest is. They are two sides of the same coin.

It would be foolish to attempt to describe the Midwest state by
state, or to follow some imaginary path winding back and forth
across the region. It is too big an area, for one thing, and for the
most part it is not tourist country at all. We think it more sensible

to proceed as if one were making a colour print, starting with the entire area blank and then superimposing on it, step by step, each of the shades, the components, which all together make the multi-hued image of the American Midwest.

We will begin with the industrial Midwest, which is chiefly to be found within an imaginary band running east and west through the top of Ohio, Indiana, and Illinois, and taking in lower Michigan and the southern edge of Wisconsin as well. On the east this band starts at Pittsburgh, in Pennsylvania, and towards the west it grows paler and less distinct as it crosses Iowa, and finally fades altogether after Omaha, Nebraska.

The industrial part of the Midwest is not beautiful. Once it was all forest, a wilderness which the early explorers found romantic and peaceful. But when the settlers came, the trees were felled and the land beneath turned out to be rather flat and characterless. The Great Lakes should help to make it more attractive, but few of the cities along the lakes take proper advantage of their situation.

A notable example of a town which has wasted its situation is Cleveland, on Lake Erie in Ohio. Cleveland turns its back to the lake, and even pumps industrial waste into it so that the beaches near Cleveland have become unfit for bathing. And yet Cleveland is not entirely without virtue. It has a fine orchestra. It has an extremely good museum of art. It has one of the most interesting repertory theatres in America, the Karamu, all-Negro. Moreover, while Cleveland itself is quite ugly, it does have some pleasant suburbs, and beyond them to the south-east there is pretty, rolling, open country between Gates Mills and Hudson. Thus if one were in Cleveland on business it would be a pity not to get away from the centre of the town at least briefly. One might drive through that country to the south-east, perhaps to see the first Mormon temple, at Kirtland, Ohio, or to look at Hudson, a pretty little town which preserves its charm by keeping all its power and telephone lines underground. South-west of Cleveland, the countryside is much less attractive, but Oberlin College, in that direction, has a widely admired art gallery.

There are several other industrial centres in northern Ohio: Akron, Toledo, Youngstown, Canton, none of them tempting to tourists. The Toledo Museum of Art is in many respects even finer than that of Cleveland, but otherwise there is little to see in industrial Ohio. A few of the big plants have exhibits of one sort or another, but nothing to match the tours of the automobile plants in Detroit.

Detroit is surely the most celebrated industrial city in America. As 'Wall Street' suggests high finance, so 'Detroit' stands for assembly-line production at its most efficient. And in fact the most exciting tourist sight in Detroit is an automobile assembly line in operation.

There are three automobile plants which have tours for visitors: Cadillac, Chrysler, and Ford. The Cadillac is the most elegant product of the giant General Motors organization, while Chrysler is the costliest model turned out by the Chrysler Corporation, which also makes Plymouth and Dodge cars. The Cadillac plant is in western Detroit; the Chrysler plant is on the northern edge of the city. Most visitors to Detroit, however, choose to watch the production of an automobile both more modest and more famous, the Ford.

The Ford empire is actually not in Detroit itself, but a few miles west, in the neighboring town of Dearborn. To see the Ford works, one must go first to the Rotunda, the Ford visitors' centre, situated in open country a mile or so south of central Dearborn. There are exhibits there, and shiny new Ford cars to inspect, and there are also continuous showings of a film about various aspects of Ford history and production. In addition, during the summer, visitors to the Rotunda can go on a test drive in a Ford car. The principal attraction, however, is the free tours which start from the Rotunda on week-days, every hour in the winter and every half-hour in the summer. One is transported in buses to the Ford works to see the assembly line in operation and perhaps to see the Ford steel mill too; Ford is the only automobile company to have its own steel mill and rolling plant.

It is important to bear in mind that all the automobile assembly lines shut down at the end of the summer for two or three months, to re-tool for the next year's models. Usually this period extends from mid-August to mid-October, but it would be foolhardy to make a special trip to Detroit without first finding out the schedule for the year in question. You could write to an automobile company direct or to the Detroit Convention and Visitors Bureau.

On the whole Detroit is very much a seasonal place, at its best in the spring and early summer. The automobile plants close in late summer, and in the winter many of the other attractions either severely restrict their hours or are closed to visitors entirely. For example, one of the most handsome new constructions in the area is the Saarinen-designed General Motors Technical Center, some twelve miles north of central Detroit, in Warren. As the name indicates, this is the headquarters for General Motors' design and research operations. There are interesting tours there, but only during the summer months.

After the automobile plants, the most popular tourist attractions in Detroit are Greenfield Village and the Henry Ford Museum next to it, two or three miles from the Rotunda, south of Dearborn. These were both creations of the first Henry Ford, who compensated for his limited education with a determination and imagination which led to the Ford car and later made him an indefatigable collector. He dearly loved machinery of all sorts, from watches to steam engines, and he also had an almost superstitious reverence for history. Thus he was equally avid to acquire the chair in which Lincoln was sitting when he was assassinated, and the first model of the gramophone. The results might have been appalling had Henry Ford not been fortunate in his curators. As it is, however, the museum is positively magnificent. The collection naturally includes a superb array of old cars and engines, but it also includes silver and furniture and chronometers and covered wagons and a 'street' of old shops, all housed in an immense reproduction of Philadelphia's Independence Hall. Yet everything is splendidly ordered, bright and gay. The admission fee is hardly minimal, but one does get one's money's worth; it takes several hours to see the museum properly.

Greenfield Village adjoins the museum, but has a separate admission fee. Like the museum, Greenfield Village is a wild mixture, for Henry Ford ended by collecting buildings. Thus there is Wilbur and Orville Wright's bicycle shop, where those young men first began to work on a flying machine; Thomas Edison's laboratory, moved intact from Menlo Park in New Jersey, with even the old rubbish heap at the back carefully put into sacks and brought here for greater authenticity; early American houses of every sort; and eccentric additions like a Cotswold cottage. The buildings are grouped together to form a mock-village which is pure surrealism.

In the summer one can wander at will in Greenfield Village, but for the rest of the year one can only go through on a guided tour. Walking tours start every two hours in the winter, more frequently in spring and autumn. These walking tours, however, take two hours, lingering over every building, and they are conducted by rather unimaginative guides. It is more pleasant and comfortable to take the forty-five minute horse-drawn omnibus tour which circles through the entire village and stops at the three or four most interesting buildings. These 'carriage tours' start every fifteen or twenty minutes during the high season, but in winter they are far less frequent and are likely not to run at all on Monday and Tuesday. It would be as well to telephone ahead if one wanted to be sure of seeing Greenfield Village in that manner.

From June to September there are Gray Line bus tours from Detroit which visit both Greenfield Village and the Ford plant in the course of a five-hour trip. As for public transport, Inter-town buses running from the centre of Detroit to the Veterans Hospital, go right past the Rotunda and reasonably near the Ford Museum and Greenfield Village.

Detroit is no uglier than any other industrial centre; in fact it is better than many. Like most large American cities it suffered a blight at the heart as those who could afford to do so moved out to the suburbs and the town itself was left to decay, but now the dreary area along the river in the centre of the city has been razed and a handsome group of civic buildings has gone up there, including a spectacular auditorium. Canada lies just across the river, opposite these new buildings; the international boundary is at the middle of the bridge. Detroit is thus both a port of entry and an important stop on the St Lawrence Seaway, situated as it is between Lake Erie and Lake Huron. In the summer, a ferry plies daily between Detroit and Cleveland, across the width of Lake Erie, and there are also boats which take passengers the entire length of the lake, to Buffalo near Niagara Falls. There are public beaches not far from the centre of Detroit and an elaborate recreation area on Belle Isle in the river.

Most visitors go to Detroit to see the attractions connected with the automobile industry, but there are other interesting things there too. On Woodward Avenue, easily reached by bus from the centre of town, there are two excellent museums, the Detroit Historical Museum and the Institute of Arts. Just west of the Museums, between Cass and Second Streets, is Wayne State University. Wayne is neither venerable nor well-known outside its own area but it has 20,000 students, many of them the sons and daughters of automobile plant workers. Wayne also has several fine new buildings: the most celebrated is the graceful McGregor Memorial Conference Center, the work of a remarkable Japanese-American architect, Minoru Yamasaki. You may be told you must visit one of Detroit's large shopping centres; we found them less exciting than others we have seen, but if you do go to the Northland Shopping Center you can then see another Yamasaki design, the Reynolds Aluminium building just across the road.

North of the city is 'Cranbrook', in the pretty village of Bloomfield Hills near Birmingham. Cranbrook is several separate institutions with a common aim: 'to inculcate an appreciation of art and nature . . . with a passion for public service.' There is a boys' school, a girls' school, and a school for small children; an academy of art, a science museum, and a handsome church. These are all the result of the vision and generosity of a Detroit industrialist, George Booth, and his wife, Ellen Scripps Booth; they named their foundation after the village in Kent from which Mr Booth's parents had emigrated to America.

The first of the Cranbrook schools was begun in 1918. Since Eliel Saarinen designed many of the buildings, and his equally famous architect son, Eero Saarinen, used Cranbrook as his headquarters, many people in America know the place chiefly because of the Saarinen connexion. Europeans, on the other hand, are likely to go there to see the innumerable examples of Milles sculpture which are dotted about the handsome grounds. But there are other attractions as well. The art galleries are open to the public daily during the summer and at week-ends in the winter. And the science museum, although comparatively small, is truly superb.

Unfortunately it is impossible to get to Cranbrook by public transport; the only possibility is to take a bus from Detroit to Birmingham, and then a taxi. It is unfortunate too that once you have reached Cranbrook you find there is no place there to eat, and even picnics in the grounds are frowned upon. Barring these vicissitudes, however, you are not likely to be disappointed.

About thirty-five miles from Detroit in the opposite direction is the Enrico Fermi Atomic Power Plant near Monroe, where visitors can have a two-hour lecture-cum-film-cum-tour. And in

Battle Creek, Michigan, to go from one extreme to the other, you can tour the Kellogg cereal factory.

Detroit is a modern industrial city, very American to be sure, but with resemblances to other modern industrial cities all over the world. Chicago is far more complex. In the first place, it is much bigger. Chicago is America's second largest city, and it stretches interminably across the prairie. Moreover, except for New York, no city in America was built of so many diverse foreign elements, and while older cities absorbed their immigrants, moulding them to established patterns, Chicago was too raw and young and impressionable to do this. Thus the concentration of immigrants there in the late nineteenth century, with their inbred hatred of the police and authority and their gratitude towards anyone who would take their part, led first to the rise of a political 'machine' in control of the city government, and later to organized crime and the gangster. Other cities produced gangsters, to be sure, but if one wanted a really splendid all-purpose model, one had to turn to Chicago.

One might expect to find Chicago completely reformed now, after so many years, but this is not the case. Perhaps the trouble is that everyone rather likes it wicked. Businessmen there for meetings eagerly look forward to the night clubs, and even the most gentle of gentlewomen is inclined to ask where she can see a racketeer. Chicagoans themselves have apparently grown so accustomed to the inefficiency and the crime and the grime that they do not even notice it. For most of them, the only significance of the 'machine' is that if they know the right politician they can get a traffic ticket 'fixed'. Most of the people with money simply move outside the city; the wealth concentrated in Chicago's fashionable suburbs is incredible.

As one drives through the west side of the city today or through parts of the north side, it is still possible to trace the waves of European immigration. For a few blocks the shop names and signs will combine English with Polish, and then comes a district where German predominates, or Czech or Polish. You cross a street and you have crossed a border. People who know the city well can point to little restaurants away from the centre of the town where the food is pure Budapest or Cracow or Dubrovnik. And near the quiet parks on the far west side where elderly men sit reading foreign newspapers, one finds onion-domed churches.

Today, however, with all immigration drastically reduced, Chicago is becoming more uniform and much of the Old World flavour is gone. In its place there is a new element for Chicago's melting-pot: the Negro population there, as in Detroit, has increased tremendously since the Second World War, and the 1960 census showed that more than a quarter of the people in Chicago were Negroes, living mainly on the south side of the city.

The heart of modern Chicago is also the site of the earliest settlement, at the point at which the Chicago River meets Lake Michigan. There on the south bank of the river is the Loop, so called because the elevated trams make a circle round it. Within the square mile of the Loop are the big stores and the theatres; at its western edge, farthest from the lake, lies the financial district, mostly along La Salle Street. Across the river on the north bank is the section known as the Near North Side, with the Michigan Avenue Bridge, the most important link between the Loop and the Near North Side. Michigan Avenue is to Chicago what Fifth Avenue is to New York. It is a handsome boulevard, running parallel to the lake and frequently within sight of it. The nearness to the lake, however, means that walking along Michigan Avenue in the winter can leave one absolutely numbed with cold. As the driving snow whips around you, it is all too clear why Chicago is called 'the Windy City'.

Chicago may have her faults, but she has done better by her lake shore than any other Midwestern city. Between Michigan Avenue and the lake there are either parks or handsome skyscrapers and blocks of apartments, and along the very edge of the lake runs the Outer Drive, which makes it possible to get from one end of Chicago to the other without contending with mid-town traffic. Also along the lake shore are many public beaches and man-made harbours for small boats.

The Loop is the section most visitors to Chicago see, but it is really rather drab nowadays, suffering from competition with the new suburban shopping centres. However, you might still like to visit Marshall Field's, the enormous department store which gave birth to Selfridge's when one of its early employees went to London to see if he could duplicate Mr Field's success on the other side of the ocean. Or, for a fine view of Chicago, you could go across Michigan Avenue to the new Prudential Building to eat or have a drink at the Top of the Rock. On the opposite side of the Loop, you might also find it interesting to go to the grain exchange, 'the wheat pit', in the Chicago Board of Trade building on La Salle Street; there is a visitors' gallery.

For the best cross-section of Chicago, however, one must go to the Near North Side. Many knowledgeable people prefer the hotels there too, only a short ride from the Loop on a Michigan Avenue bus. As you cross the river, to the west are several striking new office and apartment buildings which have recently gone up at the river's edge. And just across the Michigan Avenue Bridge to the north-east is the Tribune Tower, the home of the *Chicago Tribune*, that newspaper which was for so many years the loudest trumpeter of Midwestern isolationist and anti-British sentiment. With the death of Colonel McCormick, its oracular publisher, the *Tribune* has now softened its tone a bit. It no longer showers daily maledictions on 'imperialist, war-mongering Britain', although it is still very firm about its likes and dislikes.

The Water Tower, at Chicago Avenue and Michigan, is Chicago's most famous landmark and one of the few buildings to survive the great Chicago fire in 1871. A crenellated, turreted mock-castle, built of the coarse yellow stone so characteristic of nineteenth-century Chicago, it embodies all the provincial ugliness of the town, yet it is so bad that it is endearing. Near the Water Tower along Michigan Avenue are the smartest shops, and between here and the lake are many expensive blocks of flats, the most celebrated being the two stark black metal and glass buildings designed in the 1950's by Mies van der Rohe, which stand on the Outer Drive at Oak Street.

It is enlightening to walk west from Michigan Avenue to Rush Street, perhaps along Chestnut Street. At 18 Chestnut Street is the Lincoln Book Store, long a gathering place for devotees of Midwestern Americana. It is a fine place for browsing, but we also point it out to show what a very mixed area the Near North Side is. Almost next door to this bookshop, in an area which also includes the private and prestigious Newberry Library and any number of expensive little galleries and antique shops, are the most raucous night clubs, with more corruption to the square inch than in any other part of Chicago. This is one of the principal bailiwicks of the Chicago political machine, yet it also includes some of the most fashionable addresses in the city. One sees elegantly dressed women off to an elegant lunch, and blondes with night-faces out walking their dogs with a fur coat thrown over their slacks. As you go north along Rush Street, you pass jazz clubs and clubs which exist solely to provide a setting for those girls with night-faces, but you also pass coffee bars crowded with earnest young writers and artists. Chicago had a literary renaissance in the Twenties from which sprang countless good novelists and poets; in the coffee bars of the Near North Side the hope persists that history is about to repeat itself. West of Rush Street along Division Street is one of the old Polish districts; there is nothing for tourists to see there, but it is the setting for most of Nelson Algren's stories of love and despair and death on the cold, cruel streets of Chicago. Finally, just a few minutes' walk north from the Division Street turning and the Rush Street clubs is the most fashionable hotel in Chicago, the elegant Ambassador East, at State and Goethe Streets, where the memory of Beau Nash is expensively preserved in the Pump Room, the city's best restaurant. The Pump Room is really Bath crossed with Hollywood; long before the advent of such sybaritic New York eating places as the Four Seasons and the Forum of the Twelve Caesars, the Pump Room was 'producing' food rather than merely serving it. Coloured pages with plumed turbans and satin knee-breeches dart about, narrowly missing waiters bearing flaming swords with someone's supper impaled on the end; it has become one of the tourist sights of Chicago, esteemed by all affluent visitors.

To eat less dramatically, you might look for one of the O'Connell's chain of snack bars; their sandwiches and waffles are delicious. There is an O'Connell's on Michigan Avenue south of the Water Tower, and one on Rush Street at the north end of the night-club district, and there are two or three in the Loop.

For those so inclined, one of the obvious tourist sights in Chicago used to be the Stockyards, south-west of the Loop. These days, however, much of the activity there has ceased. Advances in refrigeration now make it more economical to butcher the animals nearer home and ship the meat rather than the live cattle and hogs, and so there are no more tours of the Stockyards.

Chicago has several good museums. The Art Institute, the finest museum of art in the Midwest, is equal in many respects to those of Boston and Philadelphia. In addition to its old masters, the Art Institute has a remarkable collection of French Impressionist and Post-impressionist paintings. It also has 'Mrs Thorne's rooms', which are endlessly fascinating. These are miniature rooms, fifty or so altogether, which illustrate different decorative styles in Europe and America over the past four centuries. Some of the furniture is genuinely old, cabinet makers' samples or pieces made long ago for dolls' houses; the remaining things are meticulous copies, and there are tiny *petit-point* carpets, and hangings made from rare old silks and brocades, and exquisite miniature chandeliers and sconces. Seeing the rooms is like gazing into little sunlit corners of history.

Out on the lake shore, along the Outer Drive east of the Loop, there are three more museums grouped together: the Natural History Museum, which old Chicagoans still call the Field Museum, and an aquarium and a planetarium. All of these museums are good solid examples of their kind. The Natural History Museum is particularly noted for its natural-habitat groupings of African animals. Quite a distance south of the centre of Chicago, in that area of depressing dilapidation which also harbours the University of Chicago, is the Museum of Science and Industry. It has a captured German U-boat, a simulated coal-mine trip, and a glorious fairy-tale doll's house, all crystal and gold, with tiny fountains working in the garden. There are good scientific and mathematical sections too, but too many exhibits have been arranged by business firms, giving much of the museum the appearance of a trade fair.

Those who really want to venture from the centre of town might prefer the Chicago Historical Society. It is a far more modest museum, but it has a fine collection of Abraham Lincoln memorabilia and is pleasantly situated in Lincoln Park, just beyond the Near North Side.

If you come into Chicago from the East at night, you will see the sky filled with flames from the hearths of the steel mills at Gary, Indiana. This region just to the south-east of Chicago rivals Pittsburgh in the production of steel; there is nothing pretty about it in the daytime, but at night it has its own strange beauty. Within a hundred miles of Chicago there are many other industrial centres. Most of them are best avoided unless you have business there, but in Racine, Wisconsin, some seventy-five miles north of Chicago, there is the remarkable Johnson Wax Factory, designed by Frank Lloyd Wright. One can take tours through it.

M

Most of the cities which rear up from the vast prairies and plains in the Midwest beyond Chicago differ very little one from the other. They exist primarily to cope with the products of the farming country around them. Thus Minneapolis, Minnesota, has its great flour mills; Omaha, Nebraska, is a meatpacking centre; Kansas City, Missouri, provides a market for both livestock and grain. There has not yet been time in these cities for much besides business, although there are a few pleasant surprises. Kansas City has the excellent William Reckhill Nelson Gallery of Art. Des Moines, the largest city in the state of Iowa, has two interesting buildings, the chapel at Drake University and an Art Center designed by Eliel Saarinen. Moreover the Iowa State Fair, held at Des Moines in the last week in August, is the quintessence of the agricultural Midwest. And Minneapolis has the University of Minnesota, a fine orchestra, and two art museums; Minneapolis and its twin-city, St Paul, comprise one of the most progressive and attractive metropolitan areas in America. But on the whole the most interesting cities in the United States are those along the coasts; inland there is vigour but much less charm.

Most of the cities of the Midwest have grown from nothing in little more than a hundred years, and often in far less time. Some of them were once trading posts in the wilderness, but few have any real history. The exceptions are the cities and towns on the Ohio River and the lower Mississippi. Even there the towns are hardly ancient, of course, but they were the very earliest settlements, with the rivers the first highways. The town of Cincinnati, Ohio, for example, began on the north bank of the Ohio River in 1788. It was the first important settlement in what is now the Midwest, and at one time no foreign visitor thought his trip complete until he had seen it. Mrs Trollope, who lived in Cincinnati for a year in the 1830's, had unpleasant things to say about its citizens, but one suspects it was because they failed to patronize her bazaar, so that she had to return to England bankrupt. Moreover even Mrs Trollope admired the charming situation of the place, on the slopes of a hill above *la belle rivière*, the loveliest river in America. She said that Cincinnati only 'wanted domes, towers, and steeples' to be quite handsome, and one wishes her bazaar building had been preserved, for it would seem to have represented her own single-handed attempt to remedy Cincinnati's deficiencies. Harriet Martineau, passing through Cincinnati ten years later, reported 'Gothic windows, Grecian pillars, and a Turkish dome', the whole 'ornamented with Egyptian devices'. The impulsive citizens also did away with their original method of refuse-disposal, which was simply to let hundreds of hogs run loose through the town, to the amazement of most visitors. The hogs emptied the dustbins efficiently, and fattened themselves for market at the same time.

Today there is nothing startling to see in Cincinnati, although there are two pleasant galleries and a zoo which offers opera as well as animals in the summer. Cincinnati is simply a comfortable, agreeable town, admired for having a model police force and two or three really good restaurants in a part of America which other-wise is not notable for such assets. Cincinnati has always seemed a bit more cosmopolitan than most of the other cities in the Mid-west, partly because it is older, no doubt, and partly too because of the sort of settlers it attracted; not only old-stock Americans, but also German Social Democrats, German-Jewish intellectuals, and French refugees.

Another river town enriched by alien elements is St Louis, on the west bank of the Mississippi River just south of its meeting with that other mighty river, the Missouri. St Louis began in 1764, when a Frenchman from New Orleans came up the river and settled there; for many years it remained a small French outpost, known only to trappers and river men. Then the United States acquired the vast Louisiana Purchase lands, including St Louis, and in 1804 President Jefferson dispatched Meriwether Lewis and William Clark to explore this new territory and find a northerly route across the continent to the Pacific Ocean. Lewis and Clark assembled their little party at St Louis before setting off up the Missouri River into the unknown, and it was to St Louis they returned two and a half years later, with their neat maps and journals and their tales of the buffalo and the plains and the shin-ing mountains which led at last to the Pacific. Their expedition marked the start of a new era for that strategically situated out-post, for as the westward expansion began, Americans poured into St Louis in ever greater numbers. Today it is a large and prosperous city with many industries; it may seem foolish to claim that one can still discern its French ancestry, particularly when so many Germans have come since. But many of the old

St. Louis families are descended from the early French settlers, and St Louis has an unhurried air that seems part Southern, as of course it is, but also part Gallic deliberation and rationality. The special character of St Louis is delightfully apparent at Gaslight Square, where the sidewalk cafés and the beer gardens, the night clubs with Victorian décor and the night clubs offering satiric revues are all thronged on a summer evening.

In Forest Park in St Louis there is another of those excellent art museums one comes to expect in the leading cities of the Midwest. There is also a delightful zoo, famous for its antic chimpanzees; the zoo has a remarkable aviary too, in which exotic, brilliantly coloured birds fly around in a vast jungle setting, completely unenclosed. In the summer, there is a season of light opera in Forest Park. And the new St Louis airport is very handsome; it was designed by Yamasaki, the same architect who did the new buildings at Wayne State University in Detroit and the Science Pavillion at the Seattle World's Fair.

Cincinnati and St Louis have grown so large that one almost forgets their past as river towns. But up and down the Ohio and the Mississippi there are smaller places which still retain a special quality. One of the most attractive of these is Hannibal, in Missouri, north of St Louis. Mark Twain grew up in Hannibal, or perhaps one should say Tom Sawyer and Huckleberry Finn grew up there. Mark Twain's family house is still there, and open to the public. Every visitor to Hannibal should also be sure to go to Riverview Park, a pretty park with a lovely view over Mark Twain's Mississippi River.

The Mississippi is tremendously important in American history, a great powerful river cutting the country in two and providing an invaluable north-south waterway. But the Mississippi is not on the whole a beautiful river. The Ohio winds picturesquely through rolling green country, the broad Hudson flows majestically to the ocean between high bluffs and palisades, and the turbulent western rivers cut deep through richly coloured canyons, but 'ol' man river he just keeps flowin' along,' as the song says, muddy and sluggish and shallow. It is more impressive to go on the river than to look at it. Generally, of course, there are now bridges across it, but here and there, particularly from southern Illinois and Kentucky across to Missouri and Arkansas, there are still a few raft-like ferries which take one or two cars. For a brief moment you can be Père Marquette and Louis Joliet in 1673, probably the first white men ever to see the upper Mississippi; or Abe Lincoln taking his flat-boat loaded with hogs down to New Orleans in the 1830's; or Huckleberry Finn. In addition to the ferries, there are trips along the Ohio and the Mississippi on the *Delta Queen* which we mentioned in Chapter 6. Moreover, there are a few excursion boats on the Mississippi which take passengers on day trips, and at least one of these is a genuine old paddle-wheel steamer. There are one or two showboats left, too, which dock at a different river town each week and give old-fashioned melodramas in a theatre on board ship, as was the custom in the old days.

Far to the north of Hannibal, there is another charming little river town, Galena, in the north-west corner of Illinois. It is actually on the Galena River, not the Mississippi, but it has the proper old-fashioned river-town air, with steep streets and nice old houses. General Grant lived in Galena for many years, and his musty Victorian house is open to the public, with its horsehair furniture and antimacassars and cut glass all still in place. It seems a strangely genteel and fussy setting for that sombre, whisky-drinking soldier.

So far we have mentioned only the relatively new industrial centres and the old river towns. There are other towns in the Midwest, some large and some small, which have distinct and individual histories.

There are, for example, those parts of the Middle West which have associations with Abraham Lincoln. Lincoln was born in Kentucky, but when he was still very young his father moved the family to Indiana, and later they moved again, to Illinois. The Lincolns were a typical pioneer family, bitterly poor, scratching a bare living from fields they cleared in the wilderness, their stock at the mercy of bears and bobcats, their crops likely to be flooded out or dried up according to the mood of the violent, unpredictable Midwestern climate. Today every log cabin the Lincoln family as much as gazed upon has been turned into a shrine. We have already mentioned, in Chapter 6, the elaborate memorial park at Hodgenville, Kentucky, and the Knob Creek farm there. In Indiana there is a replica of the Lincolns' Pigeon Creek cabin at Rockport, some forty miles east of Evansville in the southern part of the state, and near by there is another memorial park, at Lincoln City. In central Illinois, about sixty miles south of the twin university towns of Champaign and Urbana, there is still preserved the last log cabin Abraham Lincoln shared with his parents and his brothers and sisters before he went off to seek his fortune. There are countless other sites, too, which make some claim to the Lincoln-admirer's attention. If Abraham Lincoln were not such a remarkable figure, all the fuss would seem ridiculous; as it is, however, a good many people reverently follow the trail from start to finish.

For most people interested in Lincoln, however, it is enough to go to New Salem and to Springfield. Springfield is the capital of Illinois, almost two hundred miles south-west of Chicago; New Salem is a few miles north-west of Springfield. The young Abraham Lincoln went to New Salem to find work in 1831. It was there that he began to teach himself law, poring over Blackstone at night, and it was as New Salem's representative that he was elected to the Illinois legislature, his first political victory. New Salem was only a small village in Lincoln's time; all of the Illinois territory was then a sparsely populated wilderness. After Lincoln's day New Salem almost disappeared entirely, abandoned in favour of more promising towns, but now it has been restored and reconstructed so that it looks exactly as it did in the 1830's: a group of log cabins and rough board buildings in wooded country on the bank of the peaceful little Sangamon River, a very satisfactory place for anyone curious about Abraham Lincoln or the life of the American frontier. Springfield is of course completely different, a large industrial town now, but it is even richer in Lincoln memories. Lincoln served in the legislature there, in a building which is now used as the Sangamon County Courthouse. In a house at 8th and Jackson Streets, he lived with his wife and growing family from 1844 until that day in 1860 when he left for Washington to be inaugurated President. And there in Springfield he is buried.

When Abraham Lincoln was a young man in New Salem, Illinois was the frontier, but ten years later, in the 1840's, covered wagons began to roll westward across the plains beyond the Mississippi. There are several towns in the Midwest which had brief moments of glory during that westward expansion.

One of these towns is Independence, Missouri, which was the assembling point and supply base for most of the wagon trains, whether they were going south-west on the Santa Fé Trail or north-west along the Oregon Trail. Today U.S. Route 50 beyond Independence follows the old Santa Fé Trail across Kansas, while U.S. Route 40 follows the Oregon Trail much of the way west. To be sure, the Oregon Trail did swing farther north at one point, into Nebraska and then across the Rockies at South Pass in Wyoming, but eventually it returned again to what is now U.S. 40, and wagon trains heading for California continued along this same time-worn path over the Sierra Nevadas all the way to San Francisco.

There are still a few buildings left in Independence from these early days, but the chief attraction there now is a very new building, the Harry Truman Library and Museum. It seems customary for an ex-President to assemble all the documents and effects of his administration in a special memorial museum, like the Franklin Delano Roosevelt collection at Hyde Park. In Harry Truman's case, Independence was the logical site since he had lived much of his life there.

Abilene, Kansas, offers the same combination of Western history and Presidential papers. General Eisenhower grew up in Abilene, and so *his* museum is there. But for four brawling, violent years, between 1867 and 1871, Abilene had a different sort of fame as the wildest town in the West. It was the first of the towns along the new railroad to be invaded by Texas cattlemen shipping their cattle east to market. Cowboys drove huge herds to Abilene all the way from the Texas ranges, many long hard weeks on the trail, and when they finally hit town they were ready to explode. There was gun-play, and there were gamblers, come to get their share of the cattle money. To maintain a vestige of law and order Wild Bill Hickok was called in as Marshal.

Meanwhile, however, Kansas was filling up with permanent settlers, earnest farmers who hated everything about the cattle drives, from the way the cowboys behaved to the way the cattle overgrazed the land along the trail and spread the dreaded Texas tick-fever. For a romaticized picture of the mutual bitterness, one need only recall the musical comedy *Oklahoma*. Conflicts occurred everywhere along the fringes of the newly settled lands. The cattle drives were thus forced to finish farther west, to avoid trouble, and Abilene's wild days came to an end. Its reputation and the men who made it moved on to Dodge City, in the western part of Kansas. It was in Dodge City that Wyatt Earp and Bat Masterson first achieved fame. Dodge City is still fun to see, for the old Front Street saloon area has been restored.

There was one other kind of wide-open town in those days: the mining town. One of the most famous, or infamous, was the gold mining boom-town of Deadwood in South Dakota, where Wild Bill Hickok met his end. Picturesquely situated in the handsome Black Hills region, Deadwood has several evocations of the old days to entertain visitors. Not far away is the town of Lead, where the Homestake Mine is still being worked. It has now produced more gold than any other mine in the United States. At both of these towns one can make tours of the mines.

Countless little towns in the Midwest were settled by some particular religious sect, or some one nationality. We have already mentioned Kirtland, in northern Ohio, where the Mormons trekking west from New York State built their first temple. More important in Mormon history was Nauvoo, in Illinois, just across the Mississippi from the south-eastern corner of Iowa. The Mormons settled at Nauvoo with every intention of remaining for ever, and they made it the most prosperous town in Illinois in the 1840's. However, an angry mob, hating and fearing the Mormon eccentricities, set upon and killed their prophet and leader, Joseph Smith. After that, most of the Mormons moved on west to Utah, but some of their buildings still stand at Nauvoo and can be visited.

New Harmony, on the Wabash River in south-western Indiana near Evansville, harboured two remarkable groups. The town was established in 1814 by an ascetic German named George Rapp, whose followers were known as Rappites. Their New Harmony was a celibate religious colony, devoted to prayer and hard work. Several of the old communal Rappite buildings are open to the public now, and even the maze is still there; its intricacies were meant to illustrate one's difficulties in achieving salvation. The Rappites abandoned New Harmony after only ten years to return to their original settlement in Pennsylvania. George Rapp sold the property to Robert Owen, a dynamic Welsh radical whose name was a household word in America in the first half of the nineteenth century. The turbulent history of Owen's New Harmony experiment in communism makes fascinating reading, and there are one or two buildings at New Harmony which date from his era too.

In Iowa there is a group of villages known as the Amana Colonies, near Cedar Rapids. The Amana settlers, again, were German, and their communal experiment has continued to this day, with some modifications. Amana Colony refrigerators and freezers are sold all over the United States, and at Amana itself, the picturesque central village, one can buy Colony-made wine and furniture, and dine on German food.

Almost everyone who grew up in the Midwest before the Second World War could tell you of some such homogeneous religious community near his own town. Today they are fast disappearing, but once there were many hundreds. In some instances the religious impulse which had caused the founding of the town was soon just a memory, but in many other cases the bonds held firm for a long time, and some little town was known not to permit smoking or dancing, and its young people were forbidden to mingle with the 'sinful' young of neighbouring towns. Often the citizens of such towns dressed differently too, and the local school was run in strict accord with their religious precepts. The most distinct example of this kind of separateness left today is the Amish. They are best known in Pennsylvania, as indicated in Chapter 3, but there are equally large settlements in Holmes County and Madison County in Ohio, and in Elkhart County in Indiana.

For that matter, the Midwest continues to attract interesting, unconventional people with lofty aims. We have already mentioned Cranbrook, in Michigan. Quite another sort of experiment was Taliesen, in the south-west corner of Wisconsin near Spring Green. Taliesen was Frank Lloyd Wright's home, and studio, and the centre for his architectural fellowship. In winter the Wrights and all the assistants and apprentices repaired to Taliesen West, in Arizona, but the Wisconsin Taliesen was the first, the original centre. Its buildings illustrate Wright's principles, and in the studio there are models of all the major Wright designs. Frank Lloyd Wright is now gone, but the fellowship is continuing for the time being, and one can still visit Taliesen.

Taliesen is in a particularly pretty part of Wisconsin, which is in turn one of the prettiest states in the country. We have said that the Midwest is not really tourist country, but one could have a very pleasant drive up along the Mississippi, seeing Hannibal and Nauvoo and Galena and then south-western Wisconsin; everything would be intensely American and yet pleasantly varied.

Wisconsin was settled by an interesting assortment of nationalities, and south-western Wisconsin reveals a good cross-section. Not far from Spring Green, for example, there is Mineral Point, an old mining town (tin and lead) settled by miners from Cornwall. The distinctive granite buildings made the Cornish heritage very obvious, and there is also a restaurant, the Pendarvis House on Shake Rag Street, which serves Cornish pasties, saffron buns, and clotted cream. It is open only during the summer, and one must usually book a table well in advance.

A few miles east of Mineral Point is the town of New Glarus, at the heart of the Swiss section of Wisconsin. Many Swiss customs are lovingly preserved there and one can visit the cheese factories.

There are a great many Norwegian settlements all over Wisconsin too; between New Glarus and Madison, for instance, there are several towns which are still preponderately Norwegian. The biggest and most concentrated 'foreign' settlement in Wisconsin, however, is the city of Milwaukee, on Lake Michigan. Milwaukee now has a sizeable Polish colony, but the dominant mood there is and always has been German, and the principal industry is the brewing of beer. Much of the best American beer comes from Milwaukee, and German taste is responsible for the fact that American beer is light and pale and dry. You can tour the breweries in Milwaukee, and have samples at the end, and then you can have a hearty German meal at any of several Milwaukee restaurants. Milwaukee is baseball-mad, too, and the local baseball park is handsome. A night game there is delightful, with the green, green playing field brilliantly lit, and vendors selling good Milwaukee beer and sausages.

In summer, car ferries run from Milwaukee and several other points in Wisconsin across the lake to Michigan. They provide a useful short-cut for travellers going from the Detroit region to the north-western Midwest.

Wisconsin is by no means the only Midwestern state which has had a varied assortment of settlers over the past hundred years. Tremendous numbers of Swedes went to Minnesota, along with Norwegians and Danes and Germans, and many Irish immigrants. Norwegians went to North Dakota too, and in addition both North Dakota and South Dakota attracted a great many Russo-Germans, people whose ancestors had gone from Germany to Russia at the urging of Catherine the Great. North Dakota even received several groups of Icelanders; there are little towns in the north-eastern corner of the state where Icelandic names and lore still abound. South Dakota drew many Finns, and so did Minnesota. Nebraska welcomed waves of Germans, and thousands of Bohemians from what is now Czechoslovakia. A classic American novel, Willa Cather's *My Antonia*, deals with the life of these Bohemian pioneers at the turn of the century. Reading *My Antonia* or Mari Sandoz's *Old Jules*, one is staggered by the hardships the early settlers had to face in these bare and dusty plains west of the Mississippi, where even today the distances and the isolation of each farm can seem unbearable, and a towering grain elevator twenty miles away across the flat prairie becomes more exciting than the Empire State Building.

It would be a sad mistake to go to these states expecting to find everyone in native dress reciting sagas to each other and speaking broken English. In many cases only the family name still gives tangible evidence of a Norwegian, or Russian, or Bohemian background, although a few old customs are sometimes continued; many Finnish farmers, for instance, have saunas – Finnish steam-bath-houses. Then too on special occasions a family out in that part of the Midwest may eat some particular traditional dish which betrays their ancestry. Otherwise the food everywhere will seem the same: 'typical American Midwestern'.

Anyone who knows Europe, however, will soon realize that 'typical American Midwestern food' is actually very like German food, or like Scandinavian food without fish. In other words, the superficial national differences may have faded from sight, but the influence of the immigrants from northern Europe has sunk deep into the life of the north-western Midwest. The great red barns one sees on every farm, for example, are really a Scandinavian contribution, as was the log cabin. Moreover, the heavy concentration of Scandinavian and German settlers in Wisconsin, Minnesota, the Dakotas, and Nebraska has had its effects on the political attitudes of that region. Conservative in many ways, the farmers of this area have nonetheless experimented with every kind of co-operative. In addition, the Progressive Party lasted longer in Wisconsin than in any other state; the city of Milwaukee for many years had a Socialist mayor, and Minnesota has voted regularly for candidates of the radical Farm-Labor Party. 'Radical', in fact, is the key word in this part of the Midwest; the voters have always favoured dynamic men with big ideas. They have also shown great willingness to back losing causes and to follow leaders down uncharted paths, like the brooding Nordic creatures so many of them are. One should not wonder that the messianic Joseph McCarthy succeeded in becoming the Senator from Wisconsin.

The rural Midwest is by no means everywhere the same. The northernmost regions are almost entirely forest, with scarcely any farms, and at the other extremity, in south-eastern Missouri, the Midwest merges with the South and the farmers grow cotton. Most of the land in the Midwest, however, is devoted to raising hogs, to dairy cattle, or to growing maize and wheat.

East of the Mississippi the farms are generally smaller than those farther west, and there is also more mixed farming, combining crops and stock. The countryside is often very attractive. Southern Indiana and southern Illinois are rolling and mellow, and Wisconsin is prettiest of all, with its black and white cows and red barns set against the green hills. In Ohio, which was settled before the rest of the Midwest, many of the little towns have charming old houses. Ohio fell heir to all the nineteenth-century architectural fancies of the East, and so one sees delightful examples of styles like Greek Revival and Carpenter's Gothic and Hudson River Bracketed.

The great corn (maize) and hog region lies at the heart of the Midwest, with Iowa the archetype. All farmers have problems these days, but the farmers here are amongst the most prosperous. Beyond, west of the rich corn lands, lie the higher, dryer grasslands of the Great Plains with the huge wheat farms of the Dakotas and western Nebraska and Kansas. This westernmost region was the dust-bowl of the 1930's, when there was a bad drought followed by nightmarish swarms of locusts. But even in good years the moisture in these parts is hardly oppressive. Winters on

the Great Plains are bitterly cold, with blizzards; it is muddy in the
spring, miserably hot in the summer, and dusty in the autumn.
And everywhere west of the Mississippi the distances are enormous; each farm is an oasis. If you have driven through this
country once, you are not likely to want to repeat the trip again
soon.

Yet everyone should see this part of the Midwest, really to
understand America. And if you found yourself near Minden,
Nebraska, on U.S. Route 6 west of Hastings, you might enjoy
stopping at the Pioneer Village, a reconstruction of the settlers'
life in this region from the days of the first covered wagons to the
coming of the aeroplane. Most of the buildings are not copies but
the real thing, moved here from the original sites. There is even an
old sod house like those in which most pioneer families lived in the
early days on the Great Plains, when there was neither timber nor
stone to be had; wildflowers grew all over the outside of sod
houses in the spring, providing one rare bright note in an otherwise grim existence. Both those of foreign birth and the old-stock
Americans who moved hopefully westward usually came to the
Great Plains as 'homesteaders'. The government had made these
lands available free, in 'homestead' portions of 160 acres apiece, to
anyone who filed a claim and lived continuously on the land for
five years. The harsh climate and the stubborn soil broke the
spirit of many a homesteader before his five years had passed;
those who stayed were truly heroic.

The small independent college is particularly characteristic of
the Midwest. In the nineteenth century they sprouted here like
mushrooms, most of them begun with church money, to train
teachers and preachers. Some of these colleges never rose beyond
their modest beginnings, but others have grown into splendid
universities-in-microcosm. There is another kind of educational
institution, however, which has been equally significant in the
development of the American Midwest. It is the comprehensive
state university.

Almost every state in America has its own university, supported by the taxpayers of that state. Like the small private colleges, some of them are extremely good and some are sadly in-
adequate. Except for the University of California, those in the
Midwest are the biggest, and some of them – the Universities of

Michigan, of Wisconsin, of Minnesota, for example – are also among the very best. All of the huge Midwestern state universities strike Europeans as incredibly diverse and informal places, and indeed they are. The agricultural colleges which they include have been largely responsible for the improvements in American farming methods over the years, and at the same time the scholarly academic core of the best of these universities has provided a constant reminder to the practical Midwesterner that the life of the mind has its points too.

One of the most attractive of the Midwestern university towns is Madison, which is both the site of the University of Wisconsin and the capital of the state; built between lakes, with the university on a hill at one end, Madison is delightful. Moreover, in the Shorewood section of Madison is one of Frank Lloyd Wright's best-known creations, the handsome, angular Unitarian Church, totally unlike Wright's spiralling Guggenheim Museum in New York.

In Madison, or at Bloomington, Indiana, or at Iowa City, Iowa, to name only three of the most typical university towns, one can get an idea of the life of an undergraduate at one of these Midwestern universities, as different from the older American universities of the East as they are from the venerable universities of Europe. For a quick look, one might begin with the Student Union building; it is usually the heart of the campus.

Since the Midwest has every American virtue and vice twice over, undergraduate football and basketball have a unique importance here, at the great state universities and the little colleges alike. Many a deserving youth has 'worked' his way through college on an athletic scholarship; for good or ill, it is a hallowed American tradition. Given the chance, you certainly should see a football game or a basketball game at one of the big universities in the Midwest. However, you must bear in mind Chesterton's wise observation that sport in America 'has the vices of a religion. . . . It is not in the least sportive'.

We have indicated that most Americans would never think of going to the Midwest on holiday. Yet that is not entirely true, for there are three parts of the Midwest which attract many visitors.

The first is the North Woods region: northern Michigan and Michigan's upper peninsula across the lake, and the northernmost sections of Wisconsin and Minnesota. Much of this country is true wilderness, with forests and lakes and a very sparse population. People own cabins there to which they go in the summer or during the autumn deer season, and there are also a good many inns and resorts scattered through the area. It is rather like the Maine woods or parts of the Canadian wilderness. As one might expect, the fishing is very good.

Somewhat different is Mackinac Island, in the straits between Lake Huron and Lake Michigan, just east of the remarkable new Mackinac Bridge. There have been settlements here ever since French Jesuits penetrated this region in the seventeenth century. Two old forts remain, and several other historic buildings. Moreover, only horse-drawn carriages and bicycles are permitted on the island: no cars.

There are few farms in the North Woods country, but some of the inhabitants make money from the maple sugar to be had from the maple trees, as in northern New England, and there are also blueberries, both wild and cultivated. In addition, Minnesota has wild rice, an exotic dark nutty rice that is superb eaten with game. It is harvested by the Chippewa Indians in the swampy parts of northern Minnesota lakes. The Indians paddle through the swamps in their canoes, threshing the rice into their boats as they go along.

Aside from summer visitors, most of the profits in the North Woods come either from lumber or mining. For obvious reasons, lumber is big business there, and there are also rich veins of copper and iron along the shores of Lake Superior. Through the years the mines have brought in a considerable variety of peoples to add to the original French-Canadian and Anglo-American settlers. A great many Finns and Slavs came to the Minnesota mining regions, and in northern Wisconsin and upper Michigan one encounters the Welsh and Cornish too.

There is something very exhilarating about these far reaches of the United States, not only in the deep woods but in the mining towns along Lake Superior as well. Life is hard and invigorating there, on the shores of the largest lake in the world. The winter is intensely cold and spring comes dramatically when the ice begins to break up and shipping can start to move again. Summer is brief but lovely, and autumn is crisp and clear, with the woods a brilliant scarlet and red and green. It is glorious then to drive along the shores of Lake Superior on a road such as U.S. Route 61 north of Duluth, Minnesota. The views of forest and lake are breathtaking, and Duluth itself, squeezed on a narrow ledge between the cliffs and the water, is one of the most interesting of the big mining towns.

Most Americans think of North and South Dakota as remote, bleak, and thoroughly uninviting, with miserably hot summers, hard winters, and few charms. Yet the western parts of these states do attract tourists, to the Badlands and the Black Hills.

Both North Dakota and South Dakota have a Badlands, and they are somewhat similar: barren areas with strangely weathered, multi-coloured rock formations. The Badlands of North Dakota are along the Little Missouri River, and they are best seen in the two sections of the Theodore Roosevelt National Memorial Park. These North Dakota Badlands were greatly admired by that earlier President Roosevelt who did so much to awaken the United States to the grandeur of its scenery and the need to take care of it. Roosevelt said that the Badlands had a special 'dismal beauty'; as a young man in the 1880's, he spent several years there on a cattle ranch he bought near Medora. These Badlands are on the borderline between North Dakota and Montana, in country more suitable for cattle than for farming, more Western than Midwestern. Thus in that same period Medora also attracted the fascinating Marquis de Mores, a Frenchman who married an American heiress and came west with a grandiose scheme involving packing plants close to the cattle ranges, with refrigerated meat to be shipped east instead of the live cattle. This is precisely the system now favoured in the West, but the unfortunate Marquis was seventy-five years ahead of his time, the venture failed, and a few years after he left Medora his deserted ice houses all burned down. You can, however, still see his 'château' just as he left it. The North Dakota Badlands boast a fine assortment of wild life too, including prairie dogs, tail-less squirrels which live underground in 'villages' and pop out of their holes whenever they are angry or excited, to stand on their hind legs and chatter away at each other.

The other Badlands, those of South Dakota, are now officially the Badlands National Monument, one hundred and fifty square miles of 'Hell with the fires burned out', astonishingly beautiful

at sunset. The Black Hills are in South Dakota too, west of the
Badlands National Monument. The name comes from the dark
pine forests with which they are covered. Within the Black Hills
are the old mining towns of Deadwood and Lead which we have
already mentioned, but these hills also boast abundant wild life,
with beavers and badgers and porcupines, elk and deer and Rocky
Mountain bighorn sheep, and coyotes. As everyone in South
Dakota will tell you over and over again, the Black Hills are older
than the Rockies, older than the Alps, older than the Himalayas.
They are not high mountains, but they have a certain grandeur,
and there are still fine unspoiled wilderness areas. There is no
'Black Hills National Park', but much of the region is nevertheless
protected by the government in one way or another. There are
National Forest areas, and one very small National Park at Wind
Cave, and there is a State Park. In addition, there is Mount Rushmore National Memorial, one of the principal attractions of the
Black Hills. At Mount Rushmore, sixty-foot portrait heads of
Washington, Jefferson, Lincoln and Theodore Roosevelt have
been carved out of the sheer granite cliffs, five hundred feet up the
side of the mountain. It is primarily the work of a sculptor named
Gutzen Borglum; it took twenty years to finish, with thirty work-
men at a time drilling away at the granite from aerial chairs or
precarious scaffolding. Illuminated at night, the Mount Rushmore heads are eerie and impressive.

The third holiday region of the Midwest is that of the Ozark
Mountains, which spread across south-western Missouri and
north-western Arkansas. The Ozarks are hills again, or low
wooded mountains, with many swift rivers and clear lakes. Much
farther south than the Black Hills and with a heavier rainfall, they
have a very different sort of flora and fauna. In the spring, people
drive hundreds of miles to see the dogwood and the redbud in
bloom in the Ozarks, and in the autumn the colours are lovely too.
Fishing is good in the Ozarks, and the climate is comparatively
mild. But this is a poor region for farming, and life in the Ozark
hills is as primitive as it is in the eastern hill country of Kentucky
and Tennessee. In fact the Ozarks were settled by the same sort of
gun-toting, Bible-quoting, Scotch-English-Irish frontier families,
and this region is equally rich in old lore and quaint ballads. Of
course the people here are no longer as isolated as they once were,

N

and there are not quite so many dilapidated shacks and barefoot, ragged children along the back roads these days, but the Ozarks will still surprise anyone who has a Hollywood picture of America.

As civilization penetrated here, the old skills began to fade, just as they have in Kentucky and Tennessee and North Carolina. Why make it yourself when you can buy it? Fortunately, however, a few people are working to preserve the best of the Ozarks crafts, and in the resort towns of the Arkansas Ozarks, like Eureka Springs and Mountain Home, you can buy charming things carved or woven by the mountain people.

SPECIAL KNOWLEDGE

The **climate** of the Midwest does not encourage visitors, since it is very cold and snowy in the winter and miserably hot in the summer everywhere but in the extreme north. October and May are all right, sometimes.

The summer heat is enough to addle the brains, and to make matters worse, time runs amuck in the Midwest. The urban areas there usually go on 'daylight saving time' in the summer, but farmers hate this and the rural areas generally refuse to adopt it. Thus a drawing of the Midwestern **time-zones** in summer looks like a crazy quilt. In most other regions of the country there is reasonable uniformity, but in the Midwest one not only crosses the fixed time-zone borders, from Eastern to Central to Mountain, but one also weaves in and out of 'standard' and 'daylight saving' time-zones. Moreover, in some areas the trains adhere to 'standard' time even during the summer, but plane schedules use 'daylight saving'.

Food in the Midwest can be simple but good, or simply terrible; it is usually cheaper than in the East.

Abilene, Kansas

EISENHOWER LIBRARY, 4th and Kuney Streets. Daily 9–5.

Battle Creek, Michigan

KELLOG CEREAL FACTORY, Monday to Friday 9–4, conducted tours every half-hour. Free. Closed holidays.

Bloomfield Hills, Michigan

CRANBROOK INSTITUTIONS, 10 miles north-west of Detroit, off U.S. Route 10. Art Galleries: 1 April to 31 October, Tuesday to Sunday 2–5; 1 November to 31 March, Saturday and Sunday 2–5. Closed holidays. Free.

MUSEUM OF SCIENCE: 15 June to 15 September, daily 10–5; 16 September to 14 June, daily 2–5. Closed holidays. Free except week-ends.

GARDENS AND PARK: 1 May to 31 October, Tuesday to Sunday 2–5.

Chicago, Illinois

AQUARIUM, Lake Shore Drive, opposite the Natural History Museum. 1 May to 31 August, daily 9–5, 1 September to 31 October, daily 10–5; 1 November to 28 February, daily 10–4; 1 March to 30 April, daily 10–5. Free Thursday, Saturday and Sunday.

ART INSTITUTE, Michigan Avenue at Adams Street. Monday to Wednesday, Friday and Saturday 9–5, Thursday 9–9.30, Sunday 12–5. Wednesday, Saturday and Sunday free.

CHICAGO HISTORICAL SOCIETY, in Lincoln Park at Clark Street and North Avenue. Monday to Saturday 9.30–4.30; Sunday and holidays 12.30–5.30. Closed Thanksgiving, 25 December and 1 January. Free except Sundays and holidays.

GRAIN EXCHANGE, 141 West Jackson Boulevard at La Salle Street. Monday to Friday 9.30–1.15.

MUSEUM OF SCIENCE AND INDUSTRY, Lake Shore Drive and 57th Street. Winter, Monday to Saturday 9.30–4; summer, Monday to Saturday 9.30–5.30. Sunday and bank holidays, 10–6.

NATURAL HISTORY MUSEUM, Lake Shore Drive and Roosevelt Road. Winter, daily 9–4; spring and autumn, daily 9–5; summer, daily 9–6. Thursday, Saturday and Sunday free.

NEWBERRY LIBRARY, 60 West Walton Place.

PLANETARIUM, Lake Shore Drive, opposite the Natural History Museum. 30 May to Labor Day, Tuesday to Sunday 9.30–9.30; Monday 9.30–5. Shows, Monday to Friday 11, 1 and 3; Saturday, Sunday and holidays 12.30, 2 and 3.30; evening shows Tuesday to Sunday 7.30. Labor Day to 29 May, Monday, Wednesday, Thursday, Saturday and Sunday, 9.30–5; Tuesday and Friday 9.30–9.30. Shows, Monday to Friday 11 and 3; evening shows Tuesday and Friday 7.30.

Cleveland, Ohio

MUSEUM OF ART, 11150 East Boulevard. Sunday 1–6, Tuesday, Thursday, Friday 10–6, Wednesday 10–10, Saturday 9–5. 1 September to 31 May, Friday 10–10. Closed holidays. Free.

Deadwood, South Dakota

BROKEN BOOT GOLD MINE, one mile west on U.S. Route 14A. 15 May to 30 September, daily guided underground tours, 6.30–6.

Dearborn, Michigan

FORD ROTUNDA, 3000 Schaefer Road. 1 June to 1 September, Monday to Friday 8.30–9 p.m., Saturday, Sunday and holidays 1–9. 2 September to 31 May, Monday to Friday 8.30–5, Sunday 1–9. Free. Test Track rides summer only. Rouge plant tour Monday to Friday, summer every half-hour, winter every hour 9–3.

GREENFIELD VILLAGE, 15 June to Labor Day, daily 9–6.30; day after Labor Day to 14 June, Monday to Friday 9–5, Saturday, Sunday and holidays 9–5.30. 1 April to 30 October, tours every half-hour; 1 November to 30 March, tours approximately every two hours.

HENRY FORD MUSEUM, 15 June to Labor Day 9–6.30; day after Labor Day to 14 June, Monday to Friday 9–5, Saturday, Sunday and holidays 9–5.30.

Des Moines, Iowa

ART CENTER, Grand Avenue at Polk Boulevard. Tuesday, Wednesday, Friday and Saturday 11–5, Thursday 11–9. Sunday and holidays 1–6.

Detroit, Michigan

DETROIT CONVENTION AND TOURIST BUREAU, 626 Book Building, Washington Boulevard at Grand River Avenue, Detroit 26, Michigan.

DETROIT HISTORICAL MUSEUM, Woodward Avenue at Kirby Avenue. Tuesday to Sunday 9–6. Closed holidays. Free.

GENERAL MOTORS TECHNICAL CENTER, 12 Mile and Mound Road, Warren. 12 June to Labor Day, Monday to Saturday 10–5.30, Sunday 12–5.30.

INSTITUTE OF ARTS, Woodward Avenue at Kirby Avenue. 1 July to 31 August, Tuesday to Sunday 9–6; 1 September to 30 June, Tuesday to Friday 1–6, Saturday and Sunday 9–10. Closed holidays. Free.

Galena, Illinois

GENERAL GRANT'S HOUSE, Bouthillier Street. Daily 9–5; closed Thanksgiving, 25 December and 1 January. Free.

Hannibal, Missouri

MARK TWAIN'S HOUSE, 206 Hill Street. 2 June to 14 September, daily 7.30–6, 15 September to 1 June, daily 8–5. Free.

Independence, Missouri

HARRY TRUMAN LIBRARY AND MUSEUM, North west, on U.S. Route 24. 1 June to 15 September, Monday to Saturday 9–4.30, Sunday 10–5; 16–31 May, Monday to Saturday 9–4.30, Sunday 2–5.

Kansas City, Missouri

WILLIAM ROCKHILL NELSON GALLERY OF ART, 45th Terrace and Oak Street. Tuesday to Saturday 10–5, Sunday 2–6. Saturday and Sunday free.

Kirtland, Ohio

KIRTLAND TEMPLE. Daily 9–5. Closed holidays. Free.

Lead, South Dakota

THE HOMESTAKE MINE, 1 June to 31 August, tours Monday to Saturday 7–5, Sunday 8–4; May, September and October, tours, Monday to Saturday 8–3.30. Closed holidays.

Mackinac Island, Michigan

Accessible by boat from St Ignace or Mackinaw City. Accommodation available 1 June to 30 September.

Madison, Wisconsin

UNITARIAN CHURCH, 900 University Bay Drive, in Shorewood. Tuesday to Saturday 9–5.

Medora, North Dakota

DE MORES 'CHÂTEAU', West of Medora and half-mile south of U.S. Route 10. Daily (weather permitting) 8–5.

Milwaukee, Wisconsin

BREWERY TOURS
SCHLITZ, 235 West Galena Avenue. Monday to Friday 9–11 and 1–4, hourly tours, more frequent during summer.
MILLER, 4002 West State Street. Monday to Friday, tours 8–4.
PABST, 917 West Juneau Avenue. Summer, Monday to Friday, tours at 10, 11, 1, 2, 3 and 4. Saturday 10 and 11. Winter, Monday to Friday, tours at 10.30, 1, 2 and 3.30.

Minden, Nebraska

HAROLD WARP'S PIONEER VILLAGE, on U.S. Route 6. Daily, 8–sunset.

Monroe, Michigan

ENRICO FERMI ATOMIC POWER PLANT, 7 miles north, off Old Dixie Highway. Tuesday to Saturday, 10–4.

Mount Rushmore National Memorial, South Dakota

WEST OF KEYSTONE. Open all year round.

New Harmony, Indiana

WORKINGMEN'S INSTITUTE. 1 May to 30 November, Monday to Saturday 11–4, Sunday 2–5. Free.

New Salem, Illinois

LINCOLN'S NEW SALEM STATE PARK, on State Routes 97 and 123. Daily 8.30–5. Pleasant restaurant at entrance.

Racine, Wisconsin

JOHNSON WAX FACTORY. Monday to Friday, hourly tours, 8.30–10.30 and 1.30–3.30.

Springfield, Illinois

LINCOLN'S HOUSE, 8th and Jackson Streets. Last Sunday in April to last Sunday in October, daily 8–6.

Spring Green, Wisconsin

TALIESEN, seven miles south, on State Route 23. May to October, Wednesday 10–5, Sunday 12–5. Visits can sometimes be arranged by telephoning ahead.

St Louis, Missouri

ST LOUIS ART MUSEUM, in Forest Park. Tuesday to Sunday 10–5, Monday 2.30–9.30. Free.

ZOOLOGICAL GARDENS, in Forest Park. Animal houses 9.30–5. 15 May to 12 October, Tuesday to Saturday, animal shows twice daily, Sunday and holidays three times daily.

Toledo, Ohio

TOLEDO MUSEUM OF ART, Monroe Street at Scottwood Avenue. Tuesday to Saturday 9–5, Sunday, Monday and holidays 1–5. Free.

8 · The Rockies

The region included in this chapter lies on either slope of the Rocky Mountains. It comprises the states of Montana, Wyoming, Idaho, Colorado, and half of Utah. The eastern section is the high plains country where first the buffalo roamed and then the longhorn steer, but towards the centre the Rockies rise like a wall, and from then on you are in the midst of mountains. In this mountainous section are four splendid National Parks.

Cynics may tell you that the West today is sure to have only synthetic colour, since the really exciting cattle-and-cowboy period ended well before the First World War. They may also warn you that many of the National Parks are now said to be completely overrun with tourists, and are thus quite spoiled. But one day, going through Colorado or Wyoming or Montana, you will come upon two or three cowboys, looking just as they ought to look, jogging along herding cattle, and you will know that the West is still all right. Or you will climb to the top of a high pass, perhaps in one of the National Parks, and be staggered by the rugged, towering mass of the Rockies around you, the continent stretching away to the east until the visible curve of the earth hides it from your sight. Then you will know that the West is not merely all right; it is still magnificent.

Most of the territory described in this chapter was not settled until the last third of the nineteenth century, and once one has seen the Rockies, it is easy to understand why settlement was so long delayed. Driving east or west through Colorado, for example, you have your choice of several passes over the Continental Divide, that invisible line along the spine of the Rockies which separates the eastern watershed in America from the western. One pass is Monarch, at 11,312 feet; another is Loveland, 11,992 feet; Wolf Creek Pass, 10,850 feet, is comparatively tame, but Independence Pass near Aspen is over 12,000 feet and quite terrifying. It is little wonder that wagon trains, which began crossing the continent to California as early as 1841, carefully avoided this forbidding region. Some of them used the Santa Fé Trail and the California Trail south of Colorado. Others did go through Wyoming, following the Oregon Trail through South Pass, the one gap in the wall of the Rockies.

The only white men who were really familiar with this region were the 'mountain men', the trappers and hunters who ranged far and wide through the Rockies in search of beaver. For fifty years, from the time the Lewis and Clark expedition in 1804 revealed the possibilities of the West until civilization finally overtook it, the Rockies belonged to the mountain men. Most of them were Americans for whom the East was now too settled, but many were French-Canadian, some English, some Irish. All of them, obviously, were fearless and infinitely resourceful. Their custom was to gather at a trading post once a year to sell their furs, see their friends, and hear news of the outside world; the rest of the year each man moved through the wilderness alone, or at most with an Indian woman to keep him company.

When parties of settlers bound for California began to come through the area around the Rockies, a mountain man was sometimes persuaded to act as guide. He was invaluable of course, knowing the terrain and the climate and the Indians as he did. But in this manner men like Jim Bridger and 'Broken Hand' Fitzpatrick, helping to map the trails and ease the crossings, were actually contributing to the destruction of their own way of life. There is a fascinating book called *A Lady's Life in the Rocky Mountains*, written by an intrepid Englishwoman, Isabella Bird, the first woman ever elected a Fellow of the Royal Geographical Society. She spent the year 1873 in the Colorado Rockies entirely on her own, and the most unforgettable character she encountered there was one Mountain Jim, a strange and romantic figure who was to be quite literally killed by encroaching civilization. At that, he had already outlasted most of his breed.

The mountain men vanished, but their mountains are still the basic fact of this part of the West. There are other things to draw one here, of course: cowboys, and ghost towns, and Mormon settlements. But over everything tower the Rockies.

Four of the finest sections of the Rockies have been made National Parks, and visiting these National Parks is the most popular way to sample what the Rockies have to offer. People with a great deal of mountain experience in the West usually prefer other, more primitive sections of the Rockies, where there are no marked trails and one can be completely on one's own, fifty miles from any other human being. Yet even the most popular National Parks still have splendid unspoiled areas for people willing to hike far from the roads and the information centres, and for anyone unfamiliar with the Rockies, the maps and brochures and advice available at the National Parks add greatly to one's enjoyment.

The National Parks were established in order to protect some of the best scenery in the country; each one has a special justification. There are now about thirty National Parks, the majority of them west of the Mississippi River since that is where one finds the most remarkable scenery. The Parks are animal refuges as well; in the wilder parts of all the Parks in the Rockies one can see moose and elk and big-horn sheep. National Parks are not the same thing as National Monuments, which are much smaller protected areas. Nor are the National Parks the same as State Parks; those are administered by the individual states, and may well be pleasant but are seldom as spectacular.

There is accommodation in all the large National Parks, including a few quite expensive hotels, many simple lodges, and cabins and camping areas; each Park differs a little in the sort of accommodation it offers. There are also places to eat and to buy food, but no other developments, nothing like the golf courses and tennis courts one finds in Canadian National Parks. The National Parks in the United States are administered by the National Park Service, under the Department of the Interior of the federal government; the hotels and lodges and eating places within the Parks are run by private concerns under government license. Each Park is staffed with Park Rangers, there to protect the wild life and to keep the trails open. In the tourist season, however, the Rangers spend most of their time answering questions and protecting tourists from their own inadequacies. Park regulations are extremely strict about picking flowers, harming the animals, and being careless with cigarettes and fires. Fire is the great scourge and peril of the Western mountains, for even when things look green this is dry country, and forest fires can and do spread with horrifying speed. Therefore there are firm regulations about where one can camp; if you wish to camp anywhere other than at a designated camp-site, you must always first get a campfire permit from a Ranger.

As mentioned in Chapter 1, anyone who contemplates a trip to one of the National Parks should write in advance either to the Park itself or to the National Park Service, asking for the brochure about that particular Park. The brochures are very well done and full of useful information.

The most famous National Park is Yellowstone, which was also the very first. It is the biggest, too: more than sixty miles long and fifty miles wide. Most of it is in Wyoming, in the north-west corner, but a little overlaps into the neighbouring states of Idaho and Montana. Well-to-do travellers were going to Yellowstone even before the turn of the century, to marvel at the geysers and exclaim at the grandeur of the vistas; it was very much the fashionable thing. These days it may not be so fashionable but it is immensely popular. Tourists pour into Yellowstone in overpowering waves all summer long, every available bed is booked weeks in advance, and the roads through the Park are choked with cars. The roads are also lined with beggar bears, which are now one of the great attractions at Yellowstone. You are warned not to feed them, but people do, and so they prowl around every camp-site and come to stand at car windows, waiting for a handout. Bears will be bears, and they are not always amiable; the rule about keeping the car windows closed is a sound one, for they have been known to reach inside and do considerable damage to unwary tourists. But they do add a special flavour to the Park. In addition, Yellowstone has lovely lakes and pine trees, beautiful waterfalls in picturesque valleys, a remarkable canyon, and the famous geysers. However, if you expect a National Park in the Rockies to be ringed by spectacular mountain peaks, you will be disappointed in Yellowstone. It is already so high that the effect is that of a great plateau, a rolling, pine-covered uplands region, and in this respect it is less dramatic than the other three Parks in the Rockies. The throngs of tourists do rather get in the way of Yellowstone's charms too. But it has the advantage of being comparatively easy to see without a car; there is good train and bus service to the Park as well as an assortment of bus tours within it, and Yellowstone is included on many organized cross-country tours. Moreover, Yellowstone's accommodation is more reasonably priced than that within Grand Teton or Glacier National Parks.

Like all of the mountain Parks, however, Yellowstone has a relatively short season: from June to September only. It is 'open' all the year round, in the sense that if you can get there you can look at it, but the bus service stops and the lodges and eating places are shut down. You need not ask why, once you have seen the snow poles along the edges of the roads in the Park; five or six feet high, they are to indicate to the men who drive snow-ploughs where they may expect to find a road beneath the drifts.

When there is no snow problem, you can get into Yellowstone at any of five entrances. The approach to the north-east entrance, by way of Red Lodge, Montana, is reputed to be the most dramatic.

Just below Yellowstone is a much newer National Park, Grand Teton, which includes most of what is known as Jackson's Hole, a valley almost completely surrounded by high mountains. In the early nineteenth century, Jackson's Hole and the Tetons above it were the favourite hunting grounds of the mountain men; later the valley became notorious as a hideout for cattle rustlers and outlaws of every sort. But once this part of the West became better known, the hapless inhabitants of Jackson's Hole had honesty and prosperity thrust upon them; the area was simply too choice to waste on ne'er-do-wells.

The Tetons are a spectacular range of the Rockies, with majestic snow-crowned peaks, and beautiful lakes along the base of the mountains. The effect is most striking if you come to Grand Teton by car, and approach the Park from the east on U.S. Route 26-287. After the desolation of the eroded Wind River country, beautiful in its way but bare and stark, you climb over a pass and suddenly there are the Tetons, with Jackson Lake a vast reflecting pool below. Grand Teton National Park is completely unlike Yellowstone. One might say that Yellowstone is horizontal and Grand Teton is vertical.

Like most National Parks, Grand Teton is best explored on foot or on a horse. Only that way can one reach the high alpine mea-dows and the glaciers, or hope to see the moose and the elk. This Park has the largest elk herd in the United States, a herd which is so big and growing so fast that in recent years the Park authorities have begun to allow limited shooting during a short period in the autumn. Perhaps we had better interject here that the designations 'moose' and 'elk' do not have the same meaning in America as in

Europe. To quote from a placard at the Natural History Museum in London:

> Moose, the largest of deer, are found in marshy forest regions of Scandinavia, East Prussia, Russia and North America. There is some confusion over the common name 'elk'. This species which is called elk in Europe is called moose in America, whereas the name elk in America denotes the wapiti which is closely related to the red deer.

The big Jackson Lake Lodge at Grand Teton is bemoaned by those who loved these mountains in their old undeveloped days, but really the building is fitted into the Park in such a way that it is hardly noticeable. Since it enjoys a spectacular view over Jackson Lake towards the towering Tetons, and it can be reached during the season by bus or a combination of train and bus, and arrangements are easily made on the spot for pack trips and hiring horses and taking bus trips to Yellowstone, the Jackson Lake Lodge makes a particularly good headquarters for visitors without a car. The lodge is quite expensive, however, like everything else in the Jackson's Hole area; most of the dude ranches near there are expensive too, and the motels. On the surface everything seems very simple and 'Western', but it is a deceptive, costly simplicity.

The Tetons offer fine climbing, and there is a special climbing school at Jackson, the town just south of the Park. Jackson itself has become rather self-conscious in recent years, and there are now too many souvenir shops, but it still retains a frontier flavour. This is partly due to the bizarre assortment of residents it has attracted: eccentrics both rich and poor, solid ranchers, ski instructors, *émigrée* countesses, writers, wilderness guides, artists. A sampling of the gay and motley crew can usually be found at the Wirt Hotel, Jackson's social centre.

Far to the north of Yellowstone and Grand Teton, on the border between Montana and the Canadian province of Alberta, is Glacier National Park, third in size among all the National Parks. Many people think that the finest National Park in the West is Yosemite, in California, but Glacier has an ardent group of admirers too. They insist that Yosemite is entirely too crowded, while Glacier is tranquil and isolated. Nonetheless you can get to the Park by train or bus as well as by car; there are convenient connexions with trans-continental services. At Glacier you can then take bus tours within the Park, and some of the tours include a visit to Waterton Park on the Canadian side.

The Going-to-the-Sun Road twists and turns for fifty miles from one side of the Park to the other, across the very heart of it, up over passes and down into valleys. It is a beautiful and exciting drive, which makes it possible to see a great deal of Glacier in one day simply by going along it and then parking from time to time to take one of the walks suggested in the Park brochure.

Glacier has glaciers. The Park is bisected north to south by the Continental Divide, and for ages ice has flowed down either slope of the Rockies here, scouring and digging at the flanks of the mountains. Thus there are hollows filled with sparkling blue mountain lakes, and alpine meadows covered with wildflowers. In the cold mountain streams, the trout fishing is superb.

There are three hotels within Glacier Park which are quite as expensive as the Jackson Lake Lodge at Grand Teton, but there are also several lodges and motels with more moderate prices. People who stay in the Park for any length of time can hike to one of the two chalets high up among the peaks; these are an especially good feature at Glacier because they have food and beds for the unequipped mountainer. There are also more primitive overnight cabins way up high, but for them one needs one's own bedding and cooking gear.

At Browning, in the Blackfeet Indian Reservation just east of Glacier Park, there is an excellent small museum devoted to the history and customs of the Plains Indians, the various Indian tribes which lived between the Mississippi River and the Rockies. The Plains Indians are the Indians of Western films, the sort who attacked the covered wagon trains, fighting on horseback, wearing buckskin and feathers. They were tall and straight, with high cheekbones and hawk-like noses. One tends to think all American Indians looked like this, but it is not true; many were short and squat, with rather flat faces; many dressed quite differently; and few other Indians were as wedded to the horse as the Plains tribes. Plains Indians had a distinctive, semi-nomadic culture entirely dependent on a plentiful supply of buffalo (bison), which furnished them with meat and with warm robes, and with hide from which to fashion their other garments and their tepees (wigwams). Unfortunately for everyone concerned, the Plains tribes were thoroughly warlike, placing a high value on stealing horses and collecting scalps, which made them something less than popular with the white man when settlers began to penetrate west of the Mississippi. Then to make matters worse, the white man too discovered the buffalo's worth, and in the 1860's and '70's uncounted thousands of buffalo were shot, stripped of their hides, and left to rot on the plains. In no time at all the buffalo was practically extinct. Naturally the Indians retaliated by attacking the white man even more ferociously than before, and the white man's government responded in turn by ordering the Indians on to newly created reservations, which they hated. The most famous encounter between the enraged and desperate Plains Indians and the United States Army was 'Custer's last stand', in 1876. In the north-west corner of what is now the Crow Indian Reservation near Billings, Montana, General Custer and 262 men were trapped and completely wiped out by a combined force of Cheyenne and Sioux led by the great Chief Sitting Bull. Yet that Battle of the Little Big Horn was not only a last stand for General Custer; it was the last stand of the Plains Indians too. After that, the United States Government made very sure the Indians stayed on their reservations; there were still sporadic outbursts for another twenty or thirty years, but never again any big battles. Most of the Plains Indians who are left today live poorly on their reservations in remote corners of their old lands; it is a miserable story.

The main road going south from Glacier towards Missoula, Montana, passes the National Bison Range, where one of the last remaining buffalo herds is carefully protected. Missoula, below, is on the route of the Lewis and Clark expedition, which came through this unknown country in the first decade of the nineteenth century; the journals of the expedition make note of camping very near the site of the present town. The Montana State University is in Missoula, but the town also has a far more unusual institution: the United States Forest Service's fire-jumping school. Since forest fires are a constant and serious danger in the West, the Forest Service has developed a corps of trained fire-fighters who can be dropped by parachute into inaccessible mountain regions at the first hint of a fire. If you happen to go through Missoula early in the summer, when the new fire-fighters are taking their practice jumps, you are allowed to watch.

The fourth of the great National Parks in the Rockies is called simply Rocky Mountain National Park, although it was once known as Estes Park. Isabella Bird, that intrepid Englishwoman mentioned earlier, thought Estes Park the most beautiful mountain valley she had ever seen:

> ... an irregular basin, lighted up by the bright waters of the rushing Thompson (River), guarded by sentinel mountains of fantastic shape and monstrous size, with Long's Peak rising above them all in unapproachable grandeur, while the Snowy Range, with its outlying spurs heavily timbered, comes down upon the park slashed by stupendous canyons lying deep in the purple gloom.

Another English traveller, Lord Dunraven, was one of the first to urge that this valley be somehow protected by the government so that its beauties would not be spoiled.

Rocky Mountain National Park has only limited accommodation within the Park itself, unless you wish to camp. There are many inns and motels in the village of Estes Park at the eastern entrance, but one can simply come out for the day from Denver by car or on a bus tour.

All the tour buses are sure to go through the Park along the Trail Ridge Road, which runs for fifteen miles at a height of more than 11,000 feet, passing over the barren tundra slopes overlooking the snow-covered peaks all around, with the valleys beneath stretching away to the eastern plains. For those who have time to stay at the Park for a few days, Rocky Mountain is a paradise for climbers. Horses can also be hired there. Or you might go on one of the organized nature walks with a Ranger, and learn where you are most likely to see the big-horn sheep for which the Park is famous. Like most National Parks, Rocky Mountain schedules group walks, and has talks given by the Rangers in the evening, but there are always maps available with which the visitor can make his own independent explorations.

In many parts of the West there are not only National Parks but also, much more frequently, areas designated as National Forests. These are not primarily for recreation, although you can ride and hike through them if you heed the restrictions, and they are fine for pack trips. The National Forests were really created to keep fine timber areas from being over-cut and certain lands from being over-grazed; despite the name, National Forests are not always covered with trees.

A rugged and beautiful state with no National Parks but magnificent National Forests is Idaho. It is a state rich in contrasts. In addition to the forest regions, there are high mountain ranges; the first really popular ski-ing resort in the United States was Sun Valley, in the Sawtooth Mountains of south central Idaho. East of Sun Valley is a strange volcanic region, fittingly called the Craters of the Moon, which has been made a National Monument. Equally forbidding but completely different is that wasteland which lies along Interstate Route 15 as it goes from Idaho Falls north to Dillon, Montana; it begins as mile after mile of flat and featureless desolation, and then near the Montana border the road climbs into great gaunt brown mountains as bleak as one's image of Central Asia. Yet just below Idaho Falls, where the Snake River flows westward across the southern part of the state, lies some of the richest farming land in the West. And then the river changes its course to flow north and form the border between Idaho on one side and Oregon and Washington on the other; it changes its mood as well, and slices a passage a mile deep through the awesome Hell's Canyon.

Engineers have long eyed Hell's Canyon hungrily, and now a series of dams is being built there despite the anguished cries of those who put a high value on unsurpassed natural beauty. The gorge of the Snake is still well worth seeing, however. There are exciting boat trips which go along other stretches of the river, for a day, or for two or three days; if the trips last overnight, the guides take care of all the camping details. Some of these trips start from Lewiston, Idaho, or Clarkston, Washington, just across the river, and others from Homestead, Oregon. The Idaho Department of Commerce and Development can furnish information about them. If you fancy hairpin bends on narrow roads at dizzying heights, and want to go along the precipitous edge of Hell's Canyon itself, you can hire jeeps at Cuprum, Idaho. There are other river trips one can make too, on the beautiful Salmon River in the protected wilderness area of eastern Idaho.

The history of the settlement of the Rockies region divides roughly into four parts, beginning with the mountain men. The next to arrive were the Mormons, who started coming into Utah in 1847 in search of an isolated paradise. Then gold and silver were discovered in Colorado and Montana, and raw towns rose every-

where in the mountains. Finally some Texas cattlemen discovered
the advantages of fattening their herds on the grass of the northern
plains before shipping them east to market, and the result was the
cattle drive and the cowboy, and more towns.

The Mormons were the first to come to this part of America
with the intention of settling down and raising families here, and
when Brigham Young led the Mormon vanguard over the Continental Divide in 1847, they hoped they were now safe at last from
the outside world. Surely no other settlers would be tempted to
follow them into the dry, unpromising Utah basin.

The Mormons considered themselves a chosen people, singled
out by God to establish a new Jerusalem; their own name for their
sect was not 'Mormon' but 'Church of Jesus Christ of the Latter-
Day Saints'. 'Mormon' refers to one of their testaments, the Book
of Mormon. Joseph Smith, the founder of the sect, said the Book
of Mormon was a lost Book of the Bible; he had a series of revela-
tions in 1830, and in the course of them he discovered the Book of
Mormon inscribed upon golden tablets on a hill near Rochester,
New York. From the very beginning Joseph Smith attracted a
large and fervent following; by the time the nucleus of the mem-
bership set out for Utah, there were already thousands of converts
in Great Britain in addition to the many thousands in America. In
fact some English Mormons were probably among those first
Utah pioneers, since many of them had emigrated in the 1840's to
join their brethren in the United States.

Leading his growing band, Joseph Smith had tried to settle in
New York, in Ohio, in Missouri, and in Illinois, but everywhere
the Saints had trouble with the unbelievers. The worst trouble
came in Illinois, when Joseph Smith was attacked and killed by
a mob. After that it was obvious that the Saints must find sanctuary in the wilderness, and so they set off towards the West, with
their new leader, the redoubtable Brigham Young. It was Brigham Young, divinely inspired he said, who led the first group of
Mormon pioneers to what is now Salt Lake City, after a trip
across the plains and the Rockies that was remarkable for its
orderliness and planning. It was Brigham Young who told his
people they must make the desert bloom, and they did; there are
no finer, harder-working farmers anywhere than the Mormons,
as the neat and prosperous farms of Utah and southern Idaho still
prove today. Brigham Young also told them where and how to

o

build temples and tabernacles; the great Tabernacle in Salt Lake City, with its vast dome and exceptional acoustics, is an extraordinary building for an isolated, agricultural community in the mid-nineteenth century.

The success of the Mormon settlements, however, did not act as a magnet for other settlers. For one thing, the country around the Rockies was lacking in rain and not particularly fertile; it was known that the Mormons had to work terribly hard for their living. Then too the Mormons themselves were most unenthusiastic about unbelievers settling anywhere near them. They were doing their best to solve the population problem unaided; by now many Mormon families were polygamous, following the example of Brigham Young, who ultimately had seventeen wives. Outsiders refused to understand them, but then the Mormons consoled themselves with the thought that outsiders were for the most part shiftless and dishonest anyway. As the years passed and more and more outsiders came through Utah, there began to be unpleasant incidents. There was also one dreadful massacre, when a band of Mormons and allied Indians fell upon a peaceful wagon train *en route* to California and killed everyone except the very smallest children. Finally there were so many incidents that federal troops were sent into Utah, and for years the territory was under virtual armed guard. Not until the very end of the nineteenth century was Utah admitted to the Union as a state; by then Brigham Young was dead, and the Mormon elders agreed to accept civil law and abandon polygamy.

Mormons today continue to dominate Utah and much of Idaho; because of them these states are much less flamboyant than most of the other Western states. On the street Mormons look just like Episcopalians or Baptists; there is nothing unusual about their dress, except in church. But their lives are centred around their religion in a way that is quite unusual today; every Mormon is prepared to drop everything at any stage in his life and rush off across the world at the behest of the Church elders. Moreover, Mormons do not drink or smoke or even allow themselves coffee and tea, and in the little towns of Utah and Idaho you will sense that you are in a temperance area. You will also notice the tidiness everywhere; Mormons are quite as uncompromising about dirt and waste and disorder as they are about spirits and sin.

Salt Lake City is still the capital of Utah and the centre of

Mormonism, and Temple Square is the spiritual centre of Salt Lake City. The Temple and the Tabernacle are there; visitors are welcome at the Tabernacle, but only Latter-Day Saints themselves are allowed into the Temple. Brigham Young's first house, known as Lion House, is near by and open to the public, and so is the Beehive House, the second of his family houses, which later became an official residence for the President of the Church.

Salt Lake City as a whole is not picturesque or quaint; it is a thoroughly modern, business-like city, but it has a fine setting below the Wasatch Mountains at the edge of the Great Salt Lake, which really is salt, like the Dead Sea. The lake was once many times as big, and as the water area shrank, its saline content, natural enough in this mineral-heavy region, became more and more concentrated. Another result of the shrinking water was the Great Salt Desert, west of the lake; many of the world's speed records for cars have been set up on the Bonneville Flat there.

Otherwise in Utah there are several little towns which have a special importance in Mormon history, but they have nothing in particular for tourists to see. One of the first Mormon temples, for example, was built in St George, at the heart of those Mormon settlements which were established in the southern part of Utah; but Mormon temples are never open to the general public. The real attraction in southern Utah is the incredible desert scenery, much of it virtually unexplored. It belongs, however, in our chapter on the Southwest.

A student doing lessons about the Rocky Mountains who had a map to colour, could now fill in Utah and Idaho. The time is 1858, just before the Civil War; Utah and Idaho are hardly overflowing with people, but they have enough settlers for their future character to be already determined. Colorado, Wyoming, and Montana, on the other hand, are still blank; now their turn is coming.

In 1858 along Cherry Creek in Colorado, on land that is today in the middle of the city of Denver, a prospector found traces of gold, and the great Colorado gold and silver rush was on. It was almost ten years after the California gold excitement had begun; during those ten years many men on their way to or from California must have poked around in the Rockies to see what they could find, and now someone had met with luck. In the years that followed, the Cherry Creek gold proved insignificant, but prospectors spread through the Colorado mountains to the west, over every pass, up every valley, panning, washing, hoping, and there was one fantastic strike after another. Mining towns appeared everywhere in the Colorado Rockies, some at formidable heights: the town of Leadville, for example, was more than 10,000 feet up. The excitement lasted for about thirty years. Then the price of silver dropped sharply, and at the same time most of the gold mines which were not already played out came to be controlled by large, impersonal corporations; the day of the wide open mining camp, every man for himself, was gone. Leadville, which had reached an official population of 30,000 at one point, dwindled to a mere 4,000, and smaller towns disappeared altogether. Through their deserted streets wandered only the little Mexican burros which had once carried some prospector's tools or pulled ore wagons in the mines; not knowing what to do with them, their owners simply turned them loose when the mines shut down.

Today, the 'ghost' mining towns are among the chief tourist attractions in Colorado: biggish places like Leadville, Central City, Cripple Creek, Georgetown, Fairplay, Silverton, and also countless tiny mining settlements which once boomed for a year or two and were then completely abandoned, leaving only a handful of lonely, crumbling cabins at the top of a mountain. The ghost town easiest to reach from Denver is Central City; it was the first of the important mining centres and in its day a serious rival to Denver, although this is hard to believe when you see the two places now. All the old mining towns are somewhat alike: crudely-made timber buildings showing little evidence of paint, several saloons, a rococo hotel, and in the bigger towns 'opera houses' which in their time purveyed operettas, plays, music hall, talks – usually almost everything but genuine opera. The remarkable thing about Central City these days is that its Opera House now does boast a season of real opera, each July. It is interesting opera too, with the leading singers recruited from New York's Metropolitan and City Center Opera Companies, and everything is especially charming in the Victorian-Western setting. Buses go out to the performances from Denver, but it is also possible to stay in Central City, at the old Teller House. Most of the mining towns in Colorado have the advantage of a magnificent situation, high up in the Rockies. Central City is not as spectacularly situated as some of the others but it is at the head of a narrow valley and is an excellent example of its kind. There are bus tours to Central City from Denver throughout the summer, and in August the Opera House has a season of plays.

The wildest mining town in Colorado was Leadville. It is situated in what must once have been a lovely and peaceful alpine meadow high in the Rockies, one hundred miles south-west of Denver. After silver was discovered in Leadville in 1875, at least 30,000 men rushed there to crowd into hastily erected hotels and boarding houses and cabins and tents. Each of them hoped to make his fortune; of those who succeeded, none had a more dramatic story than one Horace Tabor.

Tabor had come to Colorado from New England twenty years before, with his wife Augusta and a small son. He tried prospecting, without success, and in the 1870's he was running a shop in Leadville and also acting as postmaster. Actually Augusta Tabor did most of the work; her husband was amiable and popular but not noted for his acumen or industry. Then one day he 'grubstaked' two prospectors in return for a share of their future discoveries, and they promptly went out and uncovered a fantastic silver lode. From then on Tabor's luck seemed boundless; with the profits from his first lode he invested in another exploration, and then another, and in no time at all he had accumulated a fortune of $9,000,000, with more money coming in every day. In 1883 he divorced the loyal but plain Augusta and married a beautiful young blonde girl known as 'Baby Doe' who had come to Leadville determined to find a rich husband. Two daughters were born; Tabor named them Elizabeth Pearl and Silver Dollar, and he showered luxuries on them and on his young wife and on everyone he knew. Then in 1893 silver was demonetized, and Tabor was ruined; he died penniless six years later in Denver. But the story is more than the usual rise-and-fall cliché, because of Baby Doe. Everyone assumed she would leave Tabor when his fortune evaporated, but she stood by him to the end, selling her jewels and her finery, struggling to get food for the family, darning and patching and apparently never complaining. Just before Horace Tabor died he told Baby Doe she must never abandon the Matchless, his richest mine; someday silver prices would rise again and the mine would once more be valuable. So Baby Doe went back to Leadville with her little girls and there she stayed, living in a mean cabin at the entrance to the mine, dressed in rags, ekeing out a pitiful existence for almost forty years; her own death did not come until 1936.

The story has been told over and over again; one of the most interesting contemporary American operas is *The Ballad of Baby Doe,* which had its premiere, appropriately, in the old miners' Opera House at Central City. Tourists in Leadville go to see Baby Doe Tabor's cabin at the Matchless Mine, and the house Tabor lived in during the lean years with Augusta, and the Opera House he built for Leadville, which was once called the Tabor but is now called the Elks Opera House. In its day the Opera House offered the Leadville miners every sort of extravagant entertainment, from spectacles with real elephants to Oscar Wilde talking, tongue in cheek one hopes, on 'The Practical Application of the Aesthetic Theory to Exterior and Interior House Decoration, with Observations on Dress and Personal Ornament'.

Montana had its wild mining days too. The most famous strike in Montana was at Virginia City, which is often confused with another Virginia City in Nevada; both were mining boom towns. The Virginia City in Montana never became as grand and gaudy as its counterpart in Nevada; the Montana millionaires seemed to spend their fortunes out of town. But the Virginia City in Montana was more wicked; really wicked, not merely naughty. In its early days it had a sheriff named Henry Plummer who was the original of all the crooked sheriffs in Western films. He had a gang at his command who robbed stagecoaches and ore wagons, and he pocketed the loot while he pretended to be on the trail of the thieves. Sheriff Plummer flourished for quite a while in this manner, but finally some of the local men organized a Vigilantes Committee and his crimes were revealed. There had been more than a hundred unexplained, unpunished killings; now there were twenty-four hangings, and a crude peace settled over the Montana mountains.

Western Montana is still mining country, and the city of Butte is quite as extraordinary as any ghost town. It is set right in the middle of an enormous open-pit copper mine; one feels like an ant trapped at the bottom of a giant red basin. The city sprawls all over the bowl's interior, with steep streets and ramshackle buildings; it is all thoroughly picturesque. Authenticity is carried to such lengths that even the food in Butte is every bit as bad as it

was in the nineteenth-century mining camps; the only gastronomic treat is the saffron buns sold in the bakeries as a dim
memento of the Cornish miners who must once have been here.
Shooting is discouraged in Butte these days, and the last battle
was fought long ago in the War of the Copper Kings, which
determined the financial control of the mining, and ultimately of
Montana itself. But the citizens of Butte still manage to keep in
fighting trim by driving up and down the precipitous streets and
right through traffic signals at fifty and sixty miles an hour; even
now, this is no place for the faint of heart.

The dusty, grey-green cattle country lies east of the Rockies. It is
monotonous, without trees, a great billowing sea which rolls
from Texas up through Colorado and Wyoming and Montana all
the way to Canada. It is high, with dry, clear air, and you can see
for miles. When you drive across it, the mountains in the distance
seem a mirage, always there, never any nearer; it must have been
agonizing for the people in the wagon trains, the tantalizing visi-
bility. This is one part of the Great Plains which has hardly
changed at all: still a lonely infinity of tough, pale grass and sage-
brush. Topping a rise along a Wyoming road, you half expect to
come upon a band of Indians camped in the hollow, or a herd of
buffalo grazing.

We have described the early cattle drives, from Texas up to the
rail-head towns of Kansas; that was the first half of the cattle
boom, and it lasted for about twenty years. The second half was
quite different, and for a time much more lucrative. Trying
different trails to get their cattle to the railways, Texas cattlemen
discovered these vast unclaimed grasslands. In no time at all,
cattle 'spreads' were staked out all over northern Colorado and
Wyoming and Montana where so recently the buffalo had
thundered by.

The chief town of the cattlemen was Cheyenne, Wyoming,
which still has a fine cowboy air about it; studying the saddles and
boots in the shop windows there is an endless source of delight.
Moreover, the little Wyoming State Museum in Cheyenne has a
remarkable collection of branding irons and a few other scraps of
Western memorabilia, the more endearing because so few and so
ingenuous. But unhappily the building one would most like to see
is gone; the old Cheyenne Club was torn down several years ago.

It had been built in 1880: 'Some of our rich bachelors have associated themselves with a few married men for the purpose of forming an English club', reported the Cheyenne *Daily Leader* on 25 July of that year. One learns with surprise that many of the prosperous cattlemen in this second phase of the cattle boom were not weatherbeaten ranchers at all. Men in England and Scotland had been attracted by the splendid combination of profit and romance in the Western cattle business; they invested heavily, either in syndicates or as individuals. By 1886 it was estimated that the English and Scottish companies between them controlled twenty million acres of Western grazing land; 'controlled' did not precisely mean 'owned', but at the time it seemed quite good enough.

Many of these investors went West in person, or sent sons and nephews to settle out there at least temporarily. One of the most flamboyant was Moreton Frewen, a charming English plunger who acquired a huge spread in the Powder River region of northern Wyoming. In the early 1880's in the West there seemed to be no end to the profits one could squeeze from the lowly cow, and Frewen did as well as everyone else. Moreover, he went 'Western' with a vengeance and was a tremendous hit on his annual trips back to London; on one of those trips he wooed and won the beautiful and talented Clara Jerome, and thus became the uncle of little Winston Churchill. Unfortunately young Mrs Frewen never learned to share her husband's passion for her own American West, despite the piano and the carpets and the weekly order of flowers Frewen had shipped from the East. It was perhaps just as well that within a few years he over-extended himself and had to sell out.

The Cheyenne newspaper rejoiced at Moreton Frewen's departure; a strong anti-British feeling was building up in the territory. There were many reasons for it; most of them can be discovered in the memoir of John Clay, a dour Scot who was sent out to manage some of the Scottish holdings in Wyoming and ended by staying on there until his death.

> The men who came from the other side of the Atlantic were young, mostly worthless in a business way, many of them dissolute, and when you rounded them up a very moderate lot. Very few of them survived the ordeal of hard winters, overstocked ranges and other vicissitudes. . . . The ne'er-do-well at home was exported to the

West with generally disastrous results, not only to himself but more especially to the friends who were asked to take him in charge.

Mr Clay clearly wrote from bitter personal experience! But then too Mr Clay was a hard man, known for his courage and his iron will but not notable for his tolerance. The ordeals which drove so many of his compatriots out of the West were hardly negligible.

The first crisis came as a result of the winters of 1886 and 1887, when the blizzards were so bad, the snow so deep, the cold so intense that horrifying numbers of cattle starved to death or were frozen on the open plains. Until then everyone had managed to squeak by without winter feeding, relying on the tough range cattle's ability to survive, disregarding all warning about the Wyoming climate. Now, however, there was a fearful outcry, and many British investors pulled out.

The second crisis was perhaps Mr Clay's 'other vicissitudes', a superb understatement for a life and death struggle which has provided meat for Western stories and films for seventy years now. The high – or low – point of the struggle is known as 'the Johnson County War'; like the Civil War in the South, it still hovers in the air in Wyoming. To understand it, two things must be borne in mind. First, a man with a Wyoming cattle spread in the 1880's did not actually *own* much land. All he needed to buy was enough acreage for a few buildings and for enclosures in which he could bunch his cattle together once or twice a year for branding and counting and culling; the rest of the time the cattle ranged free on government land which no one else had yet claimed. Secondly, cattle rustling was always a serious problem in the West because the cattle did roam far and wide. Branding helped, but brands could be altered, and calves born late in the spring were not branded until autumn. On the other hand, what looked like rustling might be no more than someone exercising his perfect right to claim an ownerless animal, a maverick which had somehow escaped the branding iron.

These two facts became particularly important in the years right after the two hard winters, when settlers began to appear in the cattle country, come to stake out a homestead, 160 acres of unclaimed government land. At the same time the big spreads, which had suffered severe losses, were beginning to be acutely sensitive about their herd-count. A few unscrupulous cattlemen tried to scare the settlers off; there were ugly instances of violence, defenceless homesteaders shot in the back by hired gunfighters. When the homesteaders tried to market cattle of their own, the Wyoming Stock Growers Association in Cheyenne refused to recognize their brands, impounded the cattle, and said they were rustlers. Under the circumstances, it is only reasonable to assume that some of those on the settlers' side felt few qualms if a cattleman's stray steer ended up in some settler's herd, but the cattlemen did not help matters by calling all settlers 'rustlers'.

One spring day in 1892 the feud reached its climax. More than fifty men, half of them hired Texas gunfighters but the other half eminently respectable, leading cattlemen, set out for northern Wyoming to teach some of the 'rustlers' a lesson. There are those who insist the entire scheme was devised by John Clay, although he was back in Scotland on business when the invasion actually took place. In any event, he was president of the Stock Growers Association at that time, and he later said that he was proud to call the Invaders his friends. It is not surprising; due process had few supporters on the frontier. The Cheyenne newspaper which told of the founding of the Cheyenne Club in the same issue gave a laconic account of the end of a horse thief and killer who was being sent from Cheyenne to Utah for trial.

> Welcom . . . has a fear that Sheriff Turner . . . will kill him before he reaches Utah, but Mr Turner says he will take the prisoner through safely . . . However, from Utah we hear that the people are highly incensed over the murder. It will not be surprising therefore to learn of an impromptu hanging bee in a few days.

Most people in the West in those days were completely in favour of taking the law into one's own hands, as long as one was right; in the Johnson County War, the difficulty was that each side claimed to be right.

The Invaders' first objective was the town of Buffalo in Johnson County, where they planned to begin by teaching a lesson to one 'Red' Angus, a Scot of another stripe who was the Sheriff there and who persisted in taking the settlers' side. On the way, however, the Invaders stopped at a cabin which had once been part of Moreton Frewen's spread, there to besiege and kill two cowboys who had turned homesteader and become leaders among the settler group. Unfortunately for the Invaders, one of their victims was just the sort of hero Hollywood – and everyone else – loves: brave and handsome and strong and just in all his dealings. He even had a ringing name, Nate Champion, and during the siege this paragon kept a running account:

> Me and Nick was getting breakfast . . . Boys there is bullets coming in like hail . . . They are shooting from the stable and river and back of the house . . . Nick [his friend] is dead, he died about 9 o'clock . . . Boys I feel pretty lonesome just now. I wish there was someone here with me so we could watch all sides at once . . . I shot at the men in the stable just now; don't know if I got any or not . . . It don't look as if there is much show of my getting away . . . I guess they are going to fire the house . . . Good-bye boys if I never see you again.

All alone Nate Champion held off fifty men for nine hours before they finally killed him.

The Invaders' first action was their last; someone got word to Sheriff Angus, every homesteader in the county rose up, and the next day the Invaders themselves were besieged at the ranch where they were planning their next move. Only Sheriff Angus's regard for law and justice, and the intervention of the United States Army, saved the Invaders from massacre. The trial which followed was a mockery, for it was held in Cheyenne, the Invaders' own bailiwick, and in any case the Invaders were powerful men with friends in high places. Yet in the end they found they had won all the battles but lost the war. Juries now refused to convict any rustlers, no matter how guilty, and life became intolerable in so many ways for the big cattlemen that once again many left for good. It was the end of an era.

None of this violence, however, tarnished the image of the simple cowboy. The first great cowboy novel was Owen Wister's *The Virginian,* published in 1902; its hero was the cowboy we still see in films and on television. He made very little money and he had a hard life, yet by and large he remained unruffled, cheerful and pragmatic. In the early days a good cowboy changed into 'city' clothes on the rare occasions when he went into some real town, but after a while he discovered that he was much better treated in his cowboy clothes. Everyone admired him, wanted to emulate him. The cowboy world still has such appeal that today all Western farmers call themselves ranchers, and the Episcopalian Bishop of Montana delights his flock and the rest of the world by having his clericals cut cowboy-fashion and wearing black cowboy boots and a black cowboy hat.

Some of the cattle country, in Wyoming as in Texas, has now been taken over by oil interests; for miles around Casper, Wyoming, the oil rigs now go up and down, up and down in an endless minuet. But towns like Cheyenne and Buffalo in Wyoming, and Miles City in Montana, are still cowboy towns. You know it when you see the breakfasts listed on the café menus: a steak, six ranch eggs, a quarter of a pound of bacon, a pound of spuds (potatoes), a stack of hot cakes and half a gallon of java (coffee) all for one person.

The owners of some of the big ranches are quite willing to allow visitors to look over them, although this is interesting chiefly for someone who cares about pure-bred beef cattle. Cattle in the West are still branded, cowboys continue to look like cowboys, but these days the round-ups are likely to be for doling out vitamins; ranches are now thoroughly business-like places. There are frequent rodeos during the summer in the West, however, with important ones during Cheyenne's Frontier Days at the end of July, at the Montana State Fair at Great Falls at the beginning of August, and at the Colorado State Fair at the end of August at Pueblo.

Some ranches nowadays take paying guests, and there are such 'dude ranches' everywhere in the West. Some are real working ranches, with a few dudes and a great many cattle; others have very few cattle and a great many dudes. The prettiest dude ranches, in the most beautiful situations, are often the least 'genuine', if it is cowboys and cows you seek. The biggest cattle spreads are still on the open plains, far from the mountains. The dude ranches in the scenic parts often specialize in pack trips into the mountains; the 'genuine' ranches may provide no organized entertainment for their dudes but simply let them tag along after the cowboys and try their hand at ranch work. Dude ranches vary greatly in their prices, but it would be difficult to find one asking less than $12 a day all-in, and many are considerably more expensive. Lists can be obtained from the Wyoming Commerce and Industry Commission in Cheyenne, or from the Dude Ranchers Association in Billings, Montana. In addition to the established dude ranches, which rarely accept people for less than a week and prefer two weeks, there are all kinds of lodges and quasi-dude-

ranches in the West which will take people just for a night or two
and furnish horses as well.

For anyone with time for only one Rocky Mountain state,
Colorado would probably be the obvious choice and Denver the
obvious centre. Colorado has more high mountains (fifty-one
over 14,000 feet), more breathtaking passes, more remarkable
canyons than any of the other four. Within its borders you can
taste both the alpine beauties of the northern Rockies and the
golden Gothic splendours of the arid Southwest, and in one
corner of the state there is Mesa Verde, a National Park which
protects the finest ancient Indian cliff dwellings in the country.
All that Colorado lacks is pre-eminence in the great cattle and
cowboy period; there Wyoming and Montana have the edge. But
Colorado has cowboys and cattle enough to suit most people, and
there are the old mining towns as an added bonus.

The simplest way to describe the delights of Colorado is in the
form of a circular, thousand-mile trip from Denver, moving in a
counter-clockwise direction. No one bus tour includes all the
places we mention, nor would one want to crowd everything into
a single trip, even with a car. But this imaginary circular tour will
give some idea of the variety in this one state.

We have already described Rocky Mountain National Park. Let
us begin by going there, passing through the town of Boulder on
the way. Boulder is built around the University of Colorado, an
attractive university in the shadow of the Rockies, with homogeneous buildings made of the red stone of the region, and ski-ing
runs only minutes away. After Rocky Mountain Park, you would
head for Loveland Pass; by taking a minor road south from the
Park you could fit in Central City on the way.

Driving towards Loveland Pass on U.S. Route 6, you go right
past one of the most charming of the old mining towns, Georgetown, precariously perched in a narrow gorge. 'It is the only town
I have seen in America to which the epithet picturesque could be
applied,' said the perceptive Miss Bird in 1873. Georgetown still
has a special quality unique among the ghost towns of Colorado,
like a dignified old lady quietly musing on her very gay youth.
For one thing, Georgetown never suffered a severe fire; most of
these mining towns with their crudely-built frame houses crowded
close together were burnt down and rebuilt several times in the

course of their boom days. But Georgetown is almost perfectly preserved in its original state, with several delightful Victorian-gingerbread buildings and a handsome house complete with Cornish-looking granite outbuildings, the property of one of the early mine-owners. It is only regrettable that the Hotel de Paris here has recently stopped being a hostelry and become a museum instead; it would have been so pleasant to stay there. The Hotel de Paris is surely the 'good hotel declivitously situated' which Miss Bird described, 'at the end of a narrow, piled-up irregular street, crowded with miners standing in groups, or drinking and gaming under the veranda'. Miss Bird did not mention the food, but the Hotel de Paris was run by a Frenchman, Louis du Puy, who was considered an amusing eccentric because he fretted about the excellence of his table.

U.S. Route 6 over Loveland Pass is scheduled to be supplanted soon by the new Interstate Route 70, to the relief of nervous drivers. Either route, however, will bring you to a point ten miles west of the town of Dillon where you can take a slight detour and swing round through Leadville. It will only add another twenty or thirty miles to your trip. Well beyond the Leadville turning, you will come to the magnificent Glenwood Canyon, where for perhaps twenty miles the road goes between golden-red rock walls. The railway runs through here too; on the Burlington Zephyr Vistadome train to California, these Colorado canyons are among the special delights, one reason why so many people recommend that particular way of reaching the West Coast.

After Glenwood Canyon comes the town of Glenwood Springs, and a tempting turning: fifty miles south of Glenwood Springs, in a valley difficult to reach from any other direction, is Aspen. This was once just another ghost town with abandoned silver mines, but at the end of the Second World War a Chicago industrialist, who admired the way culture and history and scenery were often combined at summer festivals in Europe, decided to see what he could do with Aspen. The result is fascinating. In the winter Aspen is one of the most attractive ski-ing resorts in the United States, with a strong international flavour because so many of the ski-ing instructors are Europeans, now happily settled there. In the summer, Aspen has a superb music festival, with programmes three times a week throughout July and August, rehearsals open to the public, and usually one or two special musical events as well. One does not need to book ahead; in fact seats are sold only at concert-time. However, anyone heading for the music festival at Aspen must bear in mind that the concerts there are scheduled according to Daylight Saving Time. Aspen is the only town in Colorado to use Daylight Saving Time in summer, and the resultant confusion has led many a concert-goer to miss the first half of a programme.

Most of the artists who appear in the concerts also teach in the Aspen summer music school. The group varies from year to year but it unfailingly includes some of the best musicians in America, who delight in Aspen because there they can play what they like in relaxed and congenial surroundings. Moreover music is not Aspen's only summer attraction. There are mountains, of course, to be explored on a hired horse or one's own two feet. There is also the Aspen Institute for Humanistic Studies, which sponsors Aspen's unique 'executive seminars' for businessmen and political leaders and a related series of bi-weekly talks open to the public. And there are showings of classic films every other day or so. There are any number of places to stay in Aspen, ranging from the Victorian splendours of the Hotel Jerome to stunning contemporary lodges.

Aspen is at the head of the Roaring Fork River valley, and on the way to Aspen from Glenwood Springs one passes another turning which leads along the Frying Pan River. Both of these are handsome valleys which look just as valleys in the Rockies ought to look; along the rivers there are pale green cottonwood trees, with the darker green of spruce and pine on the slopes of the mountains on either side, and here and there, high up, stands of shivering silvery aspen trees. There are ranches in these valleys, and usually some highly photogenic cowboys about.

In western Colorado, well beyond Glenwood Springs, is Colorado National Monument, with its slashing canyons and grotesque eroded rock formations. More unusual is Dinosaur National Monument, in the north-west corner of Colorado, quite a distance to the north of our imagined circular tour. Dinosaur National Monument is a protected area because more dinosaur skeletons have been found there than anywhere else in the Western Hemisphere; anthropologists are still hard at work chipping away at the rock strata to expose more remains. As one might expect, the best skeletons have been taken to various museums, but some examples have been left embedded in the rock for visitors to see.

Heading south from the Colorado National Monument, one goes for some seventy miles through barren but beautiful high desert country to the Black Canyon of the Gunnison, another National Monument, deep and dark and forbidding, as the name implies. Traversing it is a feat only experienced rock climbers should attempt, with the advice and consent of the Rangers there; for most people, simply looking down into it is enough. Our imaginary circular tour passes the Black Canyon and heads deeper into the precipitous country of south-western Colorado; here once again you are very near the Continental Divide.

Going southward along U.S. Route 550 you come to Ouray, a little mining town already 7,000 feet up but surrounded by mountains twice that height. The road continuing south from Ouray is called the Million Dollar Highway because it cost that to blast a way up and over these forbidding mountains. Until the road was completed, many of the little towns south of Ouray could be reached only on the narrow-gauge railways built in the boom-days to carry ore from the mines. There was once an entire network of narrow-gauge lines through these mountains, but only one is still in operation; the Durango–Silverton line. Nowadays this runs from June to September, chiefly for the benefit of the tourists; there is one train a day, leaving Durango about nine in the morning and returning there at five in the afternoon after a long stop at Silverton. The train, which still boasts its original Victorian coaches and an elderly steam engine, climbs 3,000 feet on its way to Silverton, passing beautiful gorges and going through groves of shivering aspen trees. Indians dance on the platform at Durango as the train pulls out, there is frequently a mock hold-up along the way, and at Silverton there are always colourful goings-on. Silverton is one of the most photogenic of the old mining towns, and both Silverton and the train have been in use in countless films.

Durango is not far from Mesa Verde National Park and its remarkable thirteenth-century Indian cliff dwellings. No one who is in this part of Colorado should miss seeing Mesa Verde; we will leave the description of it until Chapter 10, so that we can discuss the cliff dwellings of the Southwest all together.

9 Mormon Temple and Tabernacle (*left*), Salt Lake City, Utah

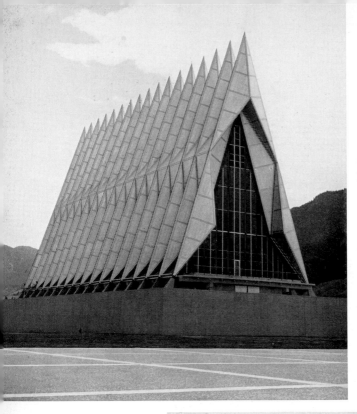

10a Air Force Academy Chapel, Colorado. Designed by Skidmore, Owings and Merrill

10b Ice Rink, Yale University. Designed by Eero Saarinen

The Trailways Bus Center in Denver offers several bus tours from Denver to Mesa Verde; their five-day tour includes a night at Durango and a trip on the narrow-gauge railway as well. At current prices, it costs about $25 a day to take this tour: roughly $20 a day for the tour itself and another $5 for meals, the one thing not included in the tour-price. This is hardly cheap; if there were two people involved, it would be no more expensive to hire a car in Denver and do the trip on one's own.

Our imaginary circular tour has halted at Durango or perhaps Mesa Verde. To follow the upward curve back towards Denver without retracing your steps, you would now have to go east along U.S. Route 160 over Wolf Creek Pass and then north on U.S. Route 285, which leads to Denver by way of Fairplay, another old mining town. Alternatively one might turn east on U.S. Route 24 and go through Cripple Creek and Colorado Springs.

Cripple Creek was the last of the wide-open mining towns; its boom came with the discovery of gold there in the 1890's, when the silver mining towns were already dying. Some of the mines at Cripple Creek are still worked, and one of them runs trips for visitors down the shafts. But most of Cripple Creek is now a highly satisfactory ghost town, with a miners' museum, and melodramas staged in the bar of the old hotel during the summer. To get from Cripple Creek to Colorado Springs, you would do well to take the minor road which goes by way of Broadmoor; the object is to avoid going into Colorado Springs on U.S. Route 24 through Manitou Springs, as depressing a stretch of road as ever there was, with its endless motels and cheap advertising.

Broadmoor is actually The Broadmoor, an enormous resort hotel with an excellent golf course and a splendid view of the mountains. It is the most celebrated but by no means the only resort hotel in the region around Colorado Springs, which has long been a holiday centre as the many tourist attractions indicate. One of the more interesting of excursions so insistently offered is the cog railway trip up to the tip of Pike's Peak at 14,110 feet. Some people love Colorado Springs but we in fact prefer places which lie deeper in the mountains; Colorado Springs is at the eastern edge. We would therefore unequivocally recommend returning to Denver by way of Fairplay, the other route, were it not for the new United States Air Force Academy which is ten or

P

fifteen miles north of Colorado Springs. The Academy is handsomely situated in the foothills of the Rockies – where it would
clearly be suicidal to attempt to land a plane. Visitors are welcome
to look over the grounds, and to eat in a pleasantly inexpensive
cafeteria in the Community Center. The principal buildings are
striking; they were designed by Skidmore Owings and Merrill,
the finest large architectural firm in America today. The chapel,
which can be visited, is a beautiful modern structure with magnificent glass.

One of the arguments for taking the Fairplay route rather than
the one through Colorado Springs is that one wants to come upon
Denver from above, dropping down from the Rockies. With all
its smart new buildings and its crisp business-like air, Denver's
chief fault is a lack of romance. There is almost nothing to remind
you of the frontier days, when the streets had a 'harlequin' look,
with

> hunters and trappers in buckskin clothing; men of the Plains with
> belts and revolvers, in great blue cloaks, relics of the war; teamsters
> in leathern suits; horsemen in fur coats and caps and buffalo-hide
> boots with the hair outside, and camping blankets behind their
> huge Mexican saddles; Broadway dandies in light kid gloves; rich
> English sporting tourists, clean, comely, and supercilious looking;
> and hundreds of Indians on their small ponies, the men wearing
> buckskin suits sewn with beads, and red blankets, with faces
> painted vermilion and hair hanging lank and straight . . .

You must therefore help things along, by approaching Denver
either from the mountains above it to the west; or from the east,
so that the city appears against the backdrop of the snow-peaked
Rockies after hundreds of miles of dusty, monotonous plains.
From the north or the south, Denver's unique situation is not so
striking.

Denver itself is not a particularly exciting town, except for the
heady optimism and the prosperity one senses there. You can go
up into the dome of the State Capitol, which is covered with gold
leaf, and have a splendid sweeping view of the Rockies. If you
have had the foresight to write well in advance for reservations,
you can tour the United States Mint. Once the gold and silver
poured out of the mountains into Denver as through a funnel, to
emerge as coin of the realm; today there are no gold coins, but the
Denver mint continues busy, producing half the United States

coinage. There are several museums in Denver too, but the East and the older parts of the Midwest are really the only places to expect good museums and galleries in America. The South has for too many years been too poor, and the West is too new; with a few exceptions, it is a great mistake to waste time on the big general museums and galleries in the Western cities. The West does not have a European sort of sophistication and it would be foolish to expect the external signs of a European culture. This is a totally different world; to get the feel of it you must stay out of doors, and spend as little time as possible in the cities. We must, however, add that many Western cities do have special museums or sections of museums especially devoted to Western American things; this of course is always interesting. In Denver, for example, there is the Colorado State Museum, with delightful, instructive dioramas about every phase of Colorado history from the Mesa Verde cliff-dwellers to the mining and cowboy days, and on the top floor of this museum husbands can look over the Western gun collection while their wives shed a few tears in front of Baby Doe Tabor's satin slippers and Silver Dollar's lace christening dress. The Denver Natural History Museum has native birds and animals artfully arranged in their natural habitat, and there you can pursue further the moose-elk-red-deer-wapiti tangle. There is also a branch of the Denver Art Museum called Chappell House where you will find an attractive presentation of the life and art of the American Indian. But you must not linger in Denver. You must go out of the town, into the mountains or across the plains.

SPECIAL KNOWLEDGE

If we were asked to pick the very **best time for a trip** through the Rockies, we would choose either the middle two weeks in June or the last two weeks in September. You could then be almost certain that snow would not be a problem, and everything would be open for the season. You would miss the worst of the crowds in the National Parks, and you could have a reasonable choice of accommodations.

We should note that one can sometimes *hire* **camping** gear in towns near the National Parks. If you wanted to try modified camping, in a camping cabin in one of the Parks, you should know that they are in great demand and the only way to get one at the height of the season is to arrive at the cabin-village very early in the morning and hope that someone will be packing up to move on.

One airline (Continental) has devised an excellent way to tour the Rockies.

When buying an airline ticket to Denver you can also book a fully-equipped **motor caravan,** to await you at the airport. Accommodating 5 adults, it costs $75 per week, plus 12 cents per mile.

Anywhere near the Rockies you are likely to be a mile above sea level, and often twice that. The sun is hot during the day, but the nights are cold. Some Americans on holiday in the West dress with dazzling informality; others simply wear sturdy, practical **clothes** suitable for hiking and mountaineering. Only in the big hotels does anyone try to look respectable at dinner, and even there it is only a relative respectability.

Food and accommodation are cheaper on the average in the West and South than in the East. Unfortunately, however, in order to seek out the least expensive accommodation it is usually necessary to have a car. At the major tourist centres, where the buses and trains disgorge their passengers, the rates are less likely to be a bargain; and distances in the West are such that one cannot simply walk somewhere else.

If the **food** is cheaper, it is also less varied. But there are always gastronomic surprises in the West. The Hotel Bonneville, for example, in remote Idaho Falls, Idaho, will give you a superb and generous lunch, course after course, for the refreshing price of 99 cents, and the OK Courts Café in Garden City, Kansas, will do the same for 97 cents. Everywhere, too, you are sure to be offered Rocky Mountain rainbow trout, delicious if it is freshly caught.

Butte is pronounced as if it were French. Not only is it a town in Montana, but also the term for a table or thumb of rock left rearing up above the surrounding plain after aeons of erosion.

Cheyenne is pronounced Shy-enn; *Sioux* is pronounced Soo.

National Parks

GLACIER NATIONAL PARK, MONTANA. Park season 15 June to 15 September. Hotel, motel and cabin reservations from Reservations Department, Glacier Park Company, East Glacier Park, Montana.

GRAND TETON NATIONAL PARK, WYOMING. Good camping grounds, cabins and amenities. Information from Park superintendent, Grand Teton National Park, Jackson, Wyoming.

ROCKY MOUNTAIN NATIONAL PARK, COLORADO. Camping grounds and cabins in the park; hotels and motels at east and west entrances. Information from the superintendent, Rocky Mountain National Park, Estes Park, Colorado.

YELLOWSTONE NATIONAL PARK, WYOMING. Park headquarters are at Mammoth Hot Springs, five miles from the north gateway. Hotel accommodation is available from early or mid-June to Labor Day or the end of September. Various types of cottages, cabins, camping grounds and eating places are open from 25 May to 1 October. Reservations from Yellowstone Park Co., Reservation Dept., Yellowstone Park, Wyoming.

Browning, Montana

MUSEUM OF THE PLAINS INDIAN, half a mile west of Browning. 1 June to 15 September. Daily 8–5. Free.

Billings, Montana

Dude Ranch information: Conna G. May, Executive Secretary, The Dude Ranchers' Association, Box 1363B, Billings, Montana.

Central City, Colorado

CENTRAL CITY OPERA HOUSE ASSOCIATION, University of Denver, Colorado Seminary, 200 W. 14th Avenue, Denver 4, Colorado. Buses and tours from Denver. For opera and theatre reservations and information, write to above address.

Cheyenne, Wyoming

WYOMING STATE MUSEUM, Central Avenue at 23rd Street. Monday to Friday 9–4.30, Sunday 12–5; 1 June to 31 August, also Saturday 9–5. Free.

Colorado Springs, Colorado

AIR FORCE ACADEMY, U.S. Route 85 and 87, thirteen miles north of Colorado Springs. Grounds open to visitors daily, 8–sunset.

PIKES PEAK COG RAILWAY, leaves from Manitou Springs. 15 May to 15 October, daily 9 and 2; 1 July to 31 August, daily 9, 2 and 5.30. Early spring and late autumn, daily 2. Advance reservation advised.

Denver, Colorado

DENVER VISITORS AND CONVENTION BUREAU, Hospitality Center, 225 Colfax, Denver 2, Colorado.

CHAPPELL HOUSE, 1300 Logan Street. Tuesday to Saturday 9–5, Sunday 2–5.

COLORADO STATE MUSEUM, 14th Avenue and Sherman Street. Monday to Friday 9–5, Saturday, Sunday and holidays 10–5. Free.

DENVER NATURAL HISTORY MUSEUM, in City Park off Colorado Boulevard. Monday to Saturday 9–5, Sunday 12–5. Free.

U.S. MINT, Colfax Avenue and Cherokee Street. Conducted tours Labor Day to 1 June, Monday to Friday 9.30 and 1; 1 July to Labor Day, Monday to Friday hourly from 7.45–2.30. Reservations must be made in advance.

STATE CAPITOL, between Colfax and 14th Avenue facing Broadway. Open daily.

TRAILWAYS BUS CENTER, Broadway, at 17th. 4 to 6-day tours to Mesa Verde.

Durango, Colorado

SILVERTON RAILWAY, Denver and Rio Grande Western Railroad Company, 479 Main Avenue, Durango, Colorado. Early June to early September, daily, departing approximately 9 and returning about 6. Reservations should be made. Operates to the end of September, approximately three times a week.

Leadville, Colorado

AUGUSTA TABOR CABIN, 116 East 5th Street. Daily 9–6.
BABY DOE TABOR'S CABIN, one mile east of Leadville. 30 May to Labor Day, daily 9–5.

Salt Lake City, Utah

BEEHIVE HOUSE, State Street at Temple Street. Being restored.
LION HOUSE, Temple Street between Main and State Street. Monday to Friday 10–4, Saturday 10–12. Free.
THE TABERNACLE, Temple Square. Open daily. Organ recitals, week-days 12, Sunday 4; summer, daily except Thursday and Sunday 7.30 p.m. Free.

Snake River Boat Trips

Information from Lewiston Chamber of Commerce, Lewiston, Idaho. There are other good rivers for boat trips in the West and for information on these one should write to the relevant State Chamber of Commerce or the State Tourist Information Bureau.

9 · The West Coast

The astonishing thing about the Pacific coast is that everything there is larger than life. One is led to expect certain grand and impressive features: mountains perhaps, and San Francisco Bay, and the sequoia trees. But no one prepares you for the fact that these are not isolated rarities, that the entire West Coast is on a Brobdingnagian scale. And so one may go there sceptical about the wonders of the region only to end by protesting that there is not nearly enough talk about the magnificence of it all.

Seattle is a case in point. It is situated in the north-western corner of the state of Washington, which is itself in the north-western corner of the United States. Because it is very near Vancouver and Victoria, many Canadians know Seattle far better than most Americans, who were hardly aware of its existence until the 1962 World's Fair. Yet Seattle should have been widely celebrated long ago, for it is a very attractive city. Like most places on the West Coast, it has grown enormously since the Second World War. The West Coast had space to spare and easy access to the sea; it was the obvious region in which to build the aircraft and armament plants needed during the war, and expansion has gone steadily on ever since.

Although more than a hundred miles from the open sea, Seattle is a major port. Ships pass through the Strait of Juan de Fuca, between Washington's Olympic Peninsula on the American side and the Canadian island of Vancouver, and then steer southward between the islands of Puget Sound. Reached at last, Seattle itself seems almost an island, squeezed between the salty Sound and the fresh-water Lake Washington; from almost any vantage point in the city one can see water. But this is not Seattle's only charm: on a clear day the great snow-crowned dome of Mount Rainier is also visible, fifty miles away to the south-east. Everywhere on the West Coast there is this sense of the outdoors pressing in, luring one off to the mountains or the sea. It is the supreme attraction of life there.

There are not a great many conventional tourist sights in Seattle proper. One is the Art Museum in Volunteer Park, small but good. Appropriately for a city which has many ties with the Orient, it has a particularly fine collection of jade, and often too there are special showings of the work of such celebrated local painters as Mark Tobey and Morris Graves. There is a Japanese Tea Garden in the Arboretum, and an experimental rose garden near the zoo. The Museum of History and Industry devotes particular attention to aeroplanes, which is as it should be since Seattle's economy is almost completely dependent on the giant Boeing Aircraft Corporation. Finally, the recent Fair has given Seattle a handsome new group of civic buildings, for the principal structures were planned as permanent additions to the city.

One of the most beautiful sights in Seattle, however, is something much more humble: it is the food section of the Pike Street Market on the waterfront, where stall after stall proffers the most glorious array imaginable of fruit and vegetables. There are all sorts of strange and wonderful varieties, but the stalls are so lovingly ordered, the produce so glistening and fresh, that even the lowly carrots are exciting. All over the West Coast one encounters magnificent fruit and vegetables and the markets are full of tempting things, but this particular one overflows with them. It has fish stalls too, offering the salmon and crabs and oysters for which the Pacific coast is famous. The Pike Street Market is not nearly as well-known as the Farmers Market in Los Angeles, but many purists prefer its simplicity. Moreover, one can eat cheaply and quite well there in the cafeterias which the stall-owners themselves patronize.

Every visitor to Seattle will want an overall picture of the city, to understand the special advantages of its situation. For a view from above, one can go to the top of the Space Needle, a souvenir of the Fair. In addition there are Gray Line sight-seeing tours, which seem an especially good idea in Seattle because of the way the town spreads up and over the hills and along the water's edge. Gray Line has an illuminating 'Discovery' bus tour all around the city, and in the summer they also offer a boat trip past the harbour and through the locks into Lake Washington.

Both of these Gray Line tours go past the University of Washington and its remarkable football stadium on the lake shore, with docks for those spectators who come to the games in their own boats – a vivid illustration of the way in which everyone in Seattle takes to the water on every possible occasion. For visitors who are interested in the theatre, the undergraduate productions at the University of Washington are known for their excellence and their experimentation. If the theatre group has something on when one is in Seattle, it is pleasant to go, particularly if they are using their unique arena stage.

But no one will want to linger long in the city in fine weather. There are too many fascinating excursions to be made. Mount Rainier, for example, gleaming in the distance in the midst of the Cascade Mountains, is a justly popular National Park area. Like many of the mountains on the West Coast, Rainier is an extinct volcano. The peak of its cone collapsed aeons ago, but it is still 14,410 feet tall, its crater filled with ice, and glaciers flowing down its sides. The Park includes hundreds of trails one can take through the forests on the lower slopes and the meadows covered with wild flowers. In the summer, moreover, it is easy to get to Mount Rainier even without a car: from late June to early September there is a regular bus service to the Park in addition to organized bus tours. There are lodges at the main visitors' centres within the Park, and there are also many camping sites, and shelter cabins for hikers.

West of Seattle, on the Olympic peninsula, there is another National Park which is quite unique. Called Olympic National Park, it is divided into two sections, the main Park and the Olympic Ocean Strip. It is much farther from Seattle than Mount Rainier; one would need three or four days even to scratch the surface, for the journey alone out on to the peninsula takes almost a day. But one is amply repaid for the time and trouble. There are mountains in this Olympic National Park too, part of the Coast Range which borders the Pacific deep into California. These mountains are not as high as those farther inland, but they are quite high enough to be impressive, and herds of elk roam their slopes. Yet in Olympic National Park it is not the mountains which excite attention so much as the remarkable rain forest.

The western flank of these mountains often gets as much as 150 inches of rain a year, and this, combined with the mild coastal climate, has resulted in a completely exotic growth of trees. It is not in the least like the rain forests of the tropics, but it is a genuine one for all that. The trees are mainly Sitka spruce, western hemlock, western red cedar, and Douglas fir, most of them staggeringly tall, 200 feet and more, with enormous trunks. All of these trees are found in other places along the West Coast, but the specimens in the Olympic rain forest include the very biggest, and nowhere else do they crowd together so densely. The floor of the forest beneath is covered with soft moss and ferns, and the whole is suffused with a pale green, luminous light. Obviously, the way to see the rain forest is to walk at least a little way along one of the trails, and the Park Service suggests the Hoh River Trail as the easiest to reach.

The Olympic Ocean Strip, the other section of Olympic National Park, is equally fine in its own way. It is a primitive and beautiful stretch of shore, which stays that way because it is rather troublesome to get to. The northern part, which is the nicest, can only be reached by footpaths which start three miles inland, either at the village of Lapush or from Lake Ozette. The Lake Ozette trails are said to be the prettiest and to lead to the better rock pools; the Lapush trails end at a splendid beach. Anyone who likes icy water is presumably free to bathe, but the chief attraction of this ocean strip is the fascinating assortment of sea life to be found in the tidal pools, and the splendid sea birds, and the seals, and the occasional deer or bear. Agate-hunters, too, do well along the shore of the peninsula, both here and on the northern coast.

There are a few Indian settlements along the ocean strip, remnants of the coastal tribes which once flourished between here and Alaska. These were the Indians who carved totem poles; they also used the enormous trees of the region to make dugout canoes which were often sixty feet long. Today, however, there is little evidence of the old Indian culture left in Washington. The island of Vancouver is much richer in this regard.

In the summer there are Gray Line bus tours into Olympic National Park from the town of Port Angeles on the northern coast of the peninsula, where the Park headquarters is, and a visitors' information centre. Unfortunately, however, there seems to be no practicable way of reaching the ocean strip section except by car. With a car, it would be pleasant to do a loop-trip from Seattle, going on to the Olympic Peninsula in a south-westerly direction past the Hood Canal, where the rhododendrons are beautiful in the spring, and then turning north to swing back finally towards Seattle along the northern coast of the peninsula, finishing with a sequence of ferries across Puget Sound from

Port Townsend to Whidbey Island and then on to the mainland.

The Puget Sound ferries are themselves one of the delights of Seattle in the summer. One can take a ferry almost anywhere among the islands, but it is particularly pleasant to go by ferry to Victoria, across the watery border between the United States and Canada by way of the fishing village of Friday Harbor on San Juan Island.

Eastern Washington, beyond the Cascades, is for the most part less interesting. The main road to the east is U.S. Route 2, which leads across the state to Spokane, Washington's second largest city. At first, between Seattle and Wenatchee, the trip is properly scenic. There are the mountains, and then along the river near Wenatchee one can watch salmon using the artificial fish ladders to go upstream to spawn. Moreover Wenatchee is at the heart of the Washington apple country; every little shop there seems to sell apple candy, and in the spring the valleys are lovely with blossom. But beyond Wenatchee the country flattens out and is far dryer, looking almost like the cattle country east of the Rockies.

The great river of the north-eastern United States is the Columbia, which begins in Canada, winds a snake-like path southward across the eastern part of the state of Washington, and then turns west to flow to the Pacific, forming the border between Washington and the state of Oregon. The Columbia is a mighty and turbulent river whose energy has now been dramatically harnessed with dams like the Grand Coulee. It is also a historic river. It was the path along which Lewis and Clark penetrated this region in 1805, the first Americans to come overland to the Pacific. Later it was thought the Columbia would become the permanent boundary between Canada and the United States; both countries claimed the territory that is now Washington and Oregon, but there were more British settlers north of the river and more Americans to the south. In the end, however, arbitration overthrew logic and the boundary was placed farther north.

The Columbia is also a beautiful river, and it makes one final spectacular gesture as it nears the Pacific: Multnomah Falls, near Portland, Oregon. Portland itself, Oregon's leading city, is handsomely situated on either side of a tributary of the Columbia, with mountains pressing close on the north and east. But the Columbia

River provides Portland's proudest sights, with Multnomah Falls and then the splendid views of the gorge one gets along the Columbia River Highway near Portland.

In much of Oregon, the climate is rather English, and so it is hardly surprising that Portland is famous for its roses and that Oregon raises a great many sheep. But there is rugged country in Oregon too. In the north-eastern part of the state there are the Blue Mountains, the Strawberry Mountains, and the Wallowa Mountains; the very names are tempting. Another beautiful mountainous section is the Klamath region of southern Oregon. The town of Ashland in that area is famous for its Shakespeare Festival, the oldest in America and tremendously popular.

Crater Lake National Park is also in southern Oregon. As its name suggests, Crater Lake lies within the cone of an extinct volcano, part of that Cascade Range to which Mount Rainier also belongs. The lake is six miles across, set deep within the cone, and the water is an incredible dark blue. There are patches of fir trees massed along the rocky rim, and here and there the surface of the lake is broken by strange little volcanic islands, cones within cones. The Indians regarded this as a sacred and fearsome place, forbidden to ordinary mortals. Today in the summer visitors who have no car can reach the park centres at Crater Lake by bus from Klamath Falls or Medford (near Ashland), and there is a lodge, and camping sites. In winter Crater Lake has become a popular ski-ing centre; there are heavy snows, which begin early in the autumn and have been known to keep the Crater Lake Rim Drive closed until July. The lowland climate of the American Pacific Coast is much milder than that of the same latitude on the Atlantic coast, but in the mountains the combination of altitude and heavy coastal moisture results in very heavy snows.

The coast of Oregon is wild and craggy, with sheer cliffs and few safe harbours. Many of the beaches both there and along the northern California coast are tempting because they are almost deserted and very beautiful, but the bathing is often extremely dangerous. U.S. Route 101, as scenic a highway as ever there was, goes through Oregon along the coast and then into California, passing many of these superb and lonely stretches of cliff and beach. The route begins in the extreme north-western corner of Oregon at the town of Astoria, near the spot at which Lewis and Clark camped for Christmas in 1805. Astoria is a very old town by

Oregon standards; it began as Fort Astor, the westernmost link in the chain of John Jacob Astor's fur stations, the American counterpart of the Hudson's Bay Company in the early nineteenth century.

There are a great many state parks along Route 101, for camping and picnicking and bathing, with the greatest concentration of parks and tourist accommodation between Depoe Bay and Florence. At Depoe Bay one can watch fishing boats slip into the rocky harbour between the cliffs, and at Neskowen, twenty miles farther on, there is unusually safe bathing. At Yachats one can take a lift down through the cliffs to see the sea-lion caves.

The distances in this part of the world are appalling: it is three hundred and eighty miles from the Oregon-California border to San Francisco. On the inland route one first eases imperceptibly into California, and then drops down into the Sacramento Valley, passing along the way more evidence of volcanic activity where the Cascade Range merges with the Sierra Nevada Mountains. Towering, glacier-capped Mount Shasta is obviously dormant, but Lassen Peak, one of several volcanic mountains in Lassen Volcanic National Park, erupted as recently as 1917. The coast road to San Francisco is completely different. It runs between giant redwood trees for so many miles that one finally becomes jaded, and claustrophobic travellers sometimes find that awe has turned to desperation.

One enters an entirely different world as one nears San Francisco. True, there are thick fogs along the rocky coast in the winter and many of the natural features continue to suggest the country farther north; one could never mistake this region for southern California. But it does lie within the boundaries of the old Spanish territory, and it represents a unique blend of many diverse California elements. Within a hundred miles of San Francisco there are landmarks illustrating every important stage in the history of the state.

Spanish explorers discovered California in the early sixteenth century and claimed it for Spain, but no one stayed to settle. In 1579, Sir Francis Drake sailed along the coast. He missed the narrow entrance to San Francisco Bay, but he did drop anchor in what is now called Drake's Bay, a few miles farther north, and he and his men were warmly received at several Indian villages in the neighbourhood. For two centuries after that, however, no one paid any attention to California. There were well-established Spanish colonies in what is now New Mexico and Texas, and in Florida, but while Spain continued to regard California as part of her territory, it was just too far away to bother with. Then in the late eighteenth century Great Britain began to show signs of pushing her claims southward along the western edge of the continent, and Russia, too, already firmly entrenched in Alaska, sent ships probing along the coast. Hastily Spain dispatched her usual combination of soldiers and missionaries to establish outposts in the California territory, and soon afterwards groups of settlers arrived. Many Spaniards amassed large ranch holdings, where they led a delightfully relaxed and pleasant life. They were a long way from real civilization, but they were blessed with an agreeable climate and a generous supply of Indian peons. Like many a new-comer since then, they became ardent 'Californios' almost overnight.

In fact they became such ardent Californios that they bitterly resented the stupidities of the colonial administration, and evinced little loyalty either towards Spain or towards Mexico, which established its independence of Madrid in 1821. In defiance of the authorities, they welcomed the trickle of Americans coming into California in the second quarter of the nineteenth century, and thus they themselves brought their pleasant way of life to an end, for the ambitious, impatient Americans were not the sort to appreciate the genial anarchy of Spanish California. The Americans promptly got together, and first declared California an independent republic and then asked the United States to admit it to the Union. The Spanish Californios raised an army and fought for a few months, but then, assured of their lands, they surrendered, and Mexico formally signed California over to the United States in 1847. It is said that the British, who had once hoped to take over California themselves, lost their chance because of a woman. There was a British agent on the scene before most of the Americans arrived, and he was popular with the Californios, and making progress. Then he shot himself over a disappointment in love, and that was the end of that.

The original Spanish settlements extended from southernmost California all the way north to Sonoma, forty or fifty miles beyond San Francisco. At Sonoma there was a Franciscan mission, the

northernmost of nineteen such missions which today comprise
the most interesting remains of the colonial period. The Sonoma
mission is not as impressive as some of those farther south, but
Sonoma itself has remained a sleepy little town basking in the
California sunshine, and the fact that the mission is still an integral
part of its square, not merely an isolated curiosity, gives it a
special charm. Moreover, about a mile west of the town is the
ranch house of Mariano Vallejo, a great landowner hereabouts in
the early nineteenth century, military governor of northern California in its Mexican period, and one of the most attractive figures
in all of California's history. He was excommunicated by the local
religious authorities for his advocacy of Rousseau, and he welcomed the Americans and made excuses for their alien ways, yet
he always remained every inch a Spaniard, and a gentleman. His
house at Sonoma is not grand by European standards, but it
represented power and wealth in the colonial period of California,
and it reflects the complex personality of the fascinating Vallejo.

North-west of Sonoma, on an isolated stretch of coast, is Fort
Ross, where Russia maintained a garrison and a trading post from
1812 to 1841. The fort has been restored and is open to the public,
and there is also a little Russian church.

Some sixty miles east of Sonoma is Sacramento, today the
capital of the state of California but once the site of Sutter's Fort.
Johann Augustus Sutter was a Swiss-German who had come to
America to seek his fortune, and then drifted west to California
when that territory was still solidly Spanish. He was given permission to build a trading post where Sacramento now stands,
and the trading post soon became a fort and the centre of an
almost feudal empire. As Sutter's Fort, it was the goal of many of
the first American settlers who came over the mountains into
California; Sutter helped them to establish themselves up and
down the Sacramento Valley. His industry was to be his undoing,
however. In 1847, he sent a company of men east of Sutter's Fort
to build a mill on the American River, and the men discovered
gold there. In the gold rush which followed, poor John Sutter
was ruined, for everyone took to the hills in search of easy money
and all of his enterprises collapsed for lack of labour. The
state of California has now reconstructed Sutter's Fort, and it too
is open to the public, in the heart of the modern city.

.   .   .   .   .

California changed dramatically with the gold rush. Five years earlier it had taken wagon trains four months to come from Missouri to California. Now the Overland Stage began to make regular runs from St Joseph, Missouri, to Sacramento in only twenty-one days. And a little village called Yerba Buena at the entrance to San Francisco Bay finally came into its own, as the port nearest the gold camps. For a booming town, Yerba Buena was a cumbersome name; the citizens decided to change it to San Francisco.

The city of San Francisco has been an exciting place ever since its re-christening. The original settlement there had been started in 1776, with a mission and a small garrison, the usual *presidio*. But it never amounted to much until the excitement over gold brought thousands of men swarming through town. San Francisco then became the logical place to spend your money if you had had a lucky strike, and also the logical place to drown your sorrows if you had been ruined.

The section along the waterfront was known as the Barbary Coast in the gold-rush days. It was a den of thieves, a haven for every vice, and a likely place for a man to be shanghaied. However, San Francisco is built on very steep hills which rise straight up from the water's edge, and it was simple for those men who were becoming millionaires overnight to shield their families from the unpleasantness along the docks. They simply put their great houses on the heights: hence 'Nob' Hill.

Most of the early San Francisco fortunes were built on California gold. Later there were the even more profitable gold and silver strikes around Virginia City, Nevada, just across the California border, and more millions to be made in California land sales, both honest and dishonest, and the additional millions to be accumulated from shipping and railroads and banking. One o the interesting things about San Francisco is the way in which all of this pyramiding wealth was firmly controlled by a mere handful of men who began with nothing and ended with a financial empire. In fact there were really only four men, Collis Huntington, Leland Stanford, Mark Hopkins, and Charles Crocker, and you still encounter their names everywhere in California. Alternating Machiavellian skill and crude force, they managed to keep almost everything in their own hands. Only when stricter federal regulations began to be applied to business dealings was their iron grip

1 San Francisco. A steep street running down to the bay, with Oakland Bridge
in the background

12a Ancient trees in the rain forests, Olympic National Park, Washington

12b On the Monterey Peninsula, California

on San Francisco and most of California finally loosened. For that
matter, San Francisco does still have the air of being a neat, con-
tainable, private world. It is not very big, really; it goes up and
down but it does not sprawl in the manner of most cities. A
delightful sort of intimacy is one of its charms. When you have
been there a day, you feel very much a part of it.

There is a freshness and excitement in San Francisco, and the
air is like wine on the clear days of summer and autumn. Tourists
there show an alarming tendency to forget they are tourists, so, in
keeping with the spirit of the place, we have only one full day of
sight-seeing within the city to suggest; after that our readers are
on their own. We will assume that they will be staying at an hotel
near Union Square, at the heart of everything.

The first thing to do is to take a cable car to Fisherman's Wharf,
for a tour of the harbour. We suggest that you go there in the
morning because San Francisco, viewed from the Bay, is at its
best then, with the sun shining towards the city and the Golden
Gate Bridge. But we must confess that one is thus restricted to
the one-hour cruise; the two-hour boat tours go only in the afternoon. The cable cars are themselves one of the great delights of
San Francisco, and they are not merely tourist attractions but very
much a part of the city transport system. Fisherman's Wharf, on
the other hand, has become very touristy. One can hardly see the
fishing boats for the souvenir shops, and the restaurants there are
very tourist-minded too. However, it is probably the logical place
to eat when one returns from the harbour trip. Abalone, sand
dabs, Rex sole, Dungeness crabs, and Olympia oysters are all
delicious West Coast fish specialties, and most of them are
available at the restaurants along Fisherman's Wharf.

After lunch, you should take a cable car back up the hill and
ask to be let off near Chinatown. Many American cities have a
Chinatown; New York City has one, and there are Chinese districts in Seattle and Los Angeles too. But San Francisco's Chinatown is deservedly the most famous. Local people will tell you
that it is not what it used to be, and that the things sold there
today are mostly Japanese because of the current embargo on
imports from Communist China. Nonetheless there is a large
Chinese colony in San Francisco, and the majority of them live
and shop in this district; Chinatown is still fascinating. It is true
that one no longer sees elderly Chinese gentlemen sporting

Q

pig-tails, but we like what one sees instead: a modern industrious people who have blended the old and the new in a practical but colourful manner, respecting tradition. One of the most engaging examples of this blending is the Ping Yuen public housing project on Pacific Avenue, thoroughly contemporary in design but with gay Chinese trimmings. The exterior decoration was added at the specific request of the Chinese community.

The only other San Francisco tourist sight we would insist on is a view from high up, best just at sunset, with the glow fading into the Pacific and the lights going on all over San Francisco and the great Bay area. The traditional place from which to enjoy this view is the Top of the Mark in the Mark Hopkins Hotel on Nob Hill, where one can have merely a drink, or dinner. The Top of the Mark, however, now has a rival in the top of the Fairmount Hotel across the way, and the Fairmount even has a special lift which runs on the outside of the building, providing an exciting view all the way up.

There is no lack of things to do at night in San Francisco. There are several exceptionally good restaurants, and while the best ones are hardly cheap, they are not nearly so expensive as the best ones in New York City or Los Angeles. Moreover there are any number of inexpensive places to eat, mostly Italian, in the North Beach district just east of Chinatown. North Beach was the original spawning-ground of the beatnik, and it is full of coffee bars and paper-back bookshops, but it is also the liveliest part of San Francisco after dark. In a good many cities, night clubs are expensive, overcrowded, smoke-filled, and frequently a deadly bore. In San Francisco they are an unmitigated delight. Some offer good jazz or witty monologuists (Mort Sahl got his start at 'the hungry i' here) or folk singers (the Kingston Trio had its first success at 'The Purple Onion'). Some are rococo and mock-sinful in the grand manner, with girls on swings flying back and forth over the customers' heads. Others are dedicated to Italian opera, with the entertainment a ceaseless flow of arias. But most of them are surprisingly inexpensive, and the custom is to stroll along Columbus Avenue and Jackson Street and Montgomery, sampling several places in one night.

San Francisco is a very sophisticated city, with smartly dressed women and a glittering opera season in the autumn. There are all sorts of tempting shops in the Union Square area. Two of the most distinctive are Gump's, which makes a specialty of expensive Oriental things and jade jewellery, and V. C. Morris, which sells china and *objets d'art* in a building designed by Frank Lloyd Wright. But San Francisco also relishes its links with California's past. The Wells Fargo Bank at the corner of Market and Montgomery Streets, not far from Union Square, has a 'history room' where visitors can inspect a Wells Fargo stagecoach, a collection of guns, samples of gold ore, and many other mementoes of the old days. It is right across the street from another thriving relic of San Francisco's past, the Palace Hotel. The original Palace, like so many of the early San Francisco landmarks, was burned in the fire which followed the 1906 earthquake. But it was rebuilt with much of the old magnificence, and it is still the favourite hotel of San Francisco traditionalists.

Other than the tiny Wells Fargo museum, San Francisco really has no museums or galleries worthy of so noble a city, and the citizens have consistently refused to vote the money necessary to house the superb Brundage collection of Oriental art, so that those treasures languish in a warehouse. There are several museums and exhibits in Golden Gate Park, on the ocean side of the city, but the collections there at present cannot be compared with those of the East.

You might like to see San Francisco's mission, familiarly known as the Mission Dolores. It is not as rich as some of the other missions farther south in California, and it is rather out of the way, but it has a fine ceiling and a lovely little garden where one still hears Spanish-speaking children at play on the other side of the wall.

San Francisco occupies only a comparatively small space right at the entrance to the Bay; beyond it and across from it are other places to be explored, and for this one would have to rely either on a bus tour or a hired car. The bus tours are not cheap, and if there were more than two people involved, one would save money hiring a car. The city itself seems not to have very heavy traffic, and so it is easy enough to drive there, except that most of the streets go at a precipitous angle up and down the hills. Anyone parking a car in San Francisco has to be very sure that his brakes are well on and his car's wheels turned into the kerb; there is a strictly enforced law about this.

For visitors who have not seen the California coast and the

giant redwood trees, one likely excursion would be to Muir
Woods and the coast beyond it. This is not at all far. Muir Woods
is in Marin County, a peninsula just across the Golden Gate Bridge
from San Francisco; it is astonishing how soon one can leave the
city behind. On the way to Muir Woods, it is pleasant to leave the
main road briefly in order to look at Sausalito, and perhaps Tiburon and Belvedere as well. Sausalito was once a picturesque fishing village; it is now a picturesque artists' colony. There are
several tempting restaurants there, but it is also a fine place to
assemble a picnic to eat later on the cliffs above the Pacific. (Any
proper San Francisco picnic must include a bottle of good California wine, a loaf of sourdough bread, and a variety of California
fruit.) Tiburon and Belvedere are less bohemian, more fashionable; the ideal place to live if one wants to be out of the city.

There are many places between which to choose after Muir
Woods and perhaps a quick look at the coast beyond it. For
example, not far away is Sonoma, with its mission and its many
associations with early California history. In addition, the best-
known section of the California wine country is in the Napa
Valley just east of Sonoma. Two of the largest vineyards there are
Christian Brothers and Louis Krug, opposite each other north of
Rutherford. The Christian Brothers' winery leans towards mass
production; the Krug wines are in general more costly, but the
best ones are really excellent. Good California wine is very good
indeed; even at its very best, it cannot be compared with the finest
French wines, but it is certainly the equal of good Italian wine. At
Louis Krug and Christian Brothers, as at most California vineyards, one can tour the caves.

The owners of one of the largest vineyards now allow the public
to share their sybaritic existence from time to time: Paul Masson
has 'Music at the Vineyards' during the summer, combining concerts with champagne suppers under the trees. Paul Masson,
however, is not in the Napa Valley but near Saratoga, in the other
important vineyard-area, south of San Francisco. Almadén, our
own favourite, lies in that direction too. Almadén is one of the
few large vineyards to combine quantity and variety with a strict
adherence to the vital traditions and a high standard. But the
Santa Clara Valley around Almadén is now being smothered in
housing developments and is thus not as attractive as the Napa
Valley.

To see Sausalito, Muir Woods, the coast, Sonoma, and the
Napa Valley vineyards all in one day would be impossible. However one could choose two or three of these points of interest, and
there might even be time to see the University of California at
Berkeley on the way back to San Francisco. It lies on the east side
of the Bay, and one would then return over the Oakland Bridge.
In American university circles the rivalry between Harvard and
the University of California is a source of endless talk. Each in its
way is unique: Harvard the venerable centre of academic excellence, steeped in New England traditions, and the University of
California, bursting with energy and new ideas, and boasting more
Nobel Prize winners than any other university in America. To see
them both is to grasp the enormous contrast between the eastern
United States and the west, for their settings and the look of the
buildings and the undergraduates are so completely different.

There are mountains all along California's spine, the towering
Sierra Nevadas. With such peaks as Mount Whitney, 14,495 feet
high, the Sierras represented the final formidable obstacle to
wagon trains heading for California in the nineteenth century.
Today, however, they supply California with much of her recreation, and in the Sierras lies Yosemite National Park. Like everyone on the West Coast, Californians are never indoors when they
can be out, surf-boarding at the beaches or climbing a mountain.
For many of them, Yosemite is now an old story. The newest
gambit is to 'pack' into the less familiar parts of the Sierras
between Yosemite and Sequoia-Kings Canyon National Park; at
towns like Bishop and Bigpine on the eastern slope of the mountains, one can hire pack-horses and a guide quite cheaply. The
guide takes you up into the high country, helps you to find a good
camp-site, and leaves you there in splendid solitude; he returns to
'pack' you out in a week or a month or whenever you say.
   But for new-comers to the Sierras, Yosemite is still the finest
introduction, with perfect mountain scenery: a deep and lovely
valley, its walls rising sheer for 4,000 feet in some places, and wild
and unspoiled high country above the valley.
   An Englishman, James Hutchings, was the first to write about
the valley, in 1856. But even more important to the future of the
Yosemite region was the proselytizing of Scottish-born John
Muir, a naturalist who came West for his health and became

tremendously excited about California, with its giant trees and its majestic mountains. Muir Woods, near San Francisco, was named in his honour, and there is also a Muir Trail in Yosemite National Park.

Like all enthusiasts, John Muir wanted people to share his pleasures, and he urged everyone to see Yosemite. In the 1880's, an hotel was built there and tourists began to come. But it was not at all like Yellowstone, where one could be driven right up to the natural wonders and perhaps even see them without stepping out of the carriage. An English guidebook of that day was clearly torn: the vistas at Yosemite were certainly impressive, but could one seriously suggest that ladies ride mules through the wilderness?

The National Park Service has now made several parts of the Park accessible by car. One can drive straight across it to the Tuolumne Meadows section of the high country, or to Glacier Point, from which there is a breathtaking view of the entire valley and its waterfalls. And one can drive into the heart of the valley. The most dramatic approach is from Merced, west of the Park, or from Fresno to the south; fortunately these are the routes which the bus services into the Park follow.

There are hotels and lodges in Yosemite as well as camp-sites, and camping equipment can be hired at the Park. There are, they say, 700 miles of trails to walk or ride along, and Yosemite, like Glacier National Park, has a series of hostels along the finest of the high trails where one can get supper and a bed and breakfast, and thus do the trail with very little in the way of camping gear.

The most remarkable stands of giant sequoia trees are to be found south of Yosemite, at Sequoia-Kings Canyon National Park, which protects another magnificent section of the Sierras. But Yosemite has three groves of sequoias too. The sequoia tree, also known as the Wellingtonia, is related to the redwoods of the coast, which are the trees in Muir Woods and along Route 101 in northern California. The Douglas fir and the Sitka spruce and the other enormously tall trees of Washington and Oregon are quite different, merely lusty specimens of 'normal' trees. Sequoias and redwoods, however, are a botanic curiosity, survivors of a prehistoric world. Logically, they should have disappeared with the brontosaurus, or have been ground to a pulp beneath the glaciers, never to rise again. Redwood trees are generally taller than sequoias; one redwood measures 368 feet, whereas sequoias usually stop just short of 300 feet. Sequoias, however, are thicker, 30 feet or more across. Sequoias also live to a riper age; the unfortunate baby redwood can only look forward to a life span of 2,000 years or so, while his sequoia cousin may live twice as long.

In the winter, most of Yosemite closes down because of snow. There is ski-ing, however, and one can still go into the valley section by way of the Merced-Arched Rock entrance. There is a bus service from Merced all the year round. Late spring is lovely at Yosemite, for the spectacular waterfalls are then at their best and the Park is not yet crowded. In the summer the hotels are likely to be booked for weeks or months ahead, and every camp-site is sure to be taken early in the day. Then in September the crowds disappear, the trees begin to turn red and gold, and Yosemite is once again not only beautiful but tranquil as well.

Anyone with time to spare could have a fine loop-trip from San Francisco, combining Yosemite with Lake Tahoe and the old gold-mining towns of the Forty-Niners. Many of the California gold camps were just tent colonies which disappeared without trace when the surface gold ran out. But others were more permanently built. None of these towns were ever as large as the great mining towns of the Colorado Rockies, but all ghost towns are somewhat alike. Here, in the lovely foothills of the Sierras, the unpainted frame houses sag, abandoned, with brave bits of wooden or iron filigree clinging to the porches, and the Wells Fargo sign still discernible on the sturdiest building in town. Appropriately, State Route 49 goes past most of these ghost towns. One of the best, Columbia, is now protected by the state, and many of its buildings are being restored.

The gold camps were along the western slope of the Sierras. Lake Tahoe is east and north of them, over the main ridge of the mountains in a valley 6,000 feet up on the California-Nevada border. It is an exceptionally beautiful lake, crystal clear and deep blue, ringed with dark pine trees and snowy mountain peaks. There are many motels and lodges at Lake Tahoe, as well as a state camping-site. In addition, just across the Nevada border is Reno, where the roulette wheels spin.

The slight cleft in the Sierras near Lake Tahoe was the usual route into California in the early days. It was hardly an easy route, but it was at least preferable to the vast desert at the southern end of the mountains, so long as one crossed before the snows came. Yet this crossing of the Sierras came at the end of many cruel trials: Indians on the Great Plains, and then the Rockies, and the waterless stretches of Utah and Nevada. For some wagon trains, the Sierras, that last test, proved too much. The grimmest example of this was the tragic Donner party, for whom the pass is named today. This party, through bad organization, was caught by the snows at the top of the Sierras and finally, after terrible privations, descended to cannibalism and murder.

The Monterey Peninsula is a very special part of California, with a strong, colourful character all its own. It is a little over a hundred miles south of San Francisco, and fortunately for visitors without a car, Gray Line runs twelve-hour bus tours there from San Francisco, three times a week for most of the year and daily in the summer.

The little town of Monterey was the Spanish capital of Alta California and the most important town in the colony right up to the moment when the American flag was raised over California. Even then it continued briefly to be the centre of things; the first state constitutional convention was held there. But after the discovery of gold, San Francisco eclipsed Monterey, and it became merely a peaceful fishing village. Retired Navy people, however, have always liked all of the Monterey peninsula, and in the 1930's, John Steinbeck's stories called additional attention to Monterey's indolent charm. Thus the town is now somewhat over-exploited. Its rich Spanish heritage is still plainly visible, however, especially in the area around the Friendly Plaza; even the town offices are housed in a handsome and historic building. Unfortunately, throngs of visitors in search of the picturesque tend to destroy whatever picturesque qualities a place may have, and the Monterey harbour is not what it used to be. But these are still the richest fishing waters of the whole California coast, and one can eat passably in the restaurants at the harbour and watch the fishing boats come in. You can go out on a fishing boat too, if you are willing to rise with the sun.

Along the peninsula beyond Monterey is Pacific Grove, a quiet community especially attractive to Monarch butterflies which winter there in vast numbers, covering the branches of the pine trees. And at Pacific Grove begins 'The 17-Mile Drive', a toll road which goes round the shore of the peninsula to Carmel. Robert Louis Stevenson is quoted as calling this peninsula 'the finest meeting place of land and water in existence'; if you take The 17-Mile Drive on a perfect day, you may be inclined to agree. The great attraction of the peninsula is the Monterey cypress, which is found only in this area. It is a cypress tree of a special sort, but in addition most specimens, clinging to the rocks along the coast, have been so warped and twisted by the winds that they look like Japanese bonsai trees seen through the wrong end of a telescope. Most of the peninsula is privately owned; there are houses here and there among the trees, and three golf clubs. But there is also a small strip of open beach and a picnic area along The 17-Mile Drive, and many viewpoints where one may park. Everything is left in its natural state, however, with no obtrusive organization or souvenir stands; a few spots are simply set aside so that the visitors themselves will be as unobtrusive as possible. The most spectacular part of the peninsula is unfortunately very private indeed, the purlieu of the Cypress Point Club. But there is a viewpoint near-by, with a telescope, so that one can see the westernmost rocks beyond the club grounds, where hundreds of sea-lions gather to sun themselves, together with pelicans and black gulls and cormorants and handsome grey gulls with pink beaks. In the early morning, even deer can sometimes be seen going over the road and across the Cypress Point golf course. At the southern end of The 17-Mile Drive there is a splendid inn, the Del Monte Lodge; it is, of course, very, very expensive to stay at but one can stop there for a drink to enjoy the view. Next to it is the celebrated Pebble Beach Golf Links, where anyone willing to pay the fee can arrange to play; much of the course is along the sea.

Just south of the Monterey Peninsula is Carmel, an extremely attractive little town. It is half retired Navy, half artists' colony, and expensively quaint; the citizens refuse to have any civic 'improvements' that would change the character of the place. There are any number of smart shops at Carmel where one can pay $20 for a gnarled piece of driftwood, but the Carmel Bach Festival in July is genuinely good, and Carmel would be a very pleasant place to spend a night at any time of the year. There are a great many inns and motels discreetly tucked away in the town and many of them are moderate in price. The Carmel beach is lovely: a curving strip of fine white sand shaded by Monterey cypresses and pines.

At Carmel there is one of the old Spanish mission churches, this one formally known as the Basilica of San Carlos Borromeo del Rio Carmelo. In many ways it is the most interesting of all the California missions today. It was the headquarters of Junipero Serra, the remarkable Franciscan who established the California mission system; Father Serra's cell and study here have been restored, and he is buried in the sanctuary. Moreover, this is certainly one of the most beautiful missions, with a striking parabolic ceiling, a splendid altar and reredos in the main church, a lovely little side chapel, a cloister, and a fine garden and setting.

On the exterior, the California mission churches are not particularly impressive. One must not expect sophisticated architecture, the splendours of colonial Mexico or something like a medieval European abbey; these are comparatively primitive adobe structures, built by the local Indians to a stock design. Moreover, the California missions lack the purity of the earlier mission churches of New Mexico, where the strong and timeless utilitarian form sometimes sets one to thinking about eighth-century Ireland or le Corbusier at Ronchamps. Nonetheless, almost all of the Spanish-Indian mission churches are worth seeing, particularly for their ingenuous and colourful interiors.

The twelve-hour Gray Line bus tour does not go beyond the Carmel mission. For anyone on the way to Los Angeles, however, more wonders lie ahead. Point Lobos, just south of Carmel along the coast, is a state park, with more of the beautiful Monterey cypress trees, more sea-lions, and more birds. While camping is not permitted there, it is an excellent place for a picnic, and the Mediterranean Market in Carmel an excellent source for picnic supplies.

The inland routes from San Francisco to Los Angeles go through fertile but rather dull country, dusty wherever it is not irrigated. The coast road, however, is spectacular. No regular buses run along this route, which helps to preserve its wild and lonely air although it is hard on the tourist without a car. However, there are guided bus tours which do go this way.

The coast road between Carmel and San Simeon, State Route 1, has been literally carved out of the side of the cliffs above the ocean in many places, yet it is not at all a frightening drive because the engineering has been so skilful. About thirty miles south of Carmel is the Big Sur region, where the coast is exceptionally rugged and craggy. The road goes inland here briefly, through a mountain valley which includes the Big Sur State Park, a fine wilderness area with camping-sites. But the coast remains the principal attraction. It is much admired by writers and artists, and one passes two or three houses clinging dramatically to the cliffs. Equally dramatic in its situation is a restaurant called Nepenthe, where the food and the view are both magnificent but the prices high. At the risk of sounding like hardened alcoholics, we again suggest that one can after all simply stop there for a drink.

After Big Sur, it is another sixty or seventy miles to San Simeon, with spectacular vistas all along the way and only a few isolated houses. San Simeon itself is a village, but it is also the name of a fantastic mock-castle on the heights above, which was the creation of William Randolph Hearst, that most powerful and eccentric of American newspaper publishers. It is an incredible place, incredibly beautiful on the outside, with terraced gardens and pools and orange and lemon trees on a peak overlooking the Pacific and the mountains, and incredible inside in quite another way. On a foggy day, when the setting is not at its best, San Simeon might seem almost grotesque, but on a fine day, with the sun sparkling on the ocean and the air heavy with the scent of the trees, San Simeon is entrancing.

San Simeon now belongs to the state, and one can see it only on a guided tour. The tours begin at the foot of the mountain; buses take groups up to the top at regular intervals, passing the little herds of zebras which are now all that is left of the San Simeon menagerie. Since the capacity of the bus is limited, the tour-groups are limited in size too, and in summer particularly it is necessary to reach San Simeon early in the day in order to be sure of a place at all. Even then one may have to wait two or three hours for one's turn. The alternative is to write well in advance for a reservation, but that costs $3 apiece instead of the normal $2.

South of San Simeon the route flattens out and is much less dramatic. There are a few pretty bays, but there are also clusters of oil wells, and towns, and people. However, just north of Santa Barbara and a few miles inland, there is the unique little settlement of Solvang. As the name suggests, this is a Danish community; it was founded only in 1912. Solvang is thoroughly Danish in appearance (and it has an excellent Danish pastry shop, fine for tea). It also boasts a Spanish mission, once almost the only thing there. Called the Mission of Santa Inés, this is not one of the more famous ones, but the interior decorations have faded to a lovely pastel which gives it a quality all its own. Many of the Spanish missions were completely abandoned in the nineteenth century, and some almost crumbled away entirely. This was not due to the Americanization of California, but to a battle between the civil and religious authorities in California's Mexican period which ended in the secularization of the missions. For a time in the nineteenth century, Santa Inés was used as a farmhouse, but the basic structure was not damaged and the Capuchins have since restored it.

There are many towns along the coast north of Los Angeles, but the biggest and most famous is Santa Barbara, long the favourite winter resort of rich and conservative people from the East. It is beautifully situated between the mountains and the sea, and no expense has been spared to keep the Spanish sections Spanish and make the nice parts nicer. Santa Barbara also has the best preserved of all the missions, a large and impressive structure which is now the mother-house of the Franciscan Order in California. It lacks the intimate charm of San Carlos Borromeo or Santa Inés, but it has its own particular attractions, not the least of them the fact that the Franciscans themselves act as guides there.

Strangers are prone to arrive in Los Angeles expecting a proper city, with a glamorous Hollywood attached to one edge, and Disneyland somewhere in between. Unhappily, things are not nearly so neat. Los Angeles has been described as fifty suburbs in search of a city, and this is painfully accurate. 'Downtown' Los Angeles is rather insignificant, sad and neglected. It is simply the place where all the freeways intersect, plaited over and under each other in a splendid futuristic tangle. It does have the Civic Center, where one might go to the Hall of Justice to see how a criminal case is tried in this most American of American cities. And it also has Olvera Street, which is not a street at all, but a colourful alleyway lined with stalls selling Mexican baskets and cafés offering Mexican food. Olvera Street is near the old Spanish plaza with its mission, and it is pleasant to spend an hour or two in this little area, still very Mexican but completely engulfed by an alien culture.

No matter what one's opinion of guided bus tours usually is, Los Angeles is the place to take them. Only the most reckless visitors would want to venture on to the freeways in a hired car; and while the city bus service tries its best, no system of public transport could possibly cope adequately with a metropolitan area that keeps doubling and tripling its population until it now sprawls for fifty miles from end to end.

However, any visitor who can beg or borrow a car in Los Angeles should some evening hie himself to the top of the hills which rear up to form the northern limits of the city. This is now considered one of the most desirable places in greater Los Angeles to live, partly because it provides such a breathtaking panorama at night, with the sea of lights stretching endlessly away. Many of the successful film people live in these hills, and many others live just below them, in Bel Air and Beverly Hills, or Westwood, or Santa Monica, three sub-divisions of greater Los Angeles which merge one into the other on the northern edge of the city. Going along Santa Monica Boulevard through Beverly Hills, one finds vendors at every corner selling 'maps to the movie stars' homes'. The stars came here because it is near Hollywood, but Hollywood itself is not really a centre of excitement any more. Many of the old studios are now devoted to television, others have moved, and in addition more and more 'Hollywood' films are actually shot on location, in other parts of America or in Europe. The only way to see the inside of a film studio these days is to take a guided bus tour which includes that among its sights; the studios themselves no longer offer tours. But one can of course make a pilgrimage to the corner of Hollywood Boulevard and Vine Street, at the heart of Hollywood, and contemplate the ornate film palaces like Grauman's Chinese Theater, imagining how exotic Hollywood must have seemed thirty years ago.

The easiest way to convey the geography of greater Los Angeles and the location of its various points of interest is to pre-tend that the centre of the city is the centre point of a clock dial, with 12 o'clock due north. Santa Monica, the nearest attractive seaside area, is then at 9 o'clock, twenty miles from the centre of town, and Beverly Hills and Hollywood are 10 o'clock and 11 respectively. At 10.30, so to speak, and not quite so far out, is the

Farmers' Market at Fairfax and Third Streets. We mentioned it earlier in connexion with the Pike Street Market in Seattle. The Los Angeles market is much bigger, and its wares no longer bear much relation to its name. There are handsome vegetables there, to be sure, and splendid fruit, including every imaginable variety of date from the California desert country. But there are also cheeses from all over the world and exotic groceries of every kind, and a large separate building with shops selling everything from Guatemalan blouses to Swedish Christmas-tree ornaments. There are restaurants too, and stalls which sell cooked food to eat on the spot: Chinese, Mexican, Italian.

About ten blocks south of the Farmers' Market, at Fairfax and Wilshire Boulevard, is something new in Los Angeles: a Japanese department store. Called Seibu, it is owned by a Tokyo firm. The West Coast has recently become tremendously excited about Japanese décor and design, and this is one of the results. Ten blocks would not normally be considered very close, but in Los Angeles it seems almost miraculous to find one attraction actually within walking distance of another. And once one reaches Wilshire Boulevard, there is direct bus service either back to central Los Angeles or out to the smart shops of Beverly Hills.

At 1 o'clock on our imaginary dial is Forest Lawn Memorial Park, that fantastically organized cemetery which Evelyn Waugh dissected in *The Loved One*. It may seem a most unlikely tourist attraction but in fact Gray Line runs special trips there. For those whose tastes are more conventional, however, there is something else in this same direction, a little way beyond the city limits near Pasadena. It is the marvellous Huntington Library and Gallery, one of the very finest collections of rare books and pictures in the United States. The gardens at the Huntington Library are remarkable too, with a special section devoted to desert plants.

Half-way to Pasadena from central Los Angeles, just off the Pasadena Freeway, is the only other museum which deserves attention: the Southwest Museum, with its superb American Indian Collection. Surprisingly few local people seem to be aware of its riches, yet it is a fascinating place, comparable only to the Museum of the American Indian in New York City.

Los Angeles is a bizarre combination of Hollywood glitter and provincial innocence. A great many people here in southern California have come originally from small towns in the Midwest, and ever since the end of the nineteenth century the climate of this region has lured people retiring on small pensions. Moreover, California has always attracted more than its share of visionaries. It seems only fitting, therefore, that Los Angeles' bravest monument should be a strange and wonderful construction known as the Watts Towers. According to our clock-dial plan, the Watts Towers are in a six o'clock direction just off the Harbor Freeway, almost ten miles south of central Los Angeles in one of the dreariest sections of the city. But a peregrinating art critic of *The Times* has called them 'One of the oddest and most touching works of art in America, and one of the most remarkable achievements of folk art anywhere . . . part ship, part cathedral, part pleasure garden'. They are the work of a gentle Italian immigrant named Simon Rodia, who devoted thirty years of loving labour to building this great spiralling, soaring, intricate structure out of broken bits of glass and tile and tin enmeshed in a steel framework. The highest tower reaches ninety-nine feet into the air; the effect is not grotesque, as one might expect, but genuinely and innocently beautiful.

The greatest tourist attraction in the Los Angeles area today is Disneyland, Walt Disney's splendid fun-fair. It is farther from the centre of the city than any of the other places we have mentioned, in a south-easterly '4.30' direction. However, one can go there on an ordinary bus; a Disneyland Freeway Flyer starts at the main Metropolitan Transit Authority station in Los Angeles. There are also day-long Gray Line bus tours which include both Disneyland and Knott's Berry Farm. One can even get there by helicopter, from the Los Angeles airport; there is also a helicopter service to many other distant corners of the greater Los Angeles area. If one cares about getting a turn on the various rides at Disneyland without long waits, it is wise to get there early in the day, particularly at week-ends and in the summer. Note too that it is closed entirely on Monday and Tuesday in the autumn and winter months.

No matter how sophisticated one's tastes may be, everyone seems to love Disneyland. Even those who begin with a superior sniff are usually captivated sooner or later by some especially delightful bit of fantasy. One of the most pleasant aspects of Disneyland is the meticulous neatness and cleanliness. In fact the only real criticism we have heard came from one visitor who complained that Disneyland was positively antiseptic; she said she much preferred the casual disorder and confusion of Knott's Berry Farm near by, where the main attraction is a rip-roaring simulation of the old West, with stagecoach rides and a chance to pan for gold. Perhaps in deference to Knott's Berry Farm, a much older enterprise, Disneyland rather neglects the world of the cowboy and the prospector, and concentrates instead on space (Tomorrowland) and the fairytale (Fantasyland) and the quainter aspects of nineteenth-century America (Main Street and Frontierland).

There is one last tourist attraction in the greater Los Angeles area which deserves to be mentioned: Marineland, on the coast west of Disneyland and almost forty miles from central Los Angeles. Marineland is essentially an elaborate aquarium combined with a porpoise circus like the two in Florida. Like them, it is a fascinating place, and the Palos Verdes peninsula on which it is situated is also attractive, not yet over-populated, and offering a lovely view of the Pacific from its hills. On the coast near Marineland there is a small church built entirely of glass, the Wayfarers' Chapel.

Going south from Los Angeles along the coast, you pass one beach resort after another, many of them quite unattractive. One of the best is Laguna, which is also an artists' colony. Five or six miles south of Laguna is a particularly famous mission, San Juan Capistrano. Most of it now lies in ruins, but they are highly romantic ruins, with white doves perched on the crumbling arches of the cloisters. And thirty miles farther on is still another mission, San Luis Rey. This last was one of the largest missions, and it is still in use, a handsome building with a delightful, gaudy interior. Near the missions, and in the inland valleys of this region, are countless orange and lemon groves. The industrious Spanish missionaries introduced the cultivation of these fruit trees to California in the eighteenth century, and they are now an important part of the economy.

The city of San Diego, almost at the Mexican border, is a year-round resort town where the temperature is almost the same in January as in June. With an excellent harbour, San Diego is an important naval base, and it has fine beaches too. All of this one might expect, but we should also mention that the San Diego zoo is celebrated throughout the country for its innovations in animal care and the excellence of its collection.

Anyone who is in San Diego is bound to be tempted to go across the border into Mexico. This part of Mexico cannot compare with the region around Mexico City and farther south, but provided one gets beyond the border town of Tiajuana, it has its own special charm, and certainly it is completely unlike the United States.

Los Angeles can be very hot in the summer. In the winter it is never really cold, but there is good ski-ing in the mountains east of the city. Many Los Angeles people, however, do not long for snow in the winter but for a hotter sun, and so they like to go inland to the desert. A surprising amount of southern California is properly considered desert. Some of this is simply very arid land, which normally supports only cactus and desert plants but which can be made fertile with irrigation. But much of the Mojave Desert, in particular, is the kind of desert one sees in films: endless rolling seas of sand.

The Imperial Valley, in the southernmost part of California east of San Diego, is a desert which has been made fertile. It is now astonishingly rich, perhaps the richest land in all of California, interesting to see in winter, but blazing hot in the summer.

Equally unbearable in summer, and not in the least fertile, is Death Valley, due east of the Monterey Peninsula but far inland, touching the Nevada border. Many a man coming to California in the early days lost his life in Death Valley; it earned its name over and over again. Now, however, many people enjoy driving through it in the cooler months, and there is an elaborate inn there as well as a less expensive one near by. Californians are fond of pointing out that their state has tremendous variety and contrast, and it is a fact that only eighty miles separate the highest point in the United States outside Alaska, Mount Whitney in the Sierras (14,495 feet) and the very lowest point, 280 feet below sea level, in Death Valley.

The most famous desert resort in California is Palm Springs, a splendid oasis town about a hundred miles south-east of Los Angeles. Handsomely situated at the foot of some mountains, over the years it has become increasingly prosperous and dazzling, with countless hotels and motels and tempting shops. Every hotel,

R

every motel, every house seems to have its own swimming pool, and there are also several golf courses, which consume a million gallons of water a day. Date palms flourish in this vicinity too. The town of Indio, a few miles south of Palm Springs, positively overflows with dates, and one soon discovers that there are all sorts of delicious varieties undreamt of in the grocery shops of colder climes. East of Palm Springs is the Joshua Tree National Monument, a mountainous section of desert with bizarre volcanic outcroppings and many fascinating desert plants. The most remarkable is the variety after which the region is named, the Joshua tree, a giant yucca or desert lily. Joshua trees sometimes grow forty feet tall and they have enormous greenish blossoms in the spring.

If one goes to California in the midst of summer, the desert can only be hurried through in the coolest hours of the day or night and it will hardly seem very attractive. But visitors who are in California at other times of the year would be missing a great deal if they did not have at least a quick look at California's desert country.

SPECIAL KNOWLEDGE

It seems to be generally agreed that the California Zephyr between San Francisco and Chicago provides the finest of all **train rides** to the West Coast. But all the major railroads co-operate in allowing round-trips which go by one route and return by another at no extra cost. Thus one could take the California Zephyr west and then return to the east by way of Arizona and New Mexico on the Santa Fé Railroad from Los Angeles, perhaps stopping over to see the Grand Canyon on the way. Or one might head back east from Seattle across the northern United States, with the possibility of stopping to see Glacier National Park in Montana.

There are various **bus tours** available on the West Coast, including California Parlor Car Tours, which go to all the most celebrated points of interest in California. Their rates work out at almost $30 a day per person all-in. One alternative is the Avis-Tanner-Gray Line scheme for a planned but self-guided tour in a hired car, with hotel rooms booked along the way. Taking the same amount of time as the California Parlor Car Tours (three days and two nights between San Francisco and Los Angeles), this scheme also works out at about $30 a day per person, but for a party of four the cost drops to about $20 a day per person. Both tours can be stretched to five days in order to include a visit to Yosemite (pronounced Yo-sem-it-ee).

Visitors to the West Coast may be glad to know that both trailers (caravans) and tents can usually be hired there for **camping.** The National Parks are of course magnificent, but the State Park systems on the West Coast are superb too, the best in the country. Anyone who plans to do any climbing might get in touch with the Sierra Club, the biggest mountain-climbing organization in the United States.

During the driest months, one encounters 'no smoking' signs out of doors, sometimes even in the Hollywood Hills within what seems to be an almost urban area. **Fire** is a deadly menace in the West at certain times of the year, and these 'no smoking' notices apply even to people going through in cars.

When **driving** in California one can turn right on a red light after stopping to make sure the road is clear. This is something Americans from the East find hard to adjust to, for in most parts of the United States one cannot move at all on a red light.

San Francisco has a reliable economy **car hire** firm, Jack Bartlett Airways Rent-a-Car, in addition to the usual Avis and Hertz.

In both Seattle and San Francisco, taxis are expensive but eating is relatively cheap. Seattle, in particular, seems to have several inexpensive cafeterias where the **food** is much better than adequate. In Los Angeles, city of the future as it is, most of the inexpensive restaurants away from the centre of the town are designed for the restless motorist. Either one actually eats inside the car, at a super-spectacular drive-in, or else the restaurant forms the decorative centrepiece of a car park, and only the most daring non-conformist would risk arriving on foot.

All sorts of interesting things go on in Los Angeles in the way of experimental **theatre and music and art,** but the city is so spread-out and fragmented that it is hard for a stranger to cope. The easiest way to learn what's afoot is to study the entertainment section of the Los Angeles *Sunday Times*.

To learn the best **bus route** one can consult the M.T.A., the public transport system for greater Los Angeles. M.T.A. publishes an excellent bus guide but is also prepared to answer telephone inquiries: Richmond 7-4455.

Where one wants to stay in Los Angeles depends on what one wants to see, but it is well to remember that the farther inland one goes, the hotter it is in the summer, and that the infamous Los Angeles 'smog', when it comes, tends to be most intense in central Los Angeles. There are several pleasant and moderately priced **hotels** and motels near the sea in Santa Monica and near-by Westwood; close to a good beach as well as to what is left of the glamorous film world. There is also a cluster of motels around Disneyland, on the opposite side of the city. However, if one had no car and wanted easy access to the Gray Line tours and all the city bus routes, then one really would have to choose the centre of town after all.

The most glamourous **woman's shop** in any West Coast city is likely to be I. Magnin. There are eight or ten of them, each full of tantalizing clothes with the distinctive California touch.

Ashland, Oregon

OREGON SHAKESPEAREAN FESTIVAL. Reservations and information from Shakespeare, P.O. Box 27, Ashland. Nightly performances during summer.

Berkeley, California

UNIVERSITY OF CALIFORNIA, East of Oxford Street, between Hearst

Street and Bancroft Way. Bus tour Sunday 1 p.m. (arrangements through Associated Students Union on the campus). Student-conducted walking tours organized on request by office of Educational Relations at University Hall.

Carmel, California

BASILICA OF SAN CARLOS BORROMEO DEL RIO CARMELO, South of Carmel on State Route 1. 15 June to 15 September, daily 9–5.30; 16 September to 14 July, daily 9.30–5.

Fort Ross, California

FORT ROSS STATE HISTORICAL MONUMENT. Daily 9–5.

Los Angeles, California

CONVENTION AND VISITORS' BUREAU, Los Angeles County Chamber of Commerce, 404 South Bixel Street, Los Angeles 54.

METROPOLITAN TRANSIT AUTHORITY, 6th and Main Streets (Richmond 7-4555).

DISNEYLAND, 1313 Harbor Boulevard, off the Santa Ana Freeway at Anaheim. Summer, Monday to Friday 9–midnight, Saturday 9–1, Sunday 9–10. Early spring and autumn, Monday to Friday 10–6 or 7, Saturday 10–midnight, Sunday 10–9. Winter, Wednesday, Thursday, Friday 10–6, Saturday, Sunday 10–7.

FOREST LAWN MEMORIAL PARK, 1712 S. Glendale Avenue, Glendale. Daily 9–5.

HUNTINGTON LIBRARY AND GALLERY, off Huntington Drive, San Marino. 1 November to 30 September, Tuesday to Sunday 1–4.30. Free.

KNOTT'S BERRY FARM, Beach Boulevard off Santa Ana Freeway, at Buena Park. Monday to Friday 10–9.30, Saturday 10–10, Sunday 10–9.

MARINELAND, Palos Verdes Drive South at Long Point. Daily 10–sunset. Feeding times, 11.45, 1.15, 3, 5, 6.45.

SOUTHWEST MUSEUM, 234 Museum Drive. Tuesday to Sunday 4.45. Closed Mondays. Free.

WATTS TOWERS, 1765 East 107th Street. Daily 12–sunset.

Monterey Peninsula, California

GRAY LINE TOUR, Gray Line Terminal, 44 Fourth Street, San Francisco. 16 June to 15 September, daily at 8; 16 September to 15 June, Sunday, Tuesday, Thursday at 8. Tour lasts 12 hours.

Sacramento, California

SUTTER'S FORT, 28th and L Streets. Daily 10–5. Closed Thanksgiving Day, 25 December. Free.

San Diego, California

SAN DIEGO ZOOLOGICAL GARDENS, Balboa Park, off Park Boulevard.

1 July to Labor Day, 9–6; Labor Day to 31 October, and 1 March to 30 June, 9–5; 1 November to 28 February, 9–4.30.

San Francisco, California

AVIS TANNER GRAY LINE TOURS, 425 4th Street, San Francisco, and 1207 West 3rd Street, Los Angeles 17. Three- and five-day self-drive tours.

BAY CRUISE, Harbor Tours Inc., Fisherman's Wharf, Pier 45. One-hour tour: 25 May to 30 September, daily 10–5 every 45 minutes; 1 October to 24 May, daily 11–4, every 75 minutes. Two-hour tour: 25 May to 31 October, daily 2; 1 November to 24 May, Saturday and Sunday, 2.

CALIFORNIA PARLOR CAR TOURS CO., 369 Market Street, San Francisco 5. Coast tour to Los Angeles and other tours around San Francisco.

MISSION DOLORES, Dolores Street, near 16th Street. 1 May to 31 October, daily 9–5; 1 November to 30 April, daily 10–4.

SIERRA CLUB, Mills Tower, San Francisco. Mountain climbing organization.

WELLS FARGO BANK MUSEUM, Market and Montgomery Streets. Every banking day, 10–3.

San Juan Capistrano, California

MISSION SAN JUAN CAPISTRANO. Winter, daily 8–5; Summer 8–6.

San Luis Rey de Francia

MISSION SAN LUIS REY DE FRANCIA, 3½ miles east of Oceanside on State Route 76. Monday to Saturday 9–5; Sunday 11.15–5.30.

San Simeon, California

HEARST SAN SIMEON STATE HISTORICAL MONUMENT, Mid-May to mid-October, daily 9–5; rest of year daily 9–3. Tours leave by bus from the parking lot just off State Route 1. 16 October to 15 June every half-hour; 16 June to 30 June every 20 minutes; 1 July to 31 August every 12 minutes; 1 September to 15 October every 20 minutes. Reservations (which are more expensive) from: Reservation Office, Division of Beaches and Parks, P.O. Box 2390, Sacramento 11, California.

Santa Barbara, California

MISSION SANTA BARBARA, Los Olivos and Laguna Streets. Summer, Monday to Saturday 9.30–5, Sunday 12–5; winter, Monday to Saturday 9.30–4.30, Sunday 12–4.30.

Seattle, Washington

SEATTLE CONVENTION AND TOURIST BUREAU, Seattle Chamber of Commerce, Seattle 4.

GRAY LINE TOURS, Gray Line Terminal, 8th and Dearborn Streets. 'Discovery' tour: 5 June to 11 September, daily 9, 1, 2.30, 4.30; 12 September to 4 June, daily 2. Lasts 2 hours. Waterfront tour: 3 April to 4 June and 12 September to 13 November, daily 10.30. Lasts 2¼ hours. Mount

Rainier 'Horizon' tour: 5 June to 11 September, daily 10. Lasts 8 to 9 hours.

JAPANESE TEA GARDEN, in the Arboretum in Washington Park. Monday to Saturday 10–7, Sunday 12–7. Closed at sunset in winter.

MUSEUM OF HISTORY AND INDUSTRY, 2720 Lake Washington Boulevard, N. Tuesday to Friday 11–5, Saturday 10–5, Sunday 12–5. Free.

SEATTLE ART MUSEUM, Volunteer Park. Tuesday to Saturday 10–5, Sunday and holidays 12–5, Thursday evening 7–10. Free.

Solvang, California

OLD MISSION SANTA INÉS. The church is always open.

Sonoma, California

MISSION SAN FRANCISCO SOLANO DE SONOMA. Daily 10–5, in summer till 6.

VALLEJO'S RANCH HOUSE. About a mile west of the Plaza. Daily 10–5. Free.

Vineyards

ALMADEN, Santa Clara Valley. Monday to Friday 9.30–3.

CHRISTIAN BROTHERS, Napa Valley, north of Rutherford. Daily 10.30–4.30.

LOUIS KRUG, Napa Valley, north of Rutherford. Daily 9.30–4.30.

PAUL MASSON, Saratoga Avenue, north east of Saratoga. Daily 10–4. Outdoor concerts occasionally during the summer.

Yachats, Oregon

SEA LION CAVES, 15 miles south of Yachats on U.S. Route 101. Lifts work continuously.

Yosemite National Park, California

Hotels are open from about 12 May to middle of September. There are good camp grounds and cabin accommodation in various parts of the park. Reservations from Yosemite Park and Curry Co., Yosemite National Park, California; or Geary Street, San Francisco 8; or 514 South Grand Avenue, Los Angeles 17.

10 · The Southwest

'It seemed to me the oldest country I had ever seen, the real antique land, first cousin to the moon . . . Man had been here such a little time that his arrival had not yet been acknowledged . . . The giant saguaro cactus, standing like a sentinel on every knoll, was not on the lookout for us, had not heard of us yet, still waiting for trampling dinosaurs . . . This country is geology by day and astronomy by night.'

It is J. B. Priestley speaking about Arizona, in a book called *Midnight in the Desert* which he wrote in the 1930's. No visitor to this part of America has written more perceptively about it; with Jacquetta Hawkes, he went on to do another superb book about the Southwest twenty years later, *Journey Down A Rainbow*.

There is no other section of the United States as fascinating to foreign visitors as the Southwest. It is not pretty, nor pleasant, nor even immediately attractive; it is a harsh, stark, arid land, sometimes ugly. But it has qualities not to be found anywhere else in the world. As Priestley said, the first impression is that it is all so incredibly old. Yet for tourists it is very new; only in the past fifty years have people begun to come to the Southwest on holiday. Until transport became easy and quick, tourists were not likely to venture into country which must have seemed no more congenial than the Sahara.

For our purposes, we are assuming that the Southwest consists of the states of Arizona, New Mexico, Nevada, and Texas, and the southernmost sections of Colorado and Utah. Within this large area, Texas means cowboys and oil to most people, Arizona and New Mexico mean Indians and desert, and Nevada – well Nevada has gambling and quick divorces and the smallest population of any American state although it is one of the biggest in area.

Nevada is incredible. It is barren, with no major rivers and virtually no rainfall. In the West, one soon becomes conscious of 'eastern slope' versus 'western slope', and the significance of the terms. Nevada lies on the eastern slope of the towering Sierra

Nevadas, which means that any moisture the clouds have carried from the Pacific has already been jolted out of them by those mountains before the clouds reach Nevada. Bare blue sky above, bare dry land below is all one sees. It goes without saying that Nevada is hardly a rich farming state, but there are a few fertile valleys and even in the most barren parts some cattle and sheep. Where vegetation is so sparse, one may need a grazing area of a hundred acres, two hundred acres, even more, for every animal one owns, so you may not actually see any animals at all. But they are there, the sheep up in the hills in the summer, often with Basque shepherds especially imported for the lonely life.

There are only two real population centres in Nevada, one around Reno, half-way down the western border of the state, and the other in the south-western corner at Las Vegas. The Reno area is the more attractive, and there is more to do and see there. First there is the lovely Lake Tahoe, just south of Reno on the California border west of Carson City. Carson City itself is the Nevada state capital, a small town which must be the most unprepossessing state capital in America. Then between Reno and Carson City there is Virginia City (not to be confused with the Virginia City in Montana), once the most fabulous mining town of them all and now virtually a ghost town.

In the boom days of the Comstock Lode, in the 1870's, there were 30,000 people at Virginia City; this was the richest 'strike' in the history of the West, almost four hundred million dollars in gold and silver yielded up in less than twenty years. Mining riches almost never come to the dogged, lonely prospector; the great fortunes here were made by coalitions of shrewd entrepreneurs from San Francisco, mostly men who had started off in life not as struggling miners but as struggling shopkeepers and money-lenders. Many of the Comstock Lode millionaires were the very prototypes of the villainous mineowners in standard Western films, busily cheating their partners and the general public. Some of them, however, were engagingly lavish with their riches, building great palaces at Virginia City fitted with marble and gold, dressing their wives in Paris velvets, importing entire opera companies for one evening's entertainment. Occasionally one of these new millionaires would take his wife and go off to do a tour of the Continent, where they must have cut quite a swathe with their rough Western manners and their limitless supply of money. The ordinary Virginia City miner, who earned high wages for his man-killing work, had extravagant pleasures too; for once, no Hollywood version could possibly be an exaggeration. In addition to the usual girls and the cold-eyed gamblers, there were the most famous entertainers in the world, actors and singers and public speakers; Virginia City paid well, and in any case everyone was curious to see it. The local newspaper, *The Territorial Enterprise*, even had the sort of witty, courageous editor films like to attribute to all Western towns, and Mark Twain, after a brief and catastrophic try at mining, did his first successful writing for this paper. Virginia City today is a tourist attraction because of its past; the old Opera House remains but the millionaire's palaces are gone, and it is all rather sad, like a crumbling film set.

Reno, as anyone in America can tell you, is where people go to get a divorce. Actually one can get an undefended divorce anywhere in Nevada after only six weeks' residence, and quickly in several other states too, but Reno is traditional. Usually the divorce-seeker stays at one of the inns or ranches at the edge of Reno, where he or she can while away the time beside a swimming pool or on a horse. There is always gambling too, for the whole of Nevada allows every kind of gambling. In fact they insist upon it, with fruit machines in every café and bus station; to a large extent, Nevada lives off her gambling revenues.

The most famous gambling town in Nevada is Las Vegas. Reno, in comparison, is gentle and innocent; in Reno one gambler may even express open pleasure at another gambler's luck. Las Vegas, never so gauche, attracts all the 'big money boys'. You can see them getting off the evening planes from Los Angeles; sometimes they fly to Las Vegas, gamble all night, and fly back to Los Angeles the next morning. The craps tables and the roulette tables keep going twenty-four hours a day; one of the startling experiences in the big Las Vegas hotels is to wend one's way in to breakfast past the busy wheels and the rattling dice. Yet although there is nothing light-hearted about the men who are betting a thousand dollars a throw, the atmosphere in Las Vegas as a whole is gay. The croupiers are business-like, but they are not the cold automatons of Monte Carlo or Cannes, and there is certainly no formality to frighten any one away. No one cares at all whether you are wearing blue jeans or a ball dress. Nor need you fill out any forms or sign a register and you can drift from casino to casino as the mood takes you. The only problem is adjusting to the presence of burly, heavily-armed, but astoundingly casual policemen.

To lure ever more customers, the casino owners import all sorts of expensive entertainment. It is possible to find such stars as Frank Sinatra, Marlene Dietrich, and Danny Kaye all in Las Vegas at the same time, appearing in cabaret at one or another of the lavish hotels along the Strip, the road which leads from the centre of Las Vegas out to the desert.

Las Vegas is really quite small, and you can find yourself in the middle of nowhere in a few moments. In the daytime both the Strip and the centre of the town look freakish and tawdry, but at night, with all the extravagant neon against the endless blackness of the surrounding desert, the effect is quite fantastic. On the whole, Las Vegas is designed for staying up most of the night and sleeping most of the day. In daylight, once you have seen the amusing Frontier Village on the grounds of the New Frontier Hotel, there is nothing else to do but gamble again, and the darkened casinos are thoroughly depressing at midday.

You can, of course, take a trip to Hoover Dam on the Colorado River, only thirty miles away. Hoover Dam began in the 1930's as Boulder Dam; when it was built, it was one of the engineering marvels of the world, and it is still the biggest although not the highest dam in the United States. It is the more impressive if one stops first in Boulder City, the nearest little town, to see the antique film of the making of the dam, which is run every half-hour in the back room of a drugstore-cum-souvenir shop there. The makeshift theatre and the naïve, old-fashioned quality of the film somehow combine to make the building of Boulder (or Hoover) Dam seem the dedicated work of eager amateurs, and one approaches the dam itself in a very sentimental mood, only to be jolted back to reality by the awesome size of the thing as it blocks up an enormous canyon. There are tours down inside the dam structure, to see the turbines and so forth, but unless you have a passionate interest in dams or a curiosity about the newest decorator-colours for turbines, we would advise against the tour. There is scant technical enlightenment, the jokes are endless and deadly, and it is peculiarly horrible to find oneself a captive audience for an insistent humourist five hundred feet deep inside the concrete walls of Hoover Dam. Instead of taking the tour, in the warmer months it is far more enjoyable to make closer acquaintance with Lake Mead, the huge lake caused by the dam. There are camping grounds and picnic grounds along its shores, and places to bathe and boat.

From the neon world of Nevada, where man has blotted out his surroundings, you can drive in less than a day to the Grand Canyon, where man seems pitifully insignificant. The Grand Canyon is east of Las Vegas, over the border in Arizona. It is the most remarkable feature of that high and arid land of canyon and butte which runs across the top of Arizona and New Mexico and the bottom of Utah and Colorado. The centre of the region is known as the Four Corners country, because it is the only place in America where four states come thus geometrically together, and the area as a whole is known to geographers as the Colorado Plateau.

The Grand Canyon was carved out of the plateau by that same turbulent Colorado River which is now somewhat restrained by Hoover Dam. No picture can do it justice, any more than a picture can reproduce the vastness of the Pacific Ocean or the majesty of the Himalayas. It is good to meet the Grand Canyon in comparative solitude – best of all at sunrise or sunset. But if you must go there on a tour, at least try to snatch a few moments to yourself. The Canyon needs no explanation and no embellishment. To quote J. B. Priestley once more, 'I have heard rumours of visitors who were disappointed. The same people will be disappointed at the Day of Judgement.'

The Grand Canyon is not the only natural wonder in the South-west. Poor in so many ways, the Southwest is rich in startling scenery. Sometimes it can seem chill and frightening, a moon landscape, and then again, early in the morning or at sunset when it is all suffused with a golden glow, the strange rocks and spires and escarpments are exceedingly beautiful. In southern Utah there is Zion National Park, and Bryce Canyon National Park. They are close to each other, and not far from the Grand Canyon, but they are each quite distinct and special. One could do worse than simply go from one National Park to another; there were good reasons for designating each one.

Zion National Park in its 94,000 acres encompasses a deep gorge on the Virgin River. After looking from above at the

Grand Canyon, it is heady next to plunge down into Zion. The towering cliffs on either side are a dark rose intermixed with a paler pink and mauve and orange; incredible colours, and in the spring and summer there are the varied greens of the trees as well.

At Bryce Canyon National Park, one stands on the rim and looks down again, but Bryce is as unlike the Grand Canyon as it is unlike Zion. Actually Bryce Canyon is less a canyon than a giant basin, its floor covered with grotesquely eroded rock formations which look like enormous pink stalagmites. As a Park, it is only about a third the size of Zion, and they complement each other.

From the end of May to the end of September there is a lodge open at both Bryce and Zion where one can stay more reasonably than at most of the better known Parks. There are also camping cabins available all the year round at Zion, and during the summer only at Bryce. At both Bryce and Zion, as at the North Rim of the Grand Canyon, there are horses for hire, and there are any number of good trails and walks and climbs; the Rangers will supply maps and give advice.

These Parks are never as crowded as the more celebrated ones, like Yellowstone and Yosemite, and either one would be a fascinating place to spend a few days' holiday in the West. If you are travelling by car, you can drop down to Bryce and Zion from Salt Lake City, or combine them handily with the North Rim of the Grand Canyon. Without a car the only way to get to Bryce and Zion seems to be on a regular bus tour.

More weird and rugged terrain, known to very few people, lies in the area north and east of Bryce and Zion; it is desolate country which a stranger should never penetrate casually. For parts of it you need a jeep and a local driver, and you should never leave a main road here without a guide or very careful preparation, unless you really hunger for disaster. But one can stay cheaply in one of the infrequent small towns and explore places like Cathedral Valley, near Fremont, Utah. Or one can make an exciting river trip. The Colorado River and the Green River which flows into it cut through the plateau in Utah, and it is possible to go down them on boats, with guides, camping at night with equipment provided by the guides. Glen Canyon, through which the Colorado River flows just before it enters Arizona, used to be one of the high-points of a river trip, but now a huge new dam is rising there, and some day this region may support a larger population. East of Glen Canyon along the Utah-Arizona border, within the Navajo reservation, there is another exciting bit of 'desert Gothic', known as Monument Valley.

To continue with our catalogue of natural wonders, there is the Painted Desert east of the Grand Canyon; part of it is near the Petrified Forest, along U.S. Route 66. The Petrified Forest is a stretch of desert covered with fallen timber turned aeons ago into varicoloured stone, and the Painted Desert is a much vaster stretch of desert in which the rocks and the very soil itself are vividly coloured. Each of these natural wonders is striking in its way, although both of them are painfully over-advertised.

The Spanish explorers who came to the Southwest in the sixteenth century were not looking for natural wonders, but for treasure. There were rumours about Seven Cities of Gold somewhere in this part, and in 1540 Coronado came here with a great army to search for them for two years without success. There really are golden cities in the Southwest, however. Coronado saw them and dismissed them, for while they were golden in the sunlight they held no treasures to be looted. Yet they had probably been the basis for the rumours. They were ancient Indian cliff dwellings, and three or four hundred years before Coronado came, they were the centres of a flourishing civilization.

It is now a thousand years since the Four Corners region was the most populous section of what is today the United States. To the north and east there were only nomad bands of Indians, but here the Indians were a settled agricultural people, with a comparatively high standard of comfort and culture. They never reached the level of the Aztecs and the Mayas in Central America, but they were nonetheless respectable country cousins, with at least some of the same refinements. They lived in great blocks of flats which made use of and enlarged upon the natural caves in canyon walls; usually they also built free-standing apartment buildings, precursors of the modern pueblos. Why and how they left these cities, where they went, what became of them, no one knows with certainty. The usual assumption is that a drought of unusual severity drove them away. It has been established that there was such a drought, lasting twenty-three years, at the end of the thirteenth century. Moreover this may have been merely the last straw; it is possible that this entire area was appreciably greener and more fertile when they built their communities, and had been growing dryer and dryer for several generations. At any rate there is no discernible sign of violence; they seem simply to have gone away, leaving all sorts of traces to delight future generations of anthropologists. Some of the modern Indians in the Southwest must be descended from the cliff dwellers, but no one is quite sure which and how. Certainly the cultural level had dropped by the time the Spaniards came.

Three of the best groups of cliff dwellings are to be found at Mesa Verde in south-western Colorado, at Chaco Canyon north-east of Gallup, New Mexico, and at Canyon de Chelly in the heart of the Navajo Reservation. There are also several smaller 'cities', like that at Bandelier near Santa Fé. (Chaco Canyon and Canyon de Chelly unfortunately are impossible to reach without a car.) All the important cliff dwellings are now either part of a National Park, like Mesa Verde, or protected as National Monuments, which means that many of them have organized camping areas. Most of them, too, have good small museums in the grounds, with exhibits and dioramas that make the Indian history of the Southwest much clearer. Mesa Verde, the best known, is a beautiful place quite apart from the remarkable cliff dwellings; it is, as its name suggests, a high mesa, and green with spruce and juniper and the aromatic piñon. The views from the road up to it are magnificent too, the landscape below splashed with golden aspen and cotton-wood trees. The air is so clear that one can see the San Juan Mountains nearly a hundred miles away.

The Southwest is not only notable for its evidences of an Indian past. It also has much the largest concentration in the United States of modern Indians. There are of course some few colonies of Indians still living on reservations east of the Mississippi, but those Indians have abandoned many of their ancient ways, sometimes of necessity, sometimes because they chose to. Many of the eastern Indians present a sad picture, having been alternately mistreated and neglected by the white man. This is also true of most of the Plains Indians tribes who once roamed the area between the Mississippi and the Rockies.

The federal government made many different treaties with each Indian tribe in America over the years, and broke most of them.

By the end of the nineteenth century most of the Indians had been herded on to land no one else could ever imagine wanting. Some few later left the reservations, but most of them huddled together, living on a meagre federal dole, with little education for the children and scant medical attention. Then in the 1930's so many people became distressed about the plight of the Indians that things began slowly to improve, and today Indian affairs are generally much better managed. There is still a long way to go, but as more and more of the Indians themselves become doctors and lawyers and teachers and administrators, many of the tribes are solving some of their problems themselves. One of the best examples of Indians maintaining tribal forms on the reservation, and yet managing their affairs so that they are also getting some of the advantages of ordinary American life, is the great Navajo tribe in the Southwest.

The Southwest Indians are the only ones in the United States who have succeeded in holding on to a sizable portion of their old land. Discriminated against and neglected, like all Indians, they were nonetheless better off in some ways because at least they had room enough to be themselves, in country ancestrally dear to them. What saved them was the fortunate fact that no one else wanted their forbidding desert territory.

There are two major divisions of Southwest Indians, with sub-divisions: the nomad tribes (the Navajo and the Apache) and the Pueblo or village groups (the Zuni, the Hopi, and the Indians of the pueblos along the Rio Grande near Albuquerque and Santa Fé).

The Apaches now live mainly on two reservations in Arizona and two in New Mexico. In their day, the Apaches had an awesome reputation as the fiercest Indians of them all, and indeed they did go on fighting the white man longer than any other tribe. Actually, however, the Navajos were once just as predatory, as other Indian tribes could have born angry witness: the Navajos simply adjusted sooner to the new shape of things. Today there are only about 10,000 Apaches left. They have no distinctive saleable crafts with which to call attention to themselves, but they are good businessmen and run several profitable enterprises. In addition, the Apaches, together with the Zunis, have become famous as fire-fighters. When a fire rages out of control in the Western mountain timber country, fire-fighters are dropped into the area from planes; the Apaches and the Zunis have made a specialty of this dangerous work.

The Navajo are much the most numerous of the Southwest Indian groups. There are now about 90,000 of them, and the tribe is growing all the time. This is one of their great problems, for no matter how well they administer their lands they cannot adequately support so many people. They depend mainly on sheep for their livelihood, and they lead a hardy, independent life in the manner of sheepherders the world over. The Navajo do not have villages. Each family has its own hogan or group of hogans; hogan means dwelling place, and a hogan may be a crude temporary affair of brush, or a cabin of mud-plastered logs, or even a modern house. If you simply drive through the Navajo Reservation, you are not likely to see many Navajo at any one time, unless perhaps you go to the capital of the Reservation at Window Rock, almost on the Arizona–New Mexico border. The great annual tribal fair is held at Window Rock in September, and the Tribal Council meets here. Also at Window Rock is the Navajo Arts and Crafts Guild centre, the best possible place to buy Navajo work or simply to learn about it. The Navajos run their own affairs in an exemplary manner, skilfully blending progress with tradition.

Weaving and silverwork are the crafts for which the Navajo is celebrated. Originally, the rugs they wove were only for their own use, but today a Navajo is more likely to wrap up in a ready-made blanket from the trading post. The rugs they make now are sold, to be hung on the walls or put on the floor. Good Navajo rugs are lovely, and not cheap. There is a great variation in design, from the simple to the sophisticated, but traditionally the best rugs use only wool that has been dyed with vegetable colours. One interesting type is the sandpainting rug, with a pattern of stylized human figures instead of the usual geometric abstractions. It simulates the ceremonial sandpaintings Navajo medicine men make to drive the evil spirits out of an ailing body.

Navajo silver jewellery is impressive too. Once the Navajos used only turquoise and coral and shells and claws for their jewellery, but then they learned about metal-working from the white man and they took to combining the turquoise with intricately worked silver. Many trading posts not only have new jewellery to sell, but also collections of 'pawn': family heirlooms pawned by the Indians. Some of the pawn is usually for sale, but

13a Grand Teton National Park, Wyoming

13b Grand Canyon of the Colorado River

14a Zuni Indians with their pottery

14b Cowboys watering their herd

much of it the trader keeps, knowing that the owner still hopes one day to redeem it. Pawn can be particularly beautiful, rougher and heavier than modern pieces perhaps, but more eloquent too.

'Trading post' is a word used very loosely in the Southwest. Early trading posts were simply shops in the middle of nowhere which sold anything and everything, and were also willing to barter. At the trading posts on the Indian reservations, the Indians could trade the things they made for whatever they needed from outside, and this they still do. There were trading posts in the towns as well, and there still are, in Gallup and in and around Taos, for example. But these days every roadside curio shop calls itself a trading post. Even a genuine old trading post may now carry cheap souvenirs, and what looks like a second-rate curio shop may really be an historic and eminently reputable place. One simply has to develop an instinct for the true and the false. The Southwest is flooded with cheap commercial copies of every kind of Indian object. Sometimes the copy is all that you want, but if there is any appreciable amount of money involved, it is always as well to ask whether what you are considering was actually made *by hand by Indians* and if so, what tribe. The laws of New Mexico and Arizona are rightly strict on this subject.

The Navajo Reservation is enormous: roughly the same size as Ceylon and twice the size of Belgium. Within the Navajo Reservation there is a separate, smaller reservation, that of the Hopi Pueblo Indians. The Hopi and the Zuni and the Rio Grande Pueblo Indians are all related to a degree, although most of them speak different languages. But despite the language differences, all Pueblo Indians have much in common. Their religious ceremonies and dress are similar, they all live in the same sort of villages, and almost all of them make handsome pottery.

One of the Hopi pueblos, Oraibi, is celebrated because it is known to be exceedingly old; a roof timber in a dwelling there was proved to have been cut in 1370. In the spring there are often ceremonial dances at some of the Hopi pueblos at the week-end, and visitors are allowed to watch provided that they are well-behaved.

Just to the south-east of the Navajo country is the town of Gallup, an important centre of Indian activities, including the three-day Indian Inter-Tribal Ceremonial held every year in mid-August. Since August is the peak tourist month, one cannot

s

expect the Inter-Tribal Ceremonial to be pure and austere, but the Indians themselves do come in great numbers, together with the white spectators, and there are Indian dances and contests and all sorts of colourful activities.

Quite as famous as the Inter-Tribal Ceremonial, but completely different, is the ceremony known as the Shalako at the Zuni pueblo south of Gallup. The Shalako is held every year a month or so before Christmas, and outsiders are allowed to go and watch, quietly. Much of it takes place at night and the spectators get very cold, as Jacquetta Hawkes attests in *Journey Down A Rainbow*. With its dramatically masked performers, the Shalako is exciting and a little frightening. The Zunis are in many respects the most interesting Pueblo group. With only one community, far from the Hopi and the Rio Grande pueblos, they are widely known for such diverse things as the Shalako, their skill as fire-fighters, their fine pottery, and the fact that they are the only Pueblo Indians who produce distinctive jewellery. Once you have seen Zuni jewellery, you can never mistake it: the distinguishing feature is the intricate channel-inlay work, with tiny turquoise stones in delicate silver settings, quite unlike the larger-scale Navajo style.

The rest of the Pueblo Indians live farther east in New Mexico. Most of their pueblos are between Albuquerque and Taos, which means that Santa Fé, in the middle, is a good headquarters for visiting them. But there are two, Acoma and Laguna, which are loosely connected with the Rio Grande Pueblos but are by themselves, midway between Gallup and Albuquerque. Laguna, near the highway, is not interesting to visitors except for its mission church. Acoma has a celebrated mission church too, but the situation of the pueblo alone would make it famous even if the church were not there. The Acoma pueblo, 'the city in the sky', is perched on the very top of a steep, forbidding butte or mesa, at the end of fifteen miles of very rough dirt road. ('Impassable in bad weather', the maps warn, and they mean it.) The Indians at Acoma are certainly not the friendly, outgoing sort, and the climb up to their pueblo is in itself quite an experience, but once you have been there you are unlikely ever to forget it. Acoma is extremely old, perhaps as old as Oraibi in the Hopi country, and you are very conscious of its antiquity. Here more than anywhere else in the Southwest you have a sense of what the country was like when the

Spaniards came, and how mad and brave they were to think that they could tame the land or its people.

The fifteen or sixteen pueblos between Albuquerque and Taos are called the Rio Grande pueblos because they are along that river. The Taos pueblo, two miles north of the town of Taos, is the best known and the most photogenic. It is a pleasant pueblo, too, accustomed to tourists and cheerfully resigned to them. Here as at many of the pueblos there is a fee for entering and another fee for taking pictures; it seems only fair when one considers what an invasion of privacy visitors represent. Most pueblos also charge a fee for sketching, but there are some which allow no sketching at all at any price, and no photography either. One should never, never try to take pictures of an Indian or Indian things without asking permission. All of the pueblos are also more or less sensitive about visitors going near their kivas. Kivas are the sacred place, commonly a small separate building, round or square, with an entrance at the top; usually one can distinguish the kiva by looking for a ladder poking out of the top of a dome or cube. The men of the pueblos use the kiva as both club and temple, and the pueblo ceremonies centre around it.

San Ildefonso and Santa Clara, between Santa Fé and Taos near Española, are two other well-known Rio Grande pueblos, particularly celebrated for their distinctive black pottery. Most of the other pueblos produce pottery with geometric patterns in colour on a white or biscuit ground, but at San Ildefonso and Santa Clara the specialty is either solid burnished black or else a pattern of black on black, part burnished and part mat, and sometimes with the pattern deeply incised. Pueblo pottery is very hard and dense, with a fine timbre, and the black pots give an especially rich effect. Of these two pueblos, San Ildefonso is the more renowned because it is the pueblo of Maria, whose pots were the first black ones to attract wide attention; she won many awards and her son is now a San Ildefonso potter too. San Ildefonso is also noted for its particularly striking kiva, right in the middle of the plaza.

It is often the arrangement in the pueblos that the women make the pottery, the men ornament it, and the women fire it. The pueblo potters use no wheel; the wheel was the one important tool even the Mayas and the Aztecs lacked, and a thousand years later the Pueblo people continue to form their perfectly symmetrical pots coil by coil. Once, every Pueblo girl was expected to be a skilled potter, as girls in other countries are expected to know how to cook, but many of the young girls these days never learn. It is delightful to see two happy little Pueblo girls skipping through their plaza hand in hand, carrying American school books and wearing kilts, leotards, and Alice bands, but those same children can hardly help growing up dissatisfied with many of the inhibiting Pueblo traditions.

In most pueblos today, however, you still need only indicate the slightest interest in pottery in order to be surrounded by women opening up bundles of their work. It may or may not be cheaper than buying from a recognized trader; that depends on the bargaining. At any rate it is more fun.

In the colder months you will be greeted at every pueblo with the delicious odour of burning piñon wood, warming the dwellings and heating the outdoor ovens. The piñon tree also bears a tiny and delicious nut, but it is the smell of burning piñon that lingers in the memory when one knows and loves the Southwest.

The very best place to learn more about all the Indians of the Southwest is at Santa Fé, which has on the one hand the superb Museum of Navajo Ceremonial Art, and then, in the multi-building Museum of New Mexico on the Plaza, an excellent section devoted to the Pueblo Indians. The Pueblo Indian section is in the building called the Palace of the Governors, for the good and sufficient reason that that is what it once was.

As every schoolboy knows, Columbus discovered America in 1492, and his sponsors were King Ferdinand and Queen Isabella of Spain. What Columbus really discovered were some of the islands of the Caribbean, but the Spaniards were not long in extending their claims until they controlled all of South America except Brazil, and all of Central America and Mexico, and Florida, and that region which is now Texas, Arizona, New Mexico and California. The fortune in gold and precious stones which they pried away from the Indians of Central America and Mexico only whetted their appetite for more, and so they looked to the north, and Coronado's expedition in 1540 was merely the first of several Spanish attempts to find gold in the Southwest. There is a notice along the road a few miles south of Taos saying that part of Coronado's army passed this way and reached the Taos pueblo. It gives one pause to reflect that in the last years of the reign of Henry VIII, conquistadors in clanking armour were riding through this valley.

In the end, however, the Spaniards had to be content here simply with saving souls; the indefatigable Spanish missionaries established countless missions throughout the Southwest, and particularly in New Mexico. There were military outposts too, and eventually some permanent Spanish settlers. In the beginning the Indians were merely wary, with some exceptions, but gradually they tired of the Spaniards' company, and in 1680 there was a great and bloody revolt. It was secretly organized in the Taos pueblo, and every other pueblo in New Mexico joined the conspiracy. Missionaries were struck down at the altar and settlers killed in their fields until there was only a pitiful remnant of the Spanish population left to take shelter with the garrison at Santa Fé before fleeing south to Mexico. For twelve years after the revolt the Indians had their ancient lands all to themselves again, but then the Spaniards came back, better organized this time, and this time they stayed. During the next hundred and fifty years those who settled here led a quiet life in their remote corner of the world. There were big landowners with handsome ranch houses, luxuries brought from Spain and Mexico, fine orchards and vineyards, and many peons, both Spanish and Indian. There were also poorer settlers who struggled along in little colonies in the hills above the Rio Grande valley. There were missionaries again; the Church was powerful here. For everyone in New Mexico, Santa Fé was the centre of things, but even Santa Fé was only a small town, sleepy and pleasant and hospitable.

Gradually the Indians learned to pay lip service to the white man's religion and laws and yet keep their own traditions intact, undercover. Even those who really accepted Christianity usually blended its teachings with their own Indian beliefs. The fact that they had had three hundred years' practice in dealing with an alien force was undoubtedly one of the reasons the Indians of the Southwest were better able to accommodate themselves to those later changes which shattered many Indian tribes.

Mexico seceded from Spain in the early part of the nineteenth century; this territory then became Mexican. It was still not heavily populated. The area around Santa Fé was the most important; there were also a few settlements in Texas, but virtually none in

Arizona. California, quite separate, with its own administrators, was almost a thousand miles away.

Then in 1846 the United States took over the region. Mexico was having a turbulent time as an independent country, and it was forced to abandon New Mexico (which then included Arizona as well) almost without a struggle. Most of the important land-owners around Santa Fé were content with the change of govern-ment. To be sure, there were a few ugly disagreements over land grants from time to time, and the new Anglo-American settlers were inclined to look down upon the poorer Spanish-Americans and to discriminate against them. But on the whole the transition was not too painful in this area, and today all of New Mexico happily capitalizes on her Spanish-American past. Almost every building is made to look New-World-Spanish, and almost every restaurant advertises Spanish – or Mexican – food.

In Albuquerque, mostly a very new city, one is inclined to find the Spanish-ness rather tiresome because it seems so artificial. The adobe buildings of the University of New Mexico are attrac-tive, and the 'Old Town' section of the city is reasonably quaint, but in general Albuquerque is a great disappointment to anyone who goes there expecting something picturesque.

Santa Fé, on the other hand, while of course it has not stayed exactly as it once was, nonetheless still evokes a strong sense of the past. The town is a zesty mixture of artists, Spanish-Ameri-cans, the idle rich, Indians, and scientists from the neighbouring atomic research station at Los Alamos. The old Plaza in Santa Fé continues to be the gathering place. Indians are there under the arches selling beads back to the white man, and La Fonda Hotel is there, where everyone meets everyone. La Fonda is a Harvey hotel. Harvey hotels and restaurants are an institution in the South-west because they not only were the first to serve decent food many long years ago, but they also adopted the old Spanish style of building and exhibited and sold Indian crafts long before the rest of the world had come to admire these aspects of South-western life.

There are many tempting shops and galleries around the Plaza in Santa Fé, but we would like to call attention to two in parti-cular. One is a delightful little restaurant called The Shed which does ingenious things with Mexican food – and most Mexican dishes desperately need to be tampered with. The other is The

Shop, run by a woman named Eleanor Bedell; it sells handsome antique and contemporary Spanish-American things, it has an art gallery stocked with good examples of local work, and in the very back room there is a Flea-Market collection of tantalizing cast-offs.

We have already mentioned the Museum of Navajo Ceremonial Art and the Pueblo exhibits in the Palace of the Governors. We should also pay tribute to the charming little Folk Art Museum high up on the edge of town next to the Navajo Museum. Moreover, the Palace of the Governors has a fine section devoted to the Spanish past of this region in addition to its Pueblo section, and there are also two other units of the Museum of New Mexico on either side, just off the Plaza, one a museum of ethnology and the other an art gallery.

Santa Fé now has opera in the summer, and very good opera too. The company draws on such sources as the New York City Center for promising young singers, and then rehearses them far more than most opera companies in order to weld together a polished and harmonious ensemble. The repertoire includes the obvious favourites – Verdi and Puccini and so on – but they are presented with a special flair, and are interspersed with contemporary operas, Stravinsky and Hindemith, for example, with the composer himself conducting if possible. It is all splendid, but the audience need warm coats. The performances are out of doors, under the stars, and it cannot be stressed too often that the daytime warmth in these high altitudes can change almost to frost at night. Santa Fé and Taos are both very high up, almost 7,000 feet. In the daytime in the summer one can be grilled in the sun and yet frozen in the shade. Furthermore, winter comes early at this altitude, with snow a possibility in late October and a certainty in November. There is ski-ing then in the mountains behind Santa Fé and also at Taos, although this is not such fine ski-ing country as Colorado.

The town of Taos is seventy miles north of Santa Fé. It is much smaller, more isolated, simpler. In this century Taos acquired fame as the place D. H. Lawrence chose to live in, and it continues to attract writers and painters. There are some very good painters there, as the quality of work in the galleries indicates; Taos must have a higher ratio of galleries to people than any other town in the world. There are also some reliable shops on the Plaza which sell Indian crafts.

In the nineteenth century when it was a frontier town on the border between the Spanish world and the American world to the north, Taos had another resident as renowned in his day as D. H. Lawrence in ours: Kit Carson. Carson was one of those legendary figures of the West who fully deserved his fame. He began as a trapper, a mountain man, in the Rockies when trappers were the only white men there, and later he guided Fremont on two epic expeditions to find a passable trail through the Rockies and the Sierra Nevadas to California. Between adventures Kit Carson lived in Taos with his New Mexican wife. He was loved and trusted by everyone who knew him, whether Spanish-American, Anglo-American or Indian. His later military expeditions against the Navajos may appear ruthless in retrospect, but even there he was only doing what seemed right and proper at the time, and doing it as decently as possible. His Taos house is still standing, and his grave is in Taos too, in a little park shaded by cottonwood trees.

Both Santa Fé and Taos are attractive and interesting towns, yet they may repel at first. The Southwest is so uncompromising. In the Navajo Reservation you have to adjust to a decorative pattern of beer cans along the roads; there is no vegetation to hide litter. And Santa Fé and Taos have a dusty bleakness in certain seasons that can chill the heart. After a while you learn to love that very harshness, or else you continue to hate it and are never really at ease in the Southwest.

Santa Fé today is full of people who care terribly about protecting its good qualities, newcomers who ardently defend every Spanish tradition. The meanest old adobe house is lovingly restored, and expensive new houses, too, are made of adobe. But this is practical as well as sentimental, for adobe does make the perfect building material for the Southwestern climate. It is simply mud, baked into bricks or poured like concrete, and thick adobe walls keep out the heat in summer and keep it in in winter. The Indian pueblos are made of adobe too, layer upon layer of it, and since a three-foot-thick adobe wall makes an ideal fall-out shelter (provided the window openings are covered) it is possible that some day the Pueblo Indians will be able to enjoy their privacy once again, having outlasted us all.

In the meantime, however, anyone who visits New Mexico can delight in the remains of the Spanish period. The chief treasures are the churches, and there are two sorts: mission churches in the Indian pueblos, and the old parish churches of the Spanish colonists.

The church at the Acoma pueblo is one of the most famous mission churches. The very fact that it was built at all in that forbidding place is in itself remarkable. And it is a massive church, with cloisters which you can just glimpse as you are hurried along by the Acoma guide. Anyone who is at all interested in the history of New Mexico should read Willa Cather's classic *Death Comes for the Archbishop*. The scene is Santa Fé in the early nineteenth century, but there is also a fascinating chapter of reminiscence devoted to the Acoma church and its extraordinary friar-creators. Like all the old Spanish churches in the Southwest, the one at Acoma is vivid and primitive in its decoration, with a fine reredos. But the Acoma church is rarely used today, and with its great empty nave, the ultimate effect is somewhat bleak and grim. For a warmer church, with a wealth of delightful, innocent trimmings and a splendid herringbone ceiling, you must stop at the Laguna pueblo. The pueblo itself at Laguna is nothing much, but the church is fine and seems to be constantly used. When we were there, the Virgin was wearing a silk square from Liberty's as a cloak.

We have been told that the church at the pueblo of San Felipe between Santa Fé and Albuquerque is well worth seeing, but it is listed as open only from 8 to 10 on Sunday morning, and apparently there is some question even about those hours. It would obviously be a mistake to go far out of the way in the hope of seeing it, and yet it is a pity that San Felipe presents problems, for most of the other Rio Grande pueblos have relatively dull churches, rebuilt with little style in the last hundred years. Moreover, the missionaries really never succeeded in penetrating the Zuni and Hopi pueblos again after the revolt of 1680, so there you find only the ruins of churches.

Both Santa Fé and Taos have good examples of early Spanish parish churches, built for the colonists rather than the Indians. At Santa Fé there is the Church of San Miguel, which is now owned by the Christian Brothers and used as a chapel for their school. It is open to the public, and although one is locked in and subjected to a disembodied voice on a recording telling you where to stand and what to look at *now*, the church amply repays any suffering.

The Taos church, equally charming but quite different, is actually at Rancho de Taos, a mile or two south of the town of Taos. It has a striking exterior, strong and solid and plain, utterly right for this country.

You cannot be long in Santa Fé before someone asks you if you have taken the 'high road' to Taos. The low road, along the highway, is much the quickest route, and it sufficed for Coronado's men and any number of other celebrated travellers. But the high road is picturesque, and one could go to Taos one way and return the other. We have already mentioned that there are little colonies of Spanish settlers in the hills above the Rio Grande valley; the high road goes through several of the oldest villages. The people in these villages have always been poor, and until quite recently they lived almost untouched by the rest of the world, like the Anglo-Americans of the Kentucky and North Carolina mountains. Like those other mountain settlers, these Spanish-Americans have always been deeply religious. Here in New Mexico the religion of course was Roman Catholicism, and it took an extreme form up in the hills. This is the region of the Penitentes, who practised flagellation and perhaps even crucifixion during Easter Week. Some of the practices continue to this day, and no outsider really knows much about them. The Church itself has been almost powerless; these villages became virtually schismatic, with a proper Roman Catholic church and then a separate Penitente chapel. It is kept strictly secret, of course, and one certainly does not make inquiries in the villages, but you can sometimes guess which is the Penitente chapel. If you see a gloomy little building, obviously not a house, with blind windows and no external ornament whatsoever with the possible exception of a bell, that may be the Penitente chapel.

Many of the people in these villages, like people in many parts of New Mexico, speak only halting English if indeed they speak it at all. Until a very short time ago, quite a number of schools in New Mexico were still taught entirely in Spanish, and the State Legislature itself continues to use both languages. Everyone has come to realize, however, that it is better not to perpetuate a language barrier, and schools must now be conducted in English. The younger generation will not be so colourful.

To reach these villages you leave the main road from Santa Fé to Taos at Pojoaque or Española, where the 'high road' goes off to the east, as State Route 76 much of the way. It goes up into the Sangre de Cristo Mountains, and the views are magnificent. The hills present a fascinating pattern with their background of pink earth dotted with the little dark juniper and piñon trees. It is primitive country where men still use hand ploughs; deer, jack-rabbits, wild turkey, pheasant and quail abound and there are plenty of trout in the rivers. Unfortunately the old tile roofs of the village houses are gradually being replaced with ugly tin ones, but bright strings of chili still festoon the walls in the autumn. You come to the first notable Spanish church before you have climbed to the really primitive part. It is at Chimayo, a place also famous for its weaving; there is a little shop in the village which sells the local handicrafts. The church is called El Sanctuario, and it is altogether gaudy and beautiful. After Chimayo the road goes steadily up, to the village of Truchas. On the way you pass a road going off to the right to Cordova, a village with excellent wood carvers, as the statues in the church testify. Truchas has a Peni-tente chapel on the left as you enter the village, but nothing else of note. At Trampas, however, the next village, there is another splendid little Spanish church, mostly eighteenth century. Beyond Trampas are Penasco and Vadito, two more villages with a Peni-tente tradition, and then you reach State Route 3 and head down to join the main road into Taos once again.

If you go north-west from Santa Fé, instead of north-east to the Penitente country, you come to Los Alamos, the atomic research centre. While the early equipment from the University of Chicago was moved in 1942 to Oak Ridge, Tennessee, the bulk of the work on the actual bomb was done at Los Alamos. Secrecy was amazingly well preserved. Los Alamos had been picked because it was remote, and even the citizens of Santa Fé had no clue about what was going on only a few miles away.

Los Alamos used to be a closed city, but you can now drive freely through it, perhaps on the way to see the cliff dwellings at Bandelier or after a visit to the pueblo of San Ildefonso, mixing periods and moods wholesale. There really is nothing to see at Los Alamos, however. It looks like any other planned new town except that it has an unusually large number of schools, to meet the needs of all the young families there. Most of the laboratories are several miles from the town itself, isolated in lonely canyons.

So far in this chapter we have been moving more or less methodically from west to east through the upper part of the Southwest, along a great plateau which is very cold in winter, with considerable snow. This does not mean that no one can travel through here then, for the main roads are kept clear, and if it were to be the only chance in a lifetime, you might well decide to see the Grand Canyon despite the cold, and perhaps even hazard Mesa Verde or go to Santa Fé and Taos. Provided that you allowed an extra day or two so that a sudden severe snowstorm would not hopelessly tangle your plans, perhaps you would even find the upper Southwest especially attractive without all the summer visitors.

On the other hand, during the colder six months of the year most Americans would elect to cross this region farther south. Down there the country is quite different, low desert interrupted here and there by mountains, instead of high desert split with canyons and eroded into buttes.

Going from west to east across the lower Southwest, the first important city is Phoenix, Arizona. Its very name indicates its newness; neither the Spaniards nor the Indians gave names like 'Phoenix'. In fact, Phoenix could never have existed until modern times; it has risen not from ashes but from nothing at all. This part of Arizona was so arid that few Indians lived there, and the Spaniards hardly bothered with it at all. Only in our century has it been made to bloom, with vast irrigation projects which have turned the Salt River Valley in which Phoenix lies into a fertile and verdant oasis. There are oranges and lemons, olives and dates, and Phoenix, at the centre of all this, is a prosperous city with almost half a million people. The prosperity is not entirely agricultural, either. The climate in the winter here is very attractive and Phoenix is ringed by many small resort towns, and dude ranches. People now come to Phoenix to retire, too; it is becoming as popular in this way as southern California.

Just east of Phoenix is Taliesen West, the winter headquarters of Frank Lloyd Wright's architectural school and fellowship. Built before Phoenix assumed its present proportions, Taliesen West once seemed a remote and exotic flowering in the desert, its buildings one of the first significant attempts to come to terms architecturally with this kind of country. These days it is quite the thing for people to build exciting contemporary houses specially designed for desert living, but Taliesen West was once revolutionary. Despite the death of Frank Lloyd Wright, the fellowship at Taliesen West seems to be continuing, at least for the present, and the public may go there to see the buildings.

Also on the eastern side of Phoenix there is a botanical garden devoted to desert plants: the Desert Botanical Gardens, in fact. It is closed in the summer, when this southern half of the Southwest becomes incredibly hot and everyone flees who can; the best time for it, as for the desert as a whole, is spring. People who talk of seeing the desert bloom usually mean the sort of desert one finds here in southern Arizona, where the flowering of cactus and brush is a fantastic sight which occurs with a dramatic burst after one of those sudden and torrential spring rains which fill the arroyos with rushing water and turn the dirt roads to thick mud. There is no predicting exactly when the desert will bloom most richly, although late April and early May is generally the time. Even when there is no hint of flowering, however, this desert country is botanically exciting because of its great variety of cacti. Most famous, most striking, is the giant saguaro cactus, which sometimes grows to a height of fifty feet. But there are many other fascinating desert plants too, and the Botanical Gardens at Phoenix is a good place to identify them.

Tucson is south-east of Phoenix and only half as big, but unlike Phoenix it does have a history. There were never great numbers of Spaniards around here, but there were missionaries, and the mission church of San Xavier del Bac near Tucson may well be the loveliest mission church of them all. Built in the late eighteenth century, it is much more ornate and rococo on the exterior than most of the mission churches one finds in the United States. It resembles neither the California examples nor those of New Mexico; people say that it is like the best old churches in Mexico itself. The inside of the church is beautiful too, richly decorated long ago by the mission Indians directed by the Franciscan builders.

From Tucson you can go to Tombstone, one of those Western mining towns which bloomed overnight like a desert cactus and was equally spikey. Countless films have been made about Wyatt Earp's adventures as Marshal of Tombstone, and some of the famous landmarks of its wicked past have been carefully preserved. The mining here remained profitable for only a short time, but Tombstone is not entirely a ghost town, since it is not too far from Tucson and the address is irresistible to devotees of the old West.

Both Phoenix and Tucson have museums concerned with the archaeology and ethnology of the Southwest, its ancient and not-so-ancient past. At Tucson there is the Arizona State Museum in the grounds of the University of Arizona; it has graphic, illuminating exhibits. And like Phoenix, Tucson too has a desert botanic gardens. The one at Tucson, the Arizona-Sonora Desert Museum, is more complex and more lively than the Desert Botanical Gardens at Phoenix, and it has desert animals as well as plants.

As any local map will show, there are several State Parks and National Monuments in southern Arizona. (By now you will realize that National Monuments in the West are usually areas which merit protection but are not grand or vast enough to become full-fledged National Parks.) Some of the Parks and National Monuments in the Phoenix-Tucson region are notable for their geologic formations, like Chiricahua, and some, like Saguaro, for their exceptional desert vegetation.

If you were to drive east from Tucson, when you reached Las Cruces, New Mexico, you would have to decide whether to veer north-east towards the white sands of Almogordo or south-east into Texas. The first atomic bomb was tested at the White Sands Proving Grounds south of Albuquerque. White Sands National Monument is near Almogordo, farther south. It is confusing, but White Sands National Monument has no connexion with the bomb. It is simply a protected area of strange and lovely white desert which does indeed, as everyone says, look exactly like great billows and drifts of fluffy snow. Well to the east of Almogordo, along the southern border of New Mexico, are the Carlsbad Caverns, a vast and dazzling underground world. There is an unusual added attraction at the Carlsbad Caverns: an enormous bat colony lives in the caves and emerges every night at dusk, in formation.

It is possible to reach the Carlsbad Caverns from the west either by way of Almogordo or on the road which goes through El Paso, Texas. Neither way, however, is very direct, for there are mountains along there. El Paso does, as its name suggests, mark a pass, the pass through which many of the earliest Spanish expeditions came up into the Southwest from Mexico. Through the centuries a town gradually grew up here, furnishing supplies and a faint echo of civilization to men going north or south through this gap in the mountains made by the Rio Grande River. El Paso is an industrial town today, with a strong Spanish-American flavour because it is so close to Mexico. There is one Indian pueblo not far away, and on the fringes of the city there are many little Spanish-American settlements, but none with old churches.

Western Texas is that traditional Texas of cowboys and cattle which is now also the great oil-producing region. Western Texas is not beautiful, except perhaps to a cow or a cowboy or an oilman. It is flat and dusty, cold in winter and miserably hot in summer. The newly rich oil towns there are all exactly alike; and every road goes on for ever. In the far south-west corner there is a National Park, Big Bend, which is exciting in part for the very reason that it is so remote, as well as wild and unspoiled. You feel sure bands of outlaws are still hiding back in its hills, and perhaps they are. It is lonely and rugged, with bare, beautiful mountains.

Far to the east of El Paso and the Big Bend is San Antonio, the only genuinely colourful city in Texas. The little San Antonio River wanders casually right through the middle of the city and makes it obvious that San Antonio is still at heart a small and informal town. At night there are lights along the river bank, and you can walk down below, at the water's edge, and hear someone somewhere plucking at a Spanish guitar.

San Antonio has a special place in the affections of all loyal Texans, for it was here that the Republic of Texas had her baptism of blood. Texas, like New Mexico and Arizona and California, originally belonged to Spain and then became Mexican territory when Mexico seceded from Spain. But in the early nineteenth century Texas began to attract Anglo-American settlers to an extent no other Mexican colony did. The land of course, particularly in eastern Texas, was far more fertile than New Mexican land, and yet it was not as hard to get to as California. At the start, Mexico was perfectly willing for the Anglo-American settlers to come, but disillusionment set in on both sides fairly soon, and the Anglo-American Texans revolted against Mexican rule. The first serious engagement of the rebellion took place at San Antonio, when a band of one hundred and eighty Texans barricaded themselves in a building known as the Alamo. (Presumably the name came from the overhanging cottonwood trees, *los alamos*.) The Texans were surrounded by four thousand Mexican soldiers under the personal command of Santa Anna, the military dictator of Mexico. Hopelessly outnumbered, they nonetheless refused to surrender, and to a man they died, among them Davy Crockett, the Tennessee frontier hero, and Jim Bowie, the soldier of fortune from New Orleans. Those who were not killed in the fighting were overpowered and slaughtered when the Mexicans broke into the makeshift fort. A month later, crying 'Remember the Alamo', an enraged, inspired army of Texans routed the Mexican forces at the Battle of San Jacinto near Houston, and the Republic of Texas was born. Mexico had learned too late that it is a tactical error to create martyrs.

Texas continued as an independent republic for nine years, and Texans will never let you forget it. They themselves seem sometimes to forget that they finally did join the United States; their cries of pain are terrible whenever they think their sovereign rights are being infringed upon by the federal government.

The Alamo is, of course, the chief tourist attraction in San Antonio. It is a peculiar building, originally a Spanish mission church and then part of a crude fortress, but it has considerable charm. San Antonio has done very well by its old buildings, skilfully preserving and restoring them. The Spanish Governor's Palace, on Military Plaza not far from the Alamo, is a fine evocation of San Antonio's colonial past.

In the eighteenth century San Antonio was singularly rich in missions. It is hard to see why there should have been quite so many in one small area, but in addition to the one which became famous as the Alamo there are four more close together along the river outside the town. The road which one takes to see them is called Mission Road, and the second mission along that road is the jewel of the four: the Mission of San José and San Miguel de Aguayo. Its church is very handsome, with splendid baroque ornamentation, and many of the outbuildings can also still be seen. In New Mexico, the mission churches were built as part of pueblos which were already there, and many of the old California missions are now stripped neatly down to church and cloister, but at San José one can see all that an active mission once included. They were self-supporting villages, little theocratic city-states, with

15a Thirteenth century Indian cliff dwellings at Mesa Verde, Colorado

15b Monument Valley, Arizona

16a El Santuario: a mission church near Chimayo, New Mexico

16b Mission San Xavier del Bac, near Tucson, Arizona. The building was begun in about 1783

housing for the Indians and quarters for a military guard as well
as a school and the central religious buildings.

The most famous ranch in Texas has its headquarters at Kings-
ville, south of San Antonio near Corpus Christi. It is the King
Ranch, celebrated because it includes almost a million acres, but
more properly distinguished for the great work done there
through the years in cross-breeding and improving range cattle.

Western Texas is not pretty, but it is more or less what one
expects. Eastern Texas comes as a surprise. In the first place, the
most easterly section is not dry at all, but semi-tropical green like
the neighbouring state of Louisiana. And then the biggest cities,
Dallas and Houston, turn out to look like any other fast-growing
new American cities west of the Mississippi. Despite the tall tales,
you do not see weather-beaten men in cowboy hats driving Rolls-
Royces. The flamboyance is there all right, but under cover; on
the surface one sees only the arrant domesticity, the nice houses
with lovingly tended gardens. Even Nieman Marcus, that legendary Dallas department store, is in fact less glittering than many
California shops. It does have a rather startling jewellery department, but otherwise it is simply pleasant and well-run. Pity.

What the big cities of Texas do have nowadays is a multitude of
exciting new monuments to culture. One hears that rich Texans
will contribute money to a good cultural cause but will not support it in any other way; in other words, no one goes to the
museums. If that is true, those Texans are missing a great deal.
For example, there is no lovelier new gallery anywhere in the
United States than the Amon Carter Museum of Western Art in
Fort Worth. Housed in a breathtaking building by Philip Johnson,
it makes even the most jaded cowboy-hater love cowboy art. And
when we were there it was full of Texans, Texans from the country, gnarled and ill at ease, contemplating their past.

Dallas and Fort Worth, only thirty miles apart, forty minutes
from each other on one of the frequent express buses, are traditional rivals and opposite in every way. When Amon Carter was
alive, the patron saint or the evil genius of Fort Worth, the rivalry
was more often bitter than comic. These days things seem calmer,
and there is even talk of having a common airport at last. But
Fort Worth, as every hoarding proclaims, is 'where the West
begins', while Dallas strives to be polished and cosmopolitan. In
any event, Dallas shows a more sophisticated taste in culture, and

T

the most recent evidence of this is in a fine little contemporary art gallery and the Dallas Theater Center. The Theater Center was designed by Frank Lloyd Wright, the only theatre he ever did. The exterior resembles the Guggenheim Museum; inside it is handsome, but notable more because it is a Wright building than because of any radical innovation in stage design. Dallas also has an opera season. The Dallas Opera was the first in the United States to snare Joan Sutherland and, earlier, Maria Callas, who will often sing in Dallas when she is not willing to sing anywhere else.

Houston is the biggest and most varied city in Texas, rich with shipping and agricultural profits as well as oil money. It is only fitting that it should also have the biggest and most splendid museum, the Houston Museum of Fine Arts. The museum has recently expanded, adding a stark new wing designed by Mies van der Rohe, and acquiring the fine Hogg Collection of Americana, Texan and otherwise. For the time being at least the latter is still being kept in place in the Hogg house, now also owned by the museum.

There are some very striking contemporary churches in Texas. One of the finest is in Dallas: the Episcopalian Church of St Michael and All Angels, on Douglas Street at Colgate. Designed by a local architect, it combines a pure but rich simplicity and glowing modern stained glass. There is also an unusual chapel in Dallas, at the very top of the new Southland office building, a proper Texas touch.

Texans are giving lavish support to the building of several great new medical centres. Cynics will tell you it is because the new rich want to be preserved as long as possible in order to spend their money, now that they have discovered even Texans cannot take it with them. In any event, Houston and Dallas are acquiring considerable prestige in medical circles.

Of course the rodeos in Texas, at the various Stock Shows and the State Fair in October, are the biggest and the best. Texas treasures its cattle connexions, and you are seldom offered anything but steak in the restaurants.

Here and there in Texas one does come upon quite unexpected delights. The state highway people, for instance, have had the ingenious idea of sowing wild flower seed together with grass seed along the verge, so that even the most desolate expanse of road can be a riot of bloom and beauty in the spring. Only one who has known the deadly bleakness of parts of the Southwest can appreciate what a lovely and imaginative gesture this seems.

There is one final surprise we must mention, too: the liquor laws. Here in rough, tough Texas, you cannot buy a drink in a public place. You can buy beer and wine, but if you want anything stronger you must carry your own bottle with you. And this is exactly what most people do. It is perfectly legal to buy spirits by the bottle in licensed shops, and so you simply go out for the evening with your bottle in a paper bag, and then the waiter brings you glasses and soda and ice. It all seems mad.

SPECIAL KNOWLEDGE

You can get to the South Rim of **Grand Canyon** by public transport: bus, or a combination of train and bus, or even plane and bus. Better still is to go by car to the North Rim, uncrowded even during the high summer season because of its relative inaccessibility. The lodge on the North Rim is closed during the winter, when the roads are often impassable.

There are mule-back trips of varying length which one can take down into the Canyon; during the summer, reservations for this usually need to be made well in advance. Some of these trips include a night or two at the lodge on the floor of the Canyon. If no mules are available, you can always go on foot, if you are strong and do not mind a stiff climb back up. There are several inns and lodges at the South Rim; again, it is wise to book well in advance. Information about any of the facilities at Grand Canyon can be obtained from the Superintendent, Grand Canyon National Park, Arizona. The National Park Service runs a visitor's centre on the South Rim at Grand Canyon Village, and it also sponsors daily talks by Park Rangers on the geology of the canyon and the history of the region in general. For visitors without a car, there are daily bus tours along the South Rim, starting at Grand Canyon Village. There are also several tourist attractions, such as imitation Indian pueblos and a few privately-run enterprises.

The Utah Parks Company runs tours to **Bryce and Zion** which start from Cedar City, Utah; some of their tours also include the North Rim of the Grand Canyon. They are of varying length, permit stopovers, and make connexions with trains at Lund, Utah, and presumably with major bus lines as well. In addition, Trailways tours go to Bryce and Zion from Salt Lake City, but on the first and last days of their four-day tours one seems to be arriving and departing in the small hours of the morning, and the hotel accommodation is outside the Parks.

If you **drive a car through the Southwest,** you must remember that this is unusual terrain, presenting special problems. In the first place, the distances are often tremendous between one town or petrol station and the next, which means that you must think a bit about the care and feeding of your car. It is wise to get more petrol – gas – whenever the tank is down to half-full. You should always have the water checked too, for this is dry country where water evaporates quickly. In hot weather everyone urges you to carry extra water as well, lest the car boil dry. Moreover in hot weather many people plan their trips so that they travel only at night through the worst sections, regions like the Mojave Desert in California or the area covered on the southerly route across the Southwest. During the day they sleep at some pleasant air-conditioned motel which also has a swimming pool, and then they start out again, refreshed, in the cool of the evening. Of course it is a poor way to see the country, but then one really cannot enjoy the low desert parts in July and August, with the temperature perhaps 110° F. That is the time for the higher plateau regions of the Southwest.

In the spring and early summer, or if there is a sudden thaw during the winter, you must beware of flash **floods** wherever a road goes over a normally dry river bed. So many of the river beds are dry most of the year that many of the back roads pass right across them without a bridge. When there is a sudden rush of water, which can happen with almost no warning, the road simply becomes impassable until the water subsides.

U.S. Route 66 has for years been the principal road through the Southwest. It has also for years enjoyed an unenviable reputation for having the most ghastly roadside advertising and the most noxious cafés and souvenir shops of any road in America. Route 66 is now gradually being supplanted by the new Interstate Route 40, which should mean less commercialism along the way; perhaps some day the only driving distraction here will be the scenery and the tumbling tumbleweed. Meanwhile it is pleasant, if you have time and a trustworthy car, to use back roads here and there, and to stop for the night at towns some distance from Route 66.

People **driving to the Southwest** from the north-eastern United States are likely to find the trip far pleasanter if they too avoid Route 66. A much more varied and interesting way to go is Route 40 (now being improved and turned into Interstate 70) west from St Louis to Kansas City; then the Kansas Turnpike south-west to Wichita through the rolling, Wyoming-like Flint Hills cattle country; then Route 54 to Dodge City and Route 50 on to La Junta, Colorado, at which point one can either continue on towards Mesa Verde and south-western Colorado or follow the old Santa Fé Trail over the Raton Pass into New Mexico.

The remote **Four Corners region** of the Southwest used to be notorious for its poor roads, but there is now an excellently signposted route called the Navajo Trail which leads over recently improved roads from the Mesa Verde to the North Rim of the Grand Canyon by way of Monument Valley in the Navajo Reservation.

We have mentioned Willa Cather's *Death Comes for the Archbishop*, which is a **classic book** about the Southwest, part history, part romance. There are several other writers who have dealt nobly with the Southwest too. Probably the best known in America today is Oliver La Farge, sensitive and scholarly with both fiction and fact. One of the finest new writers is William Eastlake, who seems completely *of* the Southwest, part cactus and part Navajo. A visitor to the Southwest who reads either J. B. Priestley's books about this region or

Willa Cather's *Death Comes for the Archbishop*, or Oliver La Farge or William Eastlake is sure to find his visit the richer for it.

arroyo: river bed, water course, usually dry.

pueblo: in the American Southwest, an Indian village with closely connected dwelling places.

Pueblo: Indian belonging to such a village-culture group.

mesa: butte: table-land or plateau raised above the surrounding region.

Apache: is pronounced Apatchy; *Navajo:* Navaho; *Rio Grande:* Rio Grand; *Canyon de Chelly:* Canyon de Shay; *saguaro:* sayaro; *Albuquerque:* Albukerky; *Houston:* as in Euston; *Tucson:* Tooson; *Taos:* Tah-os.

National Parks and Monuments

All the following National Parks and Monuments are open daily unless otherwise stated.

BANDELIER NATIONAL MONUMENT, NEW MEXICO, 45 miles north-west of Santa Fé. Overnight accommodation and meals during summer. Inquiries to Bandelier National Monument, Santa Fé, New Mexico.

BIG BEND NATIONAL PARK, TEXAS. About 50 miles south of Marathon or Alpine, off State Route 90. Camp-sites and cabin-type accommodation available year round. Reservations from National Park Concessions Inc., Big Bend National Park, Texas. Horses and guides available for trips.

BRYCE CANYON NATIONAL PARK, UTAH. The Lodge open 10 June to Labor Day. The Inn open 15 May to 9 October. Camp-sites open year round, full facilities 15 May to 15 October. 15 June to Labor Day: Bus tours of varying length leave from Cedar City for Zion, Bryce and Grand Canyon (North Rim), the shortest including only Zion and Bryce Canyon. For reservation of accommodation and bus-tour information write to the Utah Parks Company, Cedar City, Utah.

GRAND CANYON NATIONAL PARK, ARIZONA.

SOUTH RIM. Hotel, lodges and camp-sites open year round. Apply Fred Harvey, Grand Canyon, Arizona. Frequent bus service from Flagstaff and Williams, Arizona.

NORTH RIM. Open summer only. Camp-sites. Lodge open 18 June–10 September. Cafeteria open 15 May–15 October. Reservations from Utah Parks Company, Cedar City, Utah.

MESA VERDE NATIONAL PARK, COLORADO. Lodge and campground open early May to late October; reservations from the Mesa Verde Company, Mesa Verde National Park, Colorado. Bus services daily from Durango and Cortez, Colorado: information from Trailways Bus Depot, Durango or Cortez. Four- to six-day tours by Trailways, Denver, see p. 215.

PETRIFIED FOREST AND PAINTED DESERT, ARIZONA. Open during daylight. Accessible by hired car from Gallup, New Mexico, and Holbrook and Winslow, Arizona. Restaurant in Petrified Forest and in Painted Desert.

SAGUARO NATIONAL MONUMENT, ARIZONA, 17 miles east of Tucson. Monument headquarters open daily, 8–5. Free.

ZION NATIONAL PARK, UTAH. May be reached by bus tour from Cedar City. See Bryce Canyon National Park.

Acoma, New Mexico

A guide will show you round the Mission Church and village on application in the village.

Carlsbad Caverns, New Mexico

4-hour tour covering 3 miles; 4 June to 5 September, tours begin at 7 and thereafter hourly to 2. 7 September to 3 June, tours begin at 8.30, 10, 11.30 and 1.

2-hour tour covering 1½ miles (lift in and out); 4 June to 5 September tours at 9.10, 10.10, 11.10, 12.20, 1.20, 2.10, 3.10 and 4.10. 7 September to 3 June, tours at 10.55, 12.25, 1.55 and 3.10.

Colorado River Trips

Information from Utah State Department of Publicity, Salt Lake City, Utah.

Dallas, Texas

DALLAS THEATER CENTER, 3636 Turtle Creek Boulevard. Guided tours Monday to Friday 12 and 12.30, Saturday 12.30 and 1, Sunday 1.30–4.30. Limited view tours daily 10–3.30.

DALLAS MUSEUM FOR CONTEMPORARY ARTS, 3415 Cedar Springs Road. Tuesday 11.30–9.30, Wednesday to Saturday 11.30–5.30, Sunday 2–5.

Fort Worth, Texas

AMON CARTER MUSEUM OF WESTERN ART, 3501 Camp Bowie Boulevard, Fort Worth 7. Tuesday to Saturday 10–5; Sunday 1–5.30.

Houston, Texas

HOUSTON MUSEUM OF FINE ARTS, South Main and Montrose Boulevards. Tuesday to Saturday 9.30–5, Sunday 12–6. 1 October to 30 April, Wednesday stays open till 10. Free.

Phoenix, Arizona

DESERT BOTANICAL GARDENS, 8 miles east of Phoenix. 1 September to 30 June, 9–5. Free.

San Antonio, Texas

THE ALAMO, Alamo Street at Houston Street. Week-days 9–5, Sunday and holidays 10–5. Free.

SAN JOSE AND SAN MIGUEL DE AGUAYO MISSION. On U.S. Route 281 at East White Street. Week-days, 9–6, Sunday 10–6.

SPANISH GOVERNOR'S PALACE, Military Plaza. Week-days, 9.30–5.30, Sunday and holidays, 2.30–5.30.

Santa Fé, New Mexico

CHURCH OF SAN MIGUEL, College Street at East de Vargas Street. Daily 8–11.45 and 1–5.30.

MUSEUM OF INTERNATIONAL FOLK ART, off Old Pecos Road. Monday 7 p.m. to 9 p.m., Tuesday to Saturday 9–5, Sunday 1–5, holidays 2–4. Free.

MUSEUM OF NAVAJO CEREMONIAL ART, off Old Pecos Road. Tuesday to Saturday 9–12 and 1–4.30, Sunday 2–5.

PALACE OF THE GOVERNORS. The Plaza. Week-days 9–12 and 1–5, Sunday and holidays 2–4. Free.

Taos, New Mexico

PUEBLO DE TAOS, 3½ miles north of Taos. Daily 7–6.30. Register at the Governor's Office.

Tucson, Arizona

ARIZONA-SONORA DESERT MUSEUM, Tucson Mountain Park. Daily 10–5; on Sunday in summer till sunset.

ARIZONA STATE MUSEUM, in the University grounds, near East 3rd Street entrance. Week-days 10–5, Sunday 2–5. Free.

SAN XAVIER DEL BAC MISSION, 9 miles south-west of Tucson in the Papago Indian Reservation. Tours daily 9–12 and 2–5.

Index

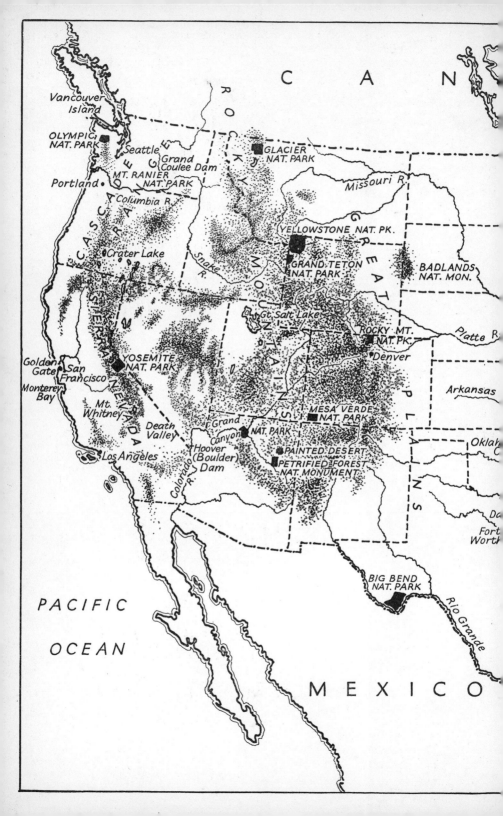